PEACEKEEPING IN EAST TIMOR

INTERNATIONAL PEACE ACADEMY
OCCASIONAL PAPER SERIES

PEACEKEEPING IN EAST TIMOR

The Path to Independence

Michael G. Smith
with Moreen Dee

LYNNE
RIENNER
PUBLISHERS

BOULDER
LONDON

This study contains the personal views of the author and not necessarily those of the United Nations or the Australian Government. The study is intended to inform those interested in peacekeeping, but does not constitute policy.

Published in the United States of America in 2003 by
Lynne Rienner Publishers, Inc.
1800 30th Street, Boulder, Colorado 80301
www.rienner.com

and in the United Kingdom by
Lynne Rienner Publishers, Inc.
3 Henrietta Street, Covent Garden, London WC2E 8LU

Library of Congress Cataloging-in-Publication Data
Smith, Michael G. (Michael Geoffrey), 1950–
    Peacekeeping in East Timor : the path to independence / Michael G. Smith with
    Moreen Dee.
       p. cm.
    Includes bibliographical references and index.
    ISBN 1-58826-142-5 (pbk. : alk. paper)
    1. East Timor—Politics and government.   2. United Nations—Peacekeeping forces—
East Timor.   I. Dee, Moreen.   II. Title.
    DS646.59.T55 S65   2002
    320.9598'6—dc21

                                                              2002029168

British Cataloguing in Publication Data
A Cataloguing in Publication record for this book
is available from the British Library.

Printed and bound in the United States of America

The paper used in this publication meets the requirements
∞ of the American National Standard for Permanence of
Paper for Printed Library Materials Z39.48-1984.

    5   4   3   2   1

To Falintil and the East Timorese People
and
To peacekeepers past, present, and future

Contents

Foreword

SERGIO VIEIRA DE MELLO

At the beginning of this study, its author and my friend, Major General Mike Smith, incorporates the standard disclaimer that the study contains nothing but his personal views and, of course, does not constitute policy. Quite right! Nonetheless, it would be foolish of any of us who are interested in international peace operations to discount what is written on these pages, for Major General Smith brings to this book a lifetime of distinguished service in the Australian Army, as well as extensive experience of that strangest of all military hybrids—international peacekeeping and enforcement.

General Mike, when I first met him in New York, was integral in both planning for the International Force in East Timor (INTERFET), the multinational force sent into East Timor to bring order amidst the chaos that was inflicted on the territory in September 1999, and in developing the military component of the United Nations Transitional Administration in East Timor (UNTAET) that took over from INTERFET in February 2000. And, of course, he served as deputy force commander of the nearly 9,000 Blue Berets from the creation of the peacekeeping force to March 2001. During this time, he repeatedly demonstrated his skills—military, diplomatic, and analytical—in helping to ensure that UNTAET has been the success that it is. Most important, he was central in helping bring to the people of East Timor that which they had for so long been denied: freedom from fear.

In this study, General Mike provides a comprehensive analysis of the many aspects of UNTAET in particular and of peacekeeping in general. Throughout, whether you agree with his position or not, he presents cogent arguments and much food for thought in an area that continually requires such stimulus in order to be able to adapt to ever changing circumstances. We continually seek to learn lessons—often painful in the last decade—from our past experiences in peacekeeping. In this work, Major General

Smith acknowledges that many of these lessons, in East Timor, were implemented. He also, more importantly, provides a salutary reminder that much more improvement is required by the international community—whether through the United Nations or by some other means—in its ability to operate quickly and effectively in future complex peace operations. The people of the East Timors of the future deserve and expect no less.

And, finally, this study amply highlights General Mike's depth of feeling for and friendship toward East Timor and its people. He rightly has deep respect for those many individuals in East Timor who worked so bravely and tirelessly to win for their country the right to independence. This new nation and its travails have consumed much of Mike's energy over the past three years. The East Timorese have certainly benefited from his dedication to their cause as, I believe, has the image of international peacekeeping, which General Mike so proudly and ably served in recent years.

I commend this study to you.

—Sergio Vieira de Mello,
Special Representative of the Secretary-General
and Transitional Administrator for East Timor

Foreword

KAY RALA XANANA GUSMÃO

After so many years of oppression, liberation came to East Timor like a whirlwind. In the midst of the Asian economic crisis of 1997 Indonesia faltered, leading to President Suharto's replacement by Dr. B. J. Habibie the following year. Against the odds, but in answer to our prayers, the new Indonesian government magnanimously offered the people of East Timor an opportunity to determine our own destiny. Through the good offices of the United Nations, who together with Portugal had helped to keep our quest for freedom alive, the historic UNAMET ballot was conducted under difficult circumstances on 30 August 1999. Almost 80 percent of our population bravely voted for their freedom, but then paid for this in blood as the militias savagely took their revenge by killing and burning, trying to destroy a nation. Still under house arrest in Jakarta, I wondered if we would recover. The following month the United Nations quickly authorized a multinational force, INTERFET, which brilliantly restored security; and then in October mandated for UNTAET to start rebuilding our country and help shepherd us to independence. These United Nations peace operations form an indelible part of our national history, and this account by Major General Mike Smith is an important contribution to that period.

We came to know General Mike both as a professional soldier and as a true friend of the people of East Timor. He was our protector in the very intense months following the reestablishment of civil society in East Timor. In that sense his contribution has a special place in our personal memories. As one learned to expect from this general, his account is honest and objective, but it fails to tell the true story of his personal contribution and commitment, and of his special role in masterminding both the transition of Falintil into a professional defense force and the establishment of a national security framework. But we in East Timor know of this, and we will not forget. This excellent written record of modern peacekeeping reveals a sol-

11

dierly devotion and General Mike's essential humanity. This is how the Timorese people came to know Mike Smith, as the abiding friend of East Timor. I commend his work to all who value the role of military profession-alism in the community of nations.

—Kay Rala Xanana Gusmão,
President of the Democratic Republic of East Timor

Acknowledgments

I am indebted to a number of people for their contribution to this study. I would like to thank the then Chief of Army, Lieutenant General Frank Hickling, for recommending my appointment as director general East Timor in March 1999, and Chief of the Defence Force Admiral Chris Barrie for appointing me to that position. My thanks also to then Minister for Defence John Moore for nominating me for the position of deputy force commander for the UN Peacekeeping Force in East Timor. Having commanded at all levels, from platoon to brigade, this appointment proved the most challenging.

In writing the study I would like to thank James Batley, Jean-Christian Cady, Professor James Cotton, James Dunn, Major General Tim Ford, Professor James Fox, Carlos Gaspar, Sue Ingram, Ian Martin, Paula Pinto, Major General Roger Powell, Jonathon Prentice, Alan Ryan, Professor Hugh Smith, Commander Dale Stephens, Sherrill Whittington, and Lieutenant Colonel Ian Wing for their useful comments and contributions. I thank Sergio Vieira de Mello and President Xanana Gusmão for the forewords they so kindly provided for this study and for their leadership and friendship. I must also acknowledge my friend Heran Song for her encouragement to complete this study. I am grateful also to General Peter Cosgrove (Australian of the Year for 2001) who, as Chief of Army, provided me with travel and research assistance following my return from East Timor. I particularly acknowledge the assistance provided by Moreen Dee, whose name rightfully appears on the title page. Moreen's international relations background and knowledge of Southeast Asia, together with her extensive research skills, greatly assisted me in writing and compiling this study. Her unfailing commitment and enthusiasm to the project were outstanding, and I could not have wanted for a more capable associate. I leave it for others to judge the usefulness of this study, but if it is worthwhile, then Moreen deserves much of the credit.

I will be forever grateful for the opportunity to work closely with the East Timorese people. The friendship and hospitality they displayed, often in the most difficult of circumstances, was testament to the spirit of a special people who have risen above the suffering inflicted on them for so long. I am touched and humbled by the experience of knowing them.

Finally, I thank my wife and our three sons for accepting so stoically the long separation while I was in New York and East Timor and for their continued support and encouragement, which enabled me to complete this study. Yet again I am indebted to their love, forbearance, and understanding. Soldiers ask a lot of their families. . . .

—Major General Mike Smith

East Timor

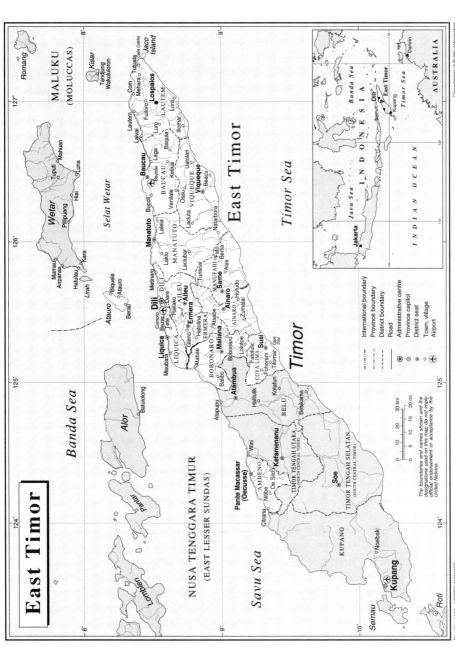

Banda Sea

MALUKU
(MOLUCCAS)

Romang

Wetar

Selat Wetar

Alor

NUSA TENGGARA TIMUR
(EAST LESSER SUNDAS)

Savu Sea

Timor

East Timor

Timor Sea

International boundary
Province boundary
District boundary
Road
⊛ **Administrative centre**
⊛ **Province capitol**
◉ **District seat**
○ **Town, village**
✈ **Airport**

0   5   10   15   20 mi
0   10   20   30 km

The boundaries and names shown and the
designations used on this map do not imply
official endorsement or acceptance by the
United Nations.

INDONESIA

Java Sea

Banda Sea

Jakarta

Dili   East Timor
Kupang
Timor Sea
Darwin

INDIAN OCEAN

AUSTRALIA

Department of Public Information
Cartographic Section

Map No. 4145   UNITED NATIONS
January 2000

1

UN Intervention
in East Timor

Peacekeeping is a 50-year-old enterprise that has evolved rapidly in the
past decade from a traditional, primarily military model of observing
ceasefires and force separations after inter-State wars, to incorporate a
complex model of many elements, military and civilian, working together
to build peace in the dangerous aftermath of civil wars.
                                            —Brahimi report, 21 August 2000[1]

THE MISSIONS

In this study, I review the United Nations' intervention in East Timor during the period 1999–2001 and specifically analyze the role of the UN
Transitional Administration in East Timor (UNTAET).[2] My analysis precedes the closure of the UNTAET mission at East Timor's independence on
20 May 2002, and necessarily represents an incomplete study. I use the
word *intervention* in the broader liberal, rather than technical, sense. In
East Timor, the UN intervened to modify the situation and shepherd a
nation to independence. The UN operated as an instrument of change, but it
did so with the approval of Indonesia as the governing power and the overwhelming majority of the East Timorese people. In the technical sense,
intervention means enforced action in the internal affairs of a state without
the consent of all major parties, and particularly that of the governing
power. This latter situation did not apply in East Timor, although it could be
argued that international pressure persuaded Indonesia to agree to a UN-
mandated multinational force (MNF) to restore security.

The international community has generally judged the UN's intervention in East Timor to have been successful, but the UNTAET mission in
particular attracted criticisms of waste and inefficiency from East Timorese
leaders, members of the mission itself, and a range of observers.[3] In fact,
the UN delivered on each of its mandates in East Timor. But for future

interventions in postconflict environments, there are obviously questions that need to be answered as to what is within the capability of the UN to provide and what improvements can be made in the UN's planning and implementation process. It must be understood, however, that the UN's involvement in East Timor went beyond traditional peacekeeping and, arguably, beyond the purpose for which the UN was originally created. In line with the trend toward more complex peace operations since the end of the Cold War, East Timor required UN assistance in the areas of governance and elections, security enforcement, and nation building. Traditional peacekeeping values of invitation, mediation, and the nonuse of force proved anachronistic and far too limiting in the case of East Timor.

Although this study focuses on the UNTAET period, it is important to understand that the UN's intervention in East Timor comprised three distinct phases and missions: the Popular Consultation, or ballot, conducted by the United Nations Mission in East Timor (UNAMET);[4] the restoration and maintenance of security, carried out by the International Force in East Timor (INTERFET);[5] and the preparation of East Timor and its people for independence, implemented by UNTAET.

Phase I, UNAMET, was a short mission of five months, commencing in June 1999. It was capably led by Ian Martin from Great Britain as the Special Representative of the Secretary-General (SRSG) for the East Timor Popular Consultation, and comprised a little over 1,000 staff. The ballot, sanctioned by Indonesia, was in the nature of a referendum that gave the East Timorese the opportunity to either accept or reject integration within the Republic of Indonesia as a special autonomous region.[6] UNAMET's role was to register eligible voters, prepare and authenticate electoral rolls, and facilitate eligible voters to secretly cast their preference.[7] UNAMET's mission culminated with the ballot on 30 August 1999, and the remaining staff were incorporated into the UNTAET mandate on 25 October 1999. There is no doubt that UNAMET's preparation and conduct of the ballot was highly professional, particularly in view of the difficult security and environmental conditions. Under its direction, and despite significant intimidation by pro-Jakarta armed militias[8] during the lead-up to the ballot, an incredible 98.6 percent of eligible voters participated in the ballot. Of these voters, a majority of 78.5 percent rejected the autonomy proposal and opted for independence. But immediately following the vote, a massive campaign of violence and destruction was inflicted by the militias, which caused the dislocation of most of the population. The Indonesian National Military (known as TNI) and Indonesian police force (POLRI), ostensibly responsible for maintaining security, failed to exert any form of control. Most of the UNAMET staff were evacuated during this period, but a small presence remained in the territory and the mission was resumed with the arrival of INTERFET.[9]

Phase II, INTERFET, was the unforecasted deployment of a UN-mandated and interim MNF to restore and maintain security until the UN could assemble a peacekeeping force (PKF).[10] INTERFET was placed under the able command of Major General Peter Cosgrove from Australia. Twenty-two nations contributed to INTERFET, and at its peak its strength was around 11,000 troops, with Australia providing the largest contingent of around 5,000. Commencing operations on 20 September 1999, INTERFET remained for five months; it progressively restored security and acted as a de facto administration until UNTAET was established in November. From that time, the MNF continued its security operations until replaced by the PKF in February 2000.

Phase III, UNTAET, was mandated on 25 October 1999 and began its difficult task on the ground in East Timor the following month.[11] UNTAET was a much larger and more complex mission than UNAMET, with the broadly defined mandate of preparing East Timor for sustainable independence. As I will show in this study, initial progress was slow and it took several months before the transitional administration became fully effective. Nonetheless, under the leadership of its experienced SRSG, Sergio Vieira de Mello from Brazil, UNTAET performed well overall. This outcome is significant given the magnitude of the task, the devastated state of East Timor's infrastructure, the absence of qualified East Timorese personnel, and the UN's lack of previous experience in such endeavors. Nevertheless, the UNTAET period revealed a number of limitations in the UN's ability to conduct this type of operation. I identify and discuss these limitations in this study.

SCOPING THE ISSUES

To provide the background to the UNTAET mission, I present in Chapter 2 an overview of East Timor's history and a brief explanation of the country's long journey to freedom. I cover the UN's intervention in 1999 in some detail, focusing on the purpose and performance of UNAMET and INTERFET. In Chapter 3 I review the purpose, structure, and performance of the UNTAET mission, emphasizing the importance of maintaining a secure environment, establishing effective governance (including the rule of law), and enabling sustainable capacity building for the world's newest state. I detail in Chapters 4 and 5 the major lessons learned from the UN's intervention. In Chapter 4, I concentrate on lessons related to overall mission planning and implementation and provide a checklist of considerations for future UN operations where transitional administrations may be contemplated. This is not a prescriptive chapter, because the East Timor situation will not necessarily apply in other postconflict situations.

Nevertheless, the lessons from East Timor are worth considering. My emphasis in Chapter 5 is on lessons specifically related to the military aspects of the operation, especially the importance of security and the need to better plan and conduct military operations in partnership with mission stakeholders. Finally, in Chapter 6, I comment on East Timor's future prospects and on the future direction of peacekeeping, emphasizing the critical support required by member states.

COALITIONS AND COMPLEX PEACE OPERATIONS

In the nuclear age, and particularly since the end of the Cold War, there has been a significant increase in subnational and transnational violence. The spectrum of violence is broad, ranging from conventional military action to extreme acts of brutality by machete-wielding mobs and sophisticated acts of terrorism and criminal activity. The weapons of war range from home-made agricultural implements to contemporary armaments and advanced munitions, explosives, and communications systems. Most of these threats are asymmetric and are underpinned by long-standing grievances that have their roots in nationalism, religion, or ethnicity. Many grievances are fueled by the growing or perceived distinction between the haves and the have-nots, the inequality of humanity, and abject poverty. As well, a number of nontraditional threats, linked with the process of globalization, are having an increased impact on conflict management. Environmental issues and unregulated mass migrations are influencing the maintenance of peace and security, and the proliferation in transnational crime challenges the capacity of nation-states to control domestic law and order.

If Operation Desert Storm—the U.S.-led international coalition to free Kuwait from Iraqi occupation in 1990—was, in contemporary rhetoric, the "mother of all battles," it was certainly not representative of the most common conflicts being confronted throughout much of the world. In 1991, the distinguished Israeli strategist and historian Martin Van Creveld clearly explained the characteristics of modern conflict in his seminal work *The Transformation of War*.[12] In 2000, U.S. Army Chief of Staff General Shinseki stated much the same on a *Panorama* program titled "The Future of War." Shinseki, then chief of the most potent mechanized force on earth, clearly indicated that the next conflicts and engagements would be more similar to Haiti, Kosovo, and East Timor than to Desert Storm.

The terrorist attacks on the World Trade Center and the Pentagon on 11 September 2001 further demonstrated that the nature of conflict had changed. President George W. Bush declared this attack to be the first war of the twenty-first century and pledged a protracted campaign of attrition well beyond surgical air strikes. This "war against terrorism" initially focused on the repressive Islamic fundamentalist Taliban regime in Kabul and the Al-Qaida headquarters of Osama bin Laden in Afghanistan, which was alleged to have masterminded the attack on the United States. But the potential for this war to extend beyond Afghanistan was real. Such a campaign raised the likelihood of friendly and civilian casualties, with high prospects for enormous civilian dislocation and suffering. This was to be a multidimensional war, transcending national boundaries, building on coalitions, employing a large military force, and permeating the world's financial system. The terrorist attacks of 11 September effectively turned the tide of public opinion throughout much of the civilized world; retribution, in the names of "justice" and "self-defense," suddenly gained public approval. In one calamitous moment as Flight 11 struck the World Trade Center, the nuclear age of deterrence was turned on its head as the world risked returning to a war of attrition of another kind. The heart of the world's only superpower had been attacked. The response was to retaliate through an international coalition, but it was also to revive dormant civil defense procedures to safeguard public movement and to prepare against possible biological, chemical, and nuclear attacks. The most immediate outcome of the operation in Afghanistan was the need to establish a credible replacement administration that could ensure security and commence the long journey of civil reconstruction. This would require a complex peace operation of mammoth proportion, well beyond that required in East Timor and more akin to that of Germany and Japan after World War II.

These developments have required nation-states to review their national security policies and to ensure that their military forces are trained and equipped for these types of threats. Many of these threats are nonconventional. While they still require many of the capabilities of conventional forces, they are gray operations and require defense forces to possess additional attributes to those of conventional warfighting. In particular, counterinsurgency doctrine is now being relearned, retitled, and adapted, because it has more relevance to many of these nonconventional conflicts, including combating terrorism, where fronts and flanks no longer have relevance in a linear sense. Almost all of these operations require the creation of coalitions—coalitions for traditional warfighting, for peace operations, for humanitarian and/or disaster relief operations, for evacuation operations, and more recently for counterterrorist operations.

History is replete with examples of coalition operations, many of which now fall into the category of complex peace operations. Increasingly, military intervention is in the pursuit of peace, humanitarian assistance, or stabilization rather than for purposes of territorial or economic conquest or for traditional power politics. This trend has increased the demand on UN capabilities. The conflicts often fall under UN authority, either directly controlled by the UN or as UN-mandated MNFs operating under Security

Council resolution. Secretary-General Boutros Boutros-Ghali recognized the implications of the challenge facing the UN in *An Agenda for Peace* (1992): "Increasingly, peacekeeping requires that civilian political officers, human rights monitors, electoral officials, refugee and humanitarian aid specialists and police play as central a role as the military."[13] Complex peace operations are thus multidimensional in character, going beyond traditional monitoring and peacekeeping to include peace enforcement, stabilization, evacuation, rescue, and humanitarian relief operations. Although Boutros-Ghali's recommendations in *An Agenda for Peace* constituted the UN's first step toward developing a broad framework for intervention that addressed this shift, many of the recommendations progressed slowly and were indeed highlighted again in the *Report on the Panel on UN Peace Operations* (2000)—more commonly referred to as the Brahimi report.[14] The UN experience in East Timor further illustrates the need for peace enforcement operations to be backed by a high level of training and preparation and by adequate funding and support from the international community. The need for coalition forces on peace operations to combat acts of terrorism in the conduct of their duties has also heightened the need to provide for force protection.

But creating effective coalitions is difficult. Carl von Clausewitz noted that war was simple, but that in war even simple things became difficult. Clausewitz was talking about the uncertainty of the battlefield and the friction that is created when two sides oppose each other. But Clausewitz was also well experienced in coalition warfare, and he understood better than most the complexities of bringing coalitions together and the inherent difficulties to be overcome. Historical, political, and cultural differences represent some of the friction points to be overcome in preparing coalitions.[15] There are differences in standards of living, gender tolerance, language, religion, and work ethic. And within military forces there are differences in competence, doctrine, training, equipment, logistics, technology, and leadership.

Coalition building is about bringing together multinational, multilingual, and multiracial forces; linking them with a common achievable mission; maintaining their loyalty and commitment; ensuring that they are properly led, trained, equipped, and supported for the tasks they have been assigned; and insisting that they behave in a way that will not discredit the coalition or create longer-term problems. Additionally, complex peace operations are inherently dangerous, cannot always be resolved quickly, and may not have long-term public support from home capitals. It is little wonder that coalition operations are so difficult. It is a consistent challenge for the various branches of an army and the various services of a national defense force to work together cohesively, let alone to meld the disparate components of a coalition force.

Three observations stand out in relation to coalitions and complex peace operations: first, both are difficult and are increasingly more likely to occur; second, most peace operations will be coalitions under UN authority, requiring increased civil–military integration and competent military and police forces; and, third, member states will need to ensure that UN peace-keeping is reformed to better conduct these operations.

THEMES

This study shows that the UN's intervention in East Timor is an important illustration of the shift from traditional peacekeeping to more complex and multifunctional peacekeeping and peace support operations. The role of peacekeeping has now expanded from the fundamental task of preserving a cessation of hostilities to include a much greater nonmilitary component to undertake the tasks of governance, humanitarian assistance, electoral super-vision, police tasks, and nation building. The scope of such operations, and the complexity of the possible "crises" inherent in each, require a wide range of military, technical, advisory, and executive skills. In the chapters that follow, I develop seven themes that emerged from the UN's interven-tion in East Timor.

Reinforcing the Brahimi Report

The first and most obvious theme is that this study confirms many of the recommendations contained in the Brahimi report, which presented its find-ings in September 2000. The report defined UN peace operations as entail-ing the three principal activities of peacemaking, peacekeeping, and peace-building and noted the challenges faced by complex missions.[16] East Timor was included for consideration by the panel, and it is noteworthy that the lessons that emerge from my analysis support and complement most of the panel's recommendations. The conclusions reached from both studies are that continued reform of the UN is essential if the challenges of complex missions are to be adequately met, and that for missions to be successful, member states must support these reforms and ensure that they are imple-mented quickly and comprehensively.

The need for reform notwithstanding, this study also emphasizes that each mission is unique and that peacekeeping templates cannot be applied uniformly among missions. Consideration of UNTAET shows that many factors interact to determine the success or failure of UN missions. But no two missions are identical and each reflects the specific conditions prevail-ing on the ground at any given time. In some cases, there may be genuine commitment by conflicting parties for the UN to bring lasting peace. In other circumstances, the UN's intervention may be only reluctantly accepted in order to gain time or avoid defeat, a fact recognized in the Brahimi report, which noted that "consent may be manipulated in many ways by the local parties. A party may give its consent to UN presence merely to gain time to retool its fighting forces and withdraw consent when the peacekeeping operation no longer serves its purpose."[17] There may also be occasions when UN intervention will not be invited but imposed—particularly where effective governance no longer exists and massive human rights violations are evident. To further complicate matters, circumstances may change during a mission's tenure, causing the Security Council to review and alter the mandate. Such variables affect the degree of complexity in carrying out UN missions and caution against templates being applied. What this East Timor case study provides, however, is a useful checklist of factors to be considered for future UN interventions. Such a checklist cannot determine whether a particular intervention should or should not occur, or whether it will succeed or fail, but rather it might assist the Security Council in considering prospects for resolving the conflict and achieving long-term peace in the troubled territory.

Improving UN Planning and Preparation

As part of its reform, the UN needs to improve its processes for the planning of and preparation for complex missions. Many of the difficulties UNTAET encountered related directly to inchoate planning and preparation within the UN Secretariat in New York. As noted in the Brahimi report, the Secretariat needs to enhance staff levels, reorganize its departments, identify personnel lists for mission deployment, establish an information (intelligence) assessment capability, and create specialized Integrated Mission Task Forces (IMTFs) to plan and coordinate complex missions effectively.[18] There is no doubt that the difficulties confronting UNTAET were magnified as a result of the massive destruction that occurred following the ballot. It is also true that the Department of Peacekeeping Operations (DPKO) was overstretched due to the withdrawal of a large number of gratis personnel coincident with the increased workload as it established several other missions.[19]

These factors help explain, but do not excuse, the lack of UN planning for a civil administration, particularly since the 5 May Agreements in 1999 identified this as a UN responsibility should integration with Indonesia be rejected. It is also axiomatic that proper planning and preparation enhances the prospects of UN missions fulfilling these mandates. While the Security Council provided strong mandates for UN intervention in East Timor, UNTAET's ability to achieve its mandate was impaired because of poor planning. With the exception of the PKF, the Electoral Division, and the

UN High Commissioner for Refugees (UNHCR), this lack of planning permeated throughout the mission, particularly affecting the areas of governance (including the establishment of the rule of law) and infrastructure development. With most effort focused on daily survival, and with inadequate strategic planning provided from the Secretariat, it proved difficult to create a coherent corporate plan to chart the mission's progress. The outcome of this meant that elements of the mission tended to operate in isolation, with a lack of shared vision and understanding as to how the objectives specified in the mandate could best be achieved.

Fostering Teamwork and Partnerships

Concomitant with better planning is the need for the UN to foster teamwork and partnerships. This process should begin during the planning phase, and it requires the early appointment of key mission personnel and the early involvement of key stakeholders. Teamwork and partnership works in three dimensions: internally within the mission, in parallel with the leaders from the host country, and externally with member states and international organizations. All these relationships are important, and the UNTAET experience suggests that more could have been achieved.

Delivering Good Governance

To have credibility and prepare a country for independence, transitional administrations such as UNTAET must be able to provide good governance and earn the respect and confidence of leaders within the host community. In turn, this is dependent on two of the earlier themes: good planning and preparation, and teamwork and partnerships. In considering the aspects of both these themes in relation to good governance, it is possible to discern a cumulative effect on the UN's performance in East Timor. In hindsight it is clear that UNTAET struggled in this area. Speedy development was difficult due to the inexperience of UNTAET personnel and the East Timorese leaders, and progress was only gradually achieved through trial and error and with the patience and understanding of the East Timorese. This study shows that it is vital for the UN to improve its understanding and expertise in this critical area of governance, which, by necessity, must include effective implementation of the rule of law.

Maintaining a Secure Environment

Maintaining a secure environment is pivotal to success in complex peace operations; without such conditions and the rule of law, community cohesion and national development will invariably fail. The only result then is a flourishing of poverty and crime. In postconflict environments, curbing violence helps provide a climate for economic recovery and sustainable development. INTERFET successfully restored security following the post-ballot violence, and the UNTAET PKF worked hard to ensure that this situation was maintained. Importantly, the prevention of large-scale militia infiltration reassured the population that their safety could be guaranteed against this potential external threat. Nonetheless, although the PKF performed to a high standard, significant lessons were learned. There is little doubt that the force could have begun operations better trained and equipped for its various tasks.

The UN civilian police (CIVPOL) contingent was certainly less effective because of even more severe limitations in these areas. Generally, lawlessness within the East Timorese community was low, but unlike the PKF, CIVPOL had difficulties winning the confidence of UNTAET and the population. The standard of many CIVPOL was not high, and it was many months before stations were opened in the subdistricts and a meaningful presence established. Nor was the coordination between the PKF and CIVPOL as robust as it should have been. Compounding the issue, the judicial and penal systems were slow to get started, causing significant problems in effectively implementing the rule of law. The UN, therefore, needs to consider security in a more holistic manner. It also needs to set higher benchmarks in doctrine and for training and to improve security mechanisms and ensure that they are practiced within missions.

Training, Training, Training

The importance of improved training for civil and military personnel, for more integration in this training, and for higher benchmarks and uniformity are other themes of this study. In 1994, A. B. Fetherston analyzed a number of complex UN peacekeeping missions.[20] Given the sharp increase in multifunctional peacekeeping since the end of the Cold War—with varying degrees of success and failure—Fetherston considered that a new paradigm was required for UN peacekeeping. She correctly assessed that "in the new international climate which is pushing the UN toward larger and more complex involvement in conflicts a much better developed and researched understanding of success is needed."[21] Although not fully articulated, her determinations were predicated on the need for better and integrated preparation and training for complex missions. Notwithstanding the improvements in training for UN operations that have occurred since 1994, the UN's intervention in East Timor confirms that more is required. The Brahimi report did not address this issue in detail, but the requirement for better training is inherent in many of the report's recommendations. This study of the East Timor experience concludes that the Secretariat needs to establish clearer benchmarks for training and that the development of integrated peacekeeping training centers (similar to the Canadian and Nordic models) needs to be encouraged and promoted.

Preparing Intelligent and Versatile Warriors

An underlying theme inferred from this study relates to the requirements for military commanders in complex peace operations. Peace operations by their very nature are multifaceted and require commanders, together with their staffs, to possess a wide range of professional and personal skills. First and foremost, commanders must ensure that they remain focused on their mission and the well-being and protection of their troops. But commanders must also be vigilant and active in developing networks with the various stakeholders, and they must be capable of influencing the decision-making process, particularly at the higher levels. Teamwork can only be built on mutual understanding, trust, and respect; and senior commanders and their staff must invest considerable time and effort in ensuring that the SRSG's and force commander's intent is fully understood and implemented. Within a multinational and multicultural setting, the need for effective communications is critical and cannot be overstated or taken for granted. The more diverse the cultures and their languages, the more challenging this task will be.

In this "information age," there is still no substitute for regular visits by senior commanders and their staff to enhance situational awareness, provide guidance to subordinate commanders, and give encouragement to deployed troops. Time senior commanders spend on the ground with one another, with UN administrators, and with local leaders is invaluable. In complex peace operations, therefore, senior commanders must be "intelligent warriors." They must possess the attributes of both the Spartans and the Athenians and know how and when to apply these qualities. Major General Joseph Kinzer, the UN force commander in Haiti, summed it up this way: "Peace operations . . . blend the attributes of soldier and statesman and apply them in the appropriate proportion at the right time and place."[22]

Nor are intelligence and versatility restricted to senior commanders. More so than in traditional warfighting, junior commanders can be required to take actions that may jeopardize the maintenance of peace, or even the prospects for reconciliation. As General Peter Cosgrove, the commander of INTERFET noted, "The decisions of junior leaders and the actions of their small teams can influence the course of international affairs."[23] The onus of such responsibility requires then that all military commanders demonstrate political, social, and military skills, determination, patience, integrity, flexibility, compassion, and excellent communication ability well beyond what may normally apply in traditional warfighting. The conclusion here seems clear enough: nations contributing troops to complex peace operations must ensure that their forces are properly trained and prepared. The benchmarks for good soldiering have now been raised beyond the requirements for warfighting to include all the constabulary and civil-military affairs (CMA)[24] tasks, cultural awareness, and negotiation skills required for third-party intervention. In other words, military forces—and by extension, CIVPOL—need to be more versatile and better trained than hitherto.

CONCLUSION

The UN's intervention in East Timor can generally be regarded as successful, but it was not without flaws that hindered the missions' tasks and progress and that could have, at any time, compounded to reverse the outcome. There are no indications that the increased requirement for the UN to undertake complex peace operations will abate. It is therefore essential for the UN to consider, and act quickly upon, the problems that arise with each particular mission. The East Timor experience reveals the need for continued reform of the UN in many areas: for better planning, preparation, teamwork, and partnerships to enhance prospects for success; for improved understanding and expertise in governance, including implementing the rule of law; for consideration of security in a more holistic manner; and for the better training of civilian, military, and police personnel.

Many of the themes identified and developed in this study have already been highlighted in examinations of peace operations since the UN Transitional Assistance Group (UNTAG) mission in Namibia in 1989–1990, the UN Operation in Somalia (UNOSOM), and the UN Transitional Authority in Cambodia (UNTAC).[25] Unfortunately, the clear analyses and practical advice to the UN by many reputable commentators, analysts, and mission commanders and specialists appeared to receive scant attention until the Brahimi report was released in September 2000. The experience of the UN operations in East Timor examined here stresses the urgency with which the UN must now face the reality of the international expectations of its role in global security, and continue the reforms necessary to competently fulfill this task. Moreover, these reforms can only be achieved with the full support of member states and with the insistence of the member states that the UN be held accountable for unsatisfactory performance.

This study is not intended to be an indictment of the UN, because many of the lessons learned in East Timor were also identified in the Brahimi report, and some are already being implemented. Rather, it is hoped that the lessons highlighted in this examination of the UN's intervention in East Timor will serve to support the Brahimi report's recommendations and further promote the body of knowledge on modern peacekeeping. This will enhance the prospects for mission success, achieving a more lasting peace, while helping to save the lives of peacekeepers and enrich the lives of those they serve.

NOTES

1. *Report of the Panel on United Nations Peace Operations* (Brahimi report), UN General Assembly Security Council, A/55/305–S/2000/809, 21 August 2000, par. 12, pp. 2–3.

2. The UNTAET mission concluded with East Timor's independence on 20 May 2002. It was replaced by the much smaller UN Mission in Support of East Timor (UNMISET).

3. See Jarat Chopra, "The UN's Kingdom of East Timor," *Survival* 42, no. 3 (2000): 27–39; James Traub, "Inventing East Timor," *Foreign Affairs* 79, no. 4 (2000): 74–89; and John McBeth, "Whose Future Is It Anyway?" *Far Eastern Economic Review* 9 (November 2000): 68–69.

4. For an account of UNAMET, see Ian Martin, *Self-Determination in East Timor: The United Nations, the Ballot, and International Intervention* (Boulder, CO: Lynne Reinner, 2001).

5. For appraisals of INTERFET, see Alan Ryan, *Primary Responsibilities and Primary Risks: Australian Defence Force Participation in the International Force East Timor,* Study Paper No. 304 (Duntroon: Land Warfare Studies Centre, 2000); Bob Breen, *Mission Accomplished East Timor* (Sydney: Allen and Unwin, 2000); and Moreen Dee, "'Coalitions of the Willing' and Humanitarian Intervention: Australia's Involvement with InterFET," *International Peacekeeping* 8, no. 3 (2001): 1–20.

6. See A/53/951; A/1999/513 Report of the Secretary-General on the Question of East Timor, 5 May 1999 (5 May Agreements), Annex II: Agreement Regarding the Modalities for the Popular Consultation of the East Timorese Through a Direct Ballot. Under Annex 1: Agreement Between the Republic of Indonesia and the Portuguese Republic on the Question of East Timor, the Indonesian government agreed to "take the constitutional steps necessary to terminate its links with East Timor thus restoring . . . the status East Timor held prior to 17 July 1976."

7. See S/RES/1246 (1999), UN Resolution 1246 (1999): Adopted by the Security Council at its 4013th Meeting, 11 June 1999.

8. A list of the pro-integration militias is attached as Annex A. A number of paramilitary-style groups existed in East Timor from the 1980s under Indonesia's civil defense doctrine. The TNI also established and supported other such groups. The foremost of these was ostensibly a social youth group, but it was closely associated with covert activities of the TNI's Special Forces. Although these groups were inactive from the mid-1990s, similar elements emerged as the new so-called militia in mid-1998 as the special autonomy proposal for East Timor became a major political issue. For further information on the militias, see John Martinkus, *A Dirty Little War* (Sydney: Random House, 2001); Harold Crouch, "The TNI and East Timor Policy," in James J. Fox and Donisio Babo Soares, eds., *Out of the Ashes: Destruction and Reconstruction of East Timor* (Adelaide: Crawford House, 2000),

pp. 151–179; and Department of Foreign Affairs and Trade (DFAT), *East Timor in Transition 1998–2000: An Australian Policy Challenge,* Brown and Wilton, Canberra, 2001, pp. 57–61.

9. See Martin, *Self-Determination in East Timor,* pp. 97–101.

10. See S/RES/1264 (1999), UN Resolution 1264 (1999): Adopted by the Security Council at its 4045th Meeting, 15 September 1999.

11. See S/RES/1272 (1999), UN Resolution 1272 (1999): Adopted by the Security Council at Its 4057th Meeting on 25 October 1999; and summary of UNTAET objectives contained in the Secretary-General's Report to the Security Council on the Situation in East Timor, S1999/1024, 4 October 1999 (Annex B). UNTAET's mandate was later extended by S/RES/1338 (2001), UN Resolution 1338 (2001), 30 January 2001.

12. Martin Van Creveld, *The Transformation of War* (New York: Free Press, 1991).

13. Boutros Boutros-Ghali, *An Agenda for Peace: Preventive Diplomacy, Peacemaking and Peacekeeping* (New York: UN Department of Public Information, 1992), pp. 30–31.

14. See footnote 1.

15. For a good overview of coalition difficulties, see Steve Bowman, "Historical and Cultural Influences on Coalition Operation," in Thomas Marshall, Phillip Kaiser, and Jon Kessmeier, eds., *Problems and Solutions in Future Coalition Operations* (Carlisle PA: US Army War College, Strategic Studies Institute, December 1997), pp. 1–21.

16. Brahimi report, par. 10, p. 2.

17. Ibid., par. 48, p. 9.

18. Ibid., pars. 65–75, pp. 12–13. An IMTF was an entity recommended by the Brahimi report as a single point of contact for missions "to turn to for the answers and support that they need, especially in the critical early months when a mission is working towards full deployment and coping with daily crises." See ibid., pars. 198–217, pp. 34–37.

19. A number of countries had provided military officers gratis for duties at UN Headquarters. The departure of these officers was followed in rapid succession by the major expansion of UNAMSIL (Lebanon) and the launches of UNMIK (Kosovo), UNAMET (East Timor), and MONUC (Congo). The Under-Secretary-General DPKO was Bernard Miyet, who was replaced by Jean-Marie Guéhenno in October 2000.

20. A. B. Fetherston, *Towards a Theory of United Nations Peacekeeping* (London: Macmillan, 1994).

21. Ibid., p. 43.

22. Major General Joseph W. Kinzer, *Success in Peacekeeping: United Nations Mission in Haiti: The Military Perspective* (Carlisle PA: U.S. Army Peacekeeping Institute, 1996), p. 1. (Kinzer was subsequently promoted to Lieutenant General.)

23. Lieutenant General Peter Cosgrove, "The Night Our Boys Stared Down the Barrel," *The Age* (Melbourne), 21 June 2000, p. 15.

24. CMA is more commonly referred to in U.S. military doctrine as civil–military cooperation (CIMIC). The term CMA was used by INTERFET and the PKF in East Timor and is therefore used in this study. The importance of CMA is discussed in more detail in subsequent chapters.

25. See F. T. Liu, "Evolution of United Nations Peacekeeping Operations," and Nick Warner, "Cambodia: Lessons of UNTAC for Future Peacekeeping

Operations," in Kevin Clements and Christine Wilson, eds., *UN Peacekeeping at the Crossroads* (Canberra: Peace Research Centre, Australian National University, 1994), pp. 60–75 and 116–131; Ramesh Thakur, "Cambodia, East Timor and the Brahimi Report," *International Peacekeeping* 8, no. 3 (2001), 115–124; and Astri Suhrke, "Peacekeepers as Nation-Builders: Dilemmas of the UN in East Timor," *International Peacekeeping* 8, no. 4 (2001): 1–20.

2

East Timor's Journey to Freedom

> If we were to try to understand why all of this happened, what happened
> to the Jews for centuries, to the Tibetans for the past fifty years, to the
> Kurdish in endless wars, to the East Timorese, I would say, we are all sac-
> rificed in the order of realpolitik, and pragmatism of states.
>
> —José Ramos-Horta[1]

The history of East Timor is marked by foreign intervention, and the struggle of the East Timorese for independence has been marked by violence.[2]
This chapter provides an overview of the major events in East Timor's
modern history, starting with Portugal's colonization and concentrating on
the involvement of the UN since 1997. It focuses on the conduct of the ballot by UNAMET and the key military and security issues in the deployment
of INTERFET.

EAST TIMOR AND ITS PEOPLE

East Timor was formerly known as Portuguese Timor. It is a small territory—19,000 square kilometers in area and approximately 265 kilometers
long and 92 kilometers wide. With a population of less than 1 million people, East Timor is one of the world's poorest countries, with mixed ethnic
groups and no common language. Its history has been greatly influenced by
Portuguese colonial rule and the consequent development of the Roman
Catholic Church.

The island of Timor is located within the Indonesian archipelago, and
East Timor shares a common border with the Indonesian province of West
Timor, which forms the major part of the Indonesian province of
Nusatenggara Timor (see map, p. 15). The Republic of Indonesia inherited
West Timor from the Dutch in 1949 as part of the decolonization process,
but Portuguese Timor continued to exist and operate as a colony. The

boundaries between the two territories were established between the Dutch and Portuguese colonial rulers, but they were not ratified until the Sentence Arbitral was signed in The Hague on 17 August 1916.[3] The colonial borders substantially remain, although delineation in places remains contested by local communities. The demarcation of the international boundary between East Timor and the Republic of Indonesia is still to be determined. East Timor comprises the eastern half of the island, the two offshore islands of Atauro (near Dili) and Jaco (at the eastern tip of the island), and the enclave of Oecussi located on the northern coast of West Timor. A number of Indonesian islands are located near East Timor's north coast. Australia is East Timor's other closest neighbor, being less than two hours flying time by commercial aircraft from Darwin.

East Timor has thirteen districts, including the Oecussi enclave.[4] The geographic peculiarity of the enclave is a result of colonial history. Originally the small town of Lifau in Oecussi was the main Portuguese settlement on Timor. Dili was established as the capital in 1769, when it was considered to offer "better natural protection against surprise attacks, as well as calmer waters for shipping."[5] In moving the capital from Lifau to Dili, it appears that the Portuguese were more fearful of attacks from the mixed race and multilingual Topass community than they were of their Dutch neighbors.[6]

Today Dili is by far the largest city, with an estimated population of around 120,000, having expanded from around 90,000 with the dislocation of the rural population following the postballot destruction in September 1999. Baucau is the next largest town, but the other district capitals have only small populations. The total population is estimated at around 800,000, having grown little since Indonesia's occupation in 1975.

Poverty is widespread among the East Timorese, with consequent low rates of literacy and high death rates. Outside the urban centers, the rural population survives mainly on subsistence farming and a few cash crops. Coffee is the main agricultural export, but the industry is in need of significant modernization. A viable fishing industry is yet to be established. Most revenue is expected to come from petroleum licenses in the Timor Sea under sharing arrangements with Australia.[7] For the foreseeable future, the new nation is likely to remain heavily reliant on international aid for its sustainment and development.

Religion plays an extremely important role in East Timor society and, reflecting Portuguese influence, more than 90 percent of the population is Roman Catholic. Most East Timorese are devout Catholics, although traditional animist practices also coexist within rural communities. East Timor's two bishops and their priests have considerable influence, and the church plays a critical social and moderating role, as it has done throughout the territory's turbulent history. The once vibrant Chinese community, which controlled much of the commerce and wealth during the Portuguese period, declined during Indonesian rule and has yet to be fully reestablished after the postballot violence. A small Muslim community of Arab origin existed in Portuguese times and was considerably enlarged in the days of Indonesian rule, at times experiencing difficulties in being accepted and assimilated by the predominantly Catholic society.[8]

East Timor's mountainous and rugged landscape is captivating and beautiful, though difficult to traverse. The climate is equatorial and tropical, with cooler and more pleasant conditions prevailing in the mountainous hinterland and eastern plateaus. There are distinctive wet and dry seasons. The dry season lasts from May to November and is more pronounced along the northern coast. The eastern and southern districts experience a longer wet season, with heavy rain not uncommon in June and July. The wetness impedes movement considerably. Roads are often cut by landslides and washaways, the rivers quickly become temporarily impassable, and flying conditions are hazardous and unpredictable.

East Timor's infrastructure is underdeveloped. Outside Dili, telecommunications coverage is poor in urban areas and nonexistent for most of the rural population.[9] The fragile road network, considerably developed and extended by the Indonesians, was not maintained in the last years of their administration and was further degraded by heavy military vehicles following the violence.[10] Air services are restricted to a handful of airports and airfields. There are only small port facilities on the north coast and none on the south coast. No rail service or government-owned public transportation system exists.[11] The inefficient power system was totally destroyed in the postballot violence and will take considerable time to be economically reestablished.

The above factors highlight the difficulties involved in maintaining governance and security and in conducting military operations in East Timor. The harsh terrain and isolation of communities helps explain why the Dutch and Portuguese experienced difficulties in totally controlling the remote parts of their colonies, why the land and maritime borders remain porous to infiltration and illegal trading, and why human rights atrocities were not easily reported and recorded. Within disaffected or isolated communities, the environment is ideal for insurgent or guerrilla activity and prone to exploitation by criminal elements. The difficulty in controlling the country also helps explain both the successful guerrilla campaign waged by Australian commandos against the Japanese in 1942 and the inability of the Indonesian military to destroy the Armed Forces for the National Liberation of East Timor (Falintil) resistance fighters during the twenty-four years of Indonesian occupation. The security challenge for the new nation, therefore, will be as much to maintain the trust and confidence of its citizens—to overcome any sense of disaffection or isolation—as it will be to demonstrate economic and social development.

FOREIGN RULERS

Until the UN-supervised ballot for self-determination on 30 August 1999, the history of East Timor reflected foreign rule. Portuguese colonization was followed by a brief Japanese interregnum, which in turn was followed by a return to Portuguese rule and finally Indonesian occupation. Portugal has had a presence in (East) Timor for more than 400 years. In the sixteenth and seventeenth centuries, Portuguese interests in Timor were mainly religious and economic, and a Portuguese military administration was not established in East Timor until the first decade of the eighteenth century. Portuguese Timor comprised a number of kingdoms with distinct traditions, and the people spoke a variety of languages belonging to one of two main language groups: Austronesian and Trans–New Guinea. The only major influence on political and economic matters in the territory, however, was exerted by a small group of Portuguese entrepreneurs, the *mestiços* (mixed-race class), and the Chinese community. Not surprisingly, Timorese heterogeneity complicated the development of a national identity and hindered prospects for achieving national unity.

For the most part, the Portuguese proved to be benign rulers, allowing the traditional system to flourish under a veneer of Portuguese administration. Portuguese was the official language, and the most common of the local languages was Tetun, which by the late nineteenth century had been promoted by the Roman Catholic Church to become the lingua franca.[12] There were occasional rebellions and uprisings against the Portuguese. A central element of Timorese culture is *funu* (struggle/conflict). The largest rebellion took place in 1911–1912 and was put down only after soldiers were sent from Africa. Generally, however, there was only limited animosity toward the colonial rulers and little evidence of the emergence of nationalism or a strong desire for independence. The only uprising against the Portuguese in the postwar period occurred in the Viqueque area in 1959 and was quickly suppressed.[13] But regardless of this acceptance of the Portuguese, evidence suggests that the colonial rulers did little to develop their colony. According to one authoritative report, "As late as 1974 . . . over 90 per cent of the East Timorese population remained illiterate, the territory had but one high school and, with the exception of some paved streets in Dili, all roads in East Timor were unsealed."[14]

Although Portugal remained neutral in World War II, Japan occupied both Dutch and Portuguese Timor during its Pacific campaign following attacks on both Kupang and Dili in February 1942. Australian forces were part of an allied force that intruded into Portuguese Timor's neutrality, ignoring the protests of the governor; these troops were sent to reinforce Timor shortly after the attack on Pearl Harbor, based on anticipation of a Japanese landing.[15] The Japanese invasion forestalled the planned arrival of Portuguese troops in Dili, and Australian troops remained in the territory as a guerrilla force. A number of Australian and Dutch soldiers who avoided capture by the Japanese following the surrender of Kupang crossed the border and joined this force.[16] The Portuguese, but more particularly the East Timorese, assisted these Australian commandos, who were fighting greatly outnumbered and with uncertain logistics support from Australia. Some of the Timorese also fought alongside the Australians. Initially these guerrilla operations were successful, inflicting heavy casualties on the Japanese, but as Japanese pressure increased, operations became more difficult. In face of the cruel retribution taken by the Japanese against the Timorese, local intelligence and support began to dry up and operations were wound down; the Australian and Dutch forces were withdrawn in early December 1942 and January 1943.[17]

Immediately following Japan's surrender to the Allies in 1945, Timor reverted to colonial rule, but the Dutch reign was short lived, with Indonesia gaining its independence in 1949, at which time Dutch Timor became part of the new Indonesian republic. Indonesia initially showed little interest in acquiring Portuguese Timor, but the Suharto regime became increasingly concerned at the prospects of instability following Portugal's Carnation Revolution on 25 April 1974, which led to the overthrow of the authoritarian regime of Marcello Caetano (successor to Oliveira Salazar). President Suharto and the military had come to power in Indonesia in 1966, following the 1965 abortive coup and its violent aftermath, which nullified the communists. The Portuguese revolution, therefore, fueled their fears of a potential left-wing communist government being established on their borders.

In late 1974, a group of senior TNI generals launched Operasi Komodo, a covert operation designed to establish the conditions to justify the incorporation of East Timor into the Republic of Indonesia.[18] Indonesia had already cultivated close relations with the small, and relatively uninfluential, Timorese Popular Democratic Association (Apodeti), which advocated integration with Indonesia. From early 1975, however, Indonesian authorities focused their efforts on winning over the leadership of the more popular right-wing Timorese Democratic Union (UDT). The Indonesian government also indicated that it would not accept self-determination for East Timor if it meant the coming to power of the left-wing Revolutionary Front for an Independent East Timor (Fretilin) which it believed would include communist elements.

The Portuguese administration in Dili, which itself was suffering from neglect and insufficient military capability following Portugal's revolution, attempted to remain neutral between the parties. Preempting Fretilin, and in the hope of averting an Indonesian invasion, the UDT quickly orchestrated a coup and assumed power from the Portuguese administration on 11 August 1975. By 15 August, hostilities had broken out between UDT and Fretilin forces, the latter being reorganized on 20 August with the name of Falintil under Nicolau Lobato as their first commander in chief. Victory for Fretilin was swift and decisive, but in October and November, Fretilin forces came under heavy attack by Indonesian military forces supported by right-wing East Timorese elements in the Bobonaro and Ermera districts. Failing to gain international or UN recognition, and in the face of mounting Indonesian military attacks, Fretilin unilaterally declared independence on 28 November 1975, installing Xavier do Amaral as president. Independence, however, was short lived. The new Fretilin government failed to attract recognition from the other parties or the international community, and on 7 December, the TNI assaulted Dili having already received tacit approval from the United States and Australia.[19] Ignoring UN resolutions reaffirming the right of the East Timorese to self-determination—first from the General Assembly on 12 December, then from the Security Council ten days later, and again from the Security Council on 22 April 1976—Indonesia incorporated East Timor as its twenty-seventh province on 17 July 1976.

In governing their twenty-seventh province, the Indonesian authorities applied methods very different from those of their Portuguese predecessors. They invested heavily in infrastructure, extending and improving the road system, expanding the education and health sectors, and enhancing ferry and air services. Dili's population tripled to around 90,000. Bahasa Indonesia replaced Portuguese as the official language, but Tetun became more widespread. The Catholic Church was allowed to continue operating (as was the case elsewhere throughout the predominantly Muslim republic), but the traditional system, which had been allowed to coexist with the Portuguese administration, was largely subverted and replaced. Although Indonesia enhanced economic development, by 1997 East Timor remained Indonesia's poorest province. Most important, the Indonesians failed to win the confidence of the majority of the East Timorese, and their governance was based on an authoritarian and corrupt military regime that repeatedly committed human rights abuses.[20]

The international community was first alerted to such abuses by reports of the alleged murder by Indonesian-led forces of five Australian-based journalists at Balibo on 16 October 1975. Reviews of this incident occurred periodically throughout the years, partly damaging an otherwise strengthening relationship between Indonesia and Australia.[21] But by far the most concerning accounts of human rights abuses were of atrocities committed by TNI forces against the East Timorese. These reports were impossible to verify, but they were sufficiently strong for James Dunn, former Australian consul in East Timor, to conclude in 1977 that "these accounts of Indonesia's behaviour in East Timor suggest that the plight of these people may well constitute, relatively speaking, the most serious case of contravention of human rights facing the world at this time."[22] On 12 November 1991, one such incident was graphically captured on film when Indonesian troops indiscriminately fired on mourners at the Santa Cruz cemetery in Dili, killing an estimated 150–270 people.[23] Such human rights abuses prevented the Indonesians from gaining the trust and confidence of the people and strengthened East Timorese and international resentment against Indonesia's occupation of the territory. In March 1993, the UN Human Rights Commission censured Indonesia for its poor human rights record in the territory.

FALINTIL AND THE RESISTANCE

Indonesia's sovereignty over East Timor was never agreed upon by most of the international community, and the issue remained unresolved within the UN for the next twenty-four years.[24] The political challenge to Indonesia's occupation of East Timor was persistently and relentlessly mounted by the Timorese who had fled to other countries following the invasion. The best known of these was José Ramos-Horta who, together with Bishop Carlos Filipe Ximenes Belo, was awarded the Nobel Peace Prize in 1996; but there was an equally dedicated group working hard from places like Portugal, Australia, the United States, and Mozambique. The history of the diaspora is yet to be written, and many individual contributions are yet to be acknowledged publicly. Within East Timor, a hard core of patriots secretly continued to report on Indonesia's occupation, while the East Timorese Roman Catholic Church—impressively led by Bishop Carlos Belo and Bishop Basilio do Nascimento—provided spiritual and moral support to their people.

Until the mid-1980s the resistance movement suffered from divisions, especially in the diaspora, reflecting the political lineup during the civil war, as well as some rivalries based on geography. Xanana Gusmão worked hard to bring unity to the resistance in East Timor itself and to structure a nonmilitary, popular opposition to Indonesian rule in the towns and villages. In April 1998, the National Council of Timorese Resistance (CNRT) was formed with representation from almost all parties. Most important, the CNRT brought together Fretilin and the UDT, agreed upon a common strategy for the resistance movement, and selected Xanana Gusmão as its president, despite his incarceration in Jakarta. The creation of the CNRT as a political umbrella group was a significant step in confirming solidarity for the independence cause, and Gusmão's appointment unambiguously established him as the undisputed leader of the independence movement. The CNRT was to play a defining role until well after the establishment of UNTAET.

The tough military fight against the TNI was left to Falintil. The story of its resistance is quite remarkable and requires detailed historical research. In general terms, Falintil operations underwent three separate phases. The first phase involved significant clashes between TNI forces and Falintil, culminating in the massive destruction of Falintil's main position at Base de Apoio on Mount Matabean and the death of its commander, Nicolau Lobato, on 31 December 1978. During this period, Falintil's strength was reduced from around 27,000 to 5,000 as the TNI progressively cleared (from west to east) Falintil from their six major bases to their final base at Matabean. During this phase, and until its forced withdrawals, Falintil controlled much of the population and concentrated on positional defense.

The second phase was from 1979 until Falintil's formal separation from Fretilin in 1987. After a power vacuum following Lobato's death, Xanana Gusmão was promoted to commander in chief in 1981, and in March 1983, an unsuccessful cease-fire with the TNI was attempted. Throughout this phase, Falintil resorted to guerrilla operations and were supported secretly with money and provisions by a large number of the East Timorese population, known as the Rede Clandestina.[25] Unlike most guerrilla movements, however, Falintil had no external support for the provision of weapons and ammunition. In order to survive, its members infiltrated TNI units and conducted exceptionally brave ambushes against stronger forces to acquire weapons and ammunition and so continue Falintil's struggle.

The third phase was from 1987 until the ballot of 1999. At its weakest point in 1987, Falintil numbered only around 100. On 20 August 1987, Gusmão restructured the force, changing it from the armed wing of a political party (Fretilin) into a national army. A recruiting drive was conducted in 1991, but with only modest success. Through Gusmão's efforts, Falintil's strategic vision changed and its existence was reconfirmed, but its operational techniques continued by necessity to follow guerrilla principles. There were similarities between how Falintil and the Australian commandos in World War II conducted operations. Unlike the commandos, however, Falintil established impenetrable mountain bases with excellent observation posts and good communications. Aided by selected clandestine members, the key Falintil commanders also secretly developed a network of safe houses throughout the main urban areas and shifted their main operations to attract attention in Dili and the major towns. It has been estimated that (for periods of time) Indonesia deployed up to 60,000 troops to defeat Falintil. The Indonesians paid a heavy price in casualties and were forced to pursue intensive intelligence operations in order to bribe, threaten, and compromise Falintil and the clandestine sources.[26] In 1992, Gusmão himself was captured at one of the safe houses in Dili and imprisoned in Cipinang Prison in Jakarta. Falintil leadership in the field was taken over by Ma'Huno, but he was detained two months later by the TNI and was then able to continue his resistance only at the political level. Nino Konis Santana was appointed field commander, but he died in 1998 and was replaced by Taur Matan Ruak. Xanana Gusmão, however, continued as commander in chief from prison. By 1998, Falintil was still barely surviving and was operating with few fighters from four regional bases.[27]

PREPARING THE GROUND FOR SELF-DETERMINATION

As mentioned, the UN and most of the international community had not given de jure recognition to Indonesia's sovereignty over East Timor, but until the Asian economic crisis of 1997, there appeared little hope for East Timor's self-determination. The disastrous economic and social consequences to Indonesia of that crisis led directly to the fall of President Suharto and his replacement, on 21 May 1998, by a caretaker president— the somewhat unpredictable and eccentric former vice-president, B. J. Habibie.

Well before the economic crisis, however, the UN had maintained interest in East Timor. From December 1976, the General Assembly annually reaffirmed the right of the East Timorese to self-determination, but as the Cold War continued and Suharto's power strengthened, the Security Council remained disinclined to take action, and prospects for self-determination seemed increasingly remote. In 1983, complying with the General Assembly's Resolution 37/30 of the previous year, the Secretary-General instituted tripartite talks between Indonesia, Portugal, and the UN to review the prospects for settlement. These talks made little progress until after the Asian economic crisis and Suharto's fall in 1998. In February 1997, newly appointed UN Secretary-General Kofi Annan designated Ambassador Jamsheed Marker from Pakistan as his Personal Representative for East Timor. A skilled diplomat with exceptional experience, Marker proved an ideal choice to broker an agreement between Indonesia and Portugal to resolve the long-standing East Timor dilemma. Marker was ably supported in his diplomatic efforts by an energetic and committed team in the Department of Political Affairs (DPA) within the UN Secretariat, led by Francesc Vendrell from Spain, director of the Asia and Pacific Division.

Following President Habibie's statement on his appointment in May 1998 that Indonesia was considering a possible autonomy proposal for the territory, Marker and the UN became closely involved, and negotiations on East Timor intensified. Indonesian foreign minister Ali Alatas officially presented this proposal to the Secretary-General in New York shortly after. Acting quickly, Marker visited Jakarta and East Timor for high-level discussions in July, followed by a constructive tripartite session in August. In September, the UN presented a draft document on proposed autonomy for East Timor, and high-level negotiations aimed at progressing the proposal began in October and continued until late January 1999.

In the meantime, there were both encouraging and worrying signs in relation to security on the ground in East Timor. Throughout 1998 and early 1999, pro-independence activism gathered momentum as did TNI planning to thwart prospects for independence. In September 1998, the Catholic Church organized a successful reconciliation meeting at Dare (near Dili) after which pro-independence activists in the urban areas showed considerable restraint so as not to jeopardize prospects for a peaceful resolution. In the countryside, however, Falintil continued its guerrilla activities against the TNI, which had commenced strengthening the militias and announced, on 5 December, a policy to arm civilian volunteers. In early January, clashes intensified between pro-integration and pro-independence elements in Ainaro and Suai.

Then, on 27 January 1999, Habibie surprised all concerned with his announcement of a referendum for East Timor. Perhaps in a contrary response to a letter received the previous month from Australian prime minister John Howard,[28] the Indonesian government announced that the East Timorese would be offered autonomy within Indonesia and that if this offer was rejected, they would "suggest to the Peoples' Consultative Assembly (MPR), formed as a result of the next elections, to release East Timor from Indonesia."[29] There seems to have been limited discussion on this key decision either within the Indonesian cabinet or with the Indonesian military. This was later to prove crucial when security failed following the ballot. The TNI had a deep psychological and economic commitment to retaining the twenty-seventh province, where its forces had suffered many casualties and where it remained the preeminent force in business and government.[30] Habibie's decision to resolve the East Timor problem, nevertheless, negated any major outstanding issues between the tripartite parties and provided the green light for agreement.

THE 5 MAY AGREEMENTS, UNAMET, AND THE VIOLENCE

On 5 May 1999, the agreements were signed between Indonesia, Portugal, and the UN for the conduct of a UN-supervised ballot, or Popular

Consultation.[31] The ballot allowed for a simple, but secret, accept/reject vote for East Timor becoming a special autonomous region within Indonesia. The tripartite members also agreed that should the people reject the integration option, preparations would be made for East Timor to become independent. In such circumstances, it was further agreed that the UN would accept responsibility for the non–self-governing territory, enabling it to begin the process of transition to independence.[32]

UNAMET was mandated to conduct the ballot under UN Security Council Resolution 1246 on 11 June 1999. Planning was already well advanced, however, with Kofi Annan having appointed Ian Martin from Great Britain as SRSG on 21 May. Martin arrived in Dili on 1 June, ten days before the mandate had been authorized by the Security Council.[33] Despite the short time frame in which to prepare for the vote, the delays caused by security concerns, and the administrative difficulties caused by the physical harshness of the environment and the underdeveloped infrastructure, the ballot was conducted on 30 August.

In terms of planning and execution, UNAMET was an outstanding achievement. An important factor in this was the early selection and deployment of key personnel and the prior planning and preparation that had been conducted by the DPA.[34] Other factors that contributed to the mission's success were the UN's ability to support the mission logistically through assessed contributions, the immediate establishment of a UN Trust Fund, and Indonesia's determination that the ballot go ahead. But much of the credit for the electoral success went to the excellent preparatory work done by the DPA's Electoral Assistance Division, under the capable direction of Carina Perelli from Uruguay. At Perelli's request, considerable assistance was also provided by the Australian Electoral Commission, particularly by Michael Maley, director of Research and International Services. The major undertaking was to arrange the registration and voting, a process further complicated by the need to include the diaspora in a number of approved voting centers around the world. The difficult task on the ground in East Timor itself was accomplished by the chief electoral officer, Jeff Fischer, and his dedicated army of electoral staff.[35] The registration exceeded expectations, with a total of 451,792 approved voters and only 913 rejections (mainly underage). As the environment became increasingly insecure, there were some outstanding displays of professionalism and courage by UNAMET personnel. The real heroes, however, were the East Timorese people, who supported the UN's involvement and voted overwhelmingly for their freedom in the full knowledge that the TNI and POLRI might fail to guarantee their security against pro-Jakarta militia elements.

Given the uncertain security situation in East Timor prior to the ballot, important security questions were raised in the international media and considered by the UN and the CNRT. If security could not be ensured by

Indonesia, then should a PKF be deployed before the ballot? On this issue Indonesia had made it very clear that no foreign troops would be allowed in East Timor. Under the 5 May Agreements, it was Indonesia's responsibility to maintain security, and it remained unwilling to countenance military assistance from others. The role of CIVPOL was purely an advisory one to the Indonesian police, and they were also to supervise the escort of ballot papers and boxes to and from the polling sites. A considerable and protracted effort expended by the DPKO, and ultimately pressed by Marker, finally gained Indonesia's agreement to the deployment of a small number of unarmed military liaison officers (MLOs) as part of UNAMET. This was a hard-won concession, as Indonesia would not even agree to the usual title "military observers" being used, let alone having a PKF deployed alongside its forces. If the preemptive deployment of a PKF was not possible, would it have been better to postpone the ballot until after the election of a new president—one who might exact more commitment from the TNI and POLRI? On this issue there was common agreement between the UN and the CNRT (as well as the core group of interested nations) that to postpone the ballot indefinitely would be to jeopardize it occurring at all. Ian Martin was required to play a mediatory role in overcoming opposition to this view within UNAMET. Gusmão, with the support of the bishops, also succeeded in overcoming any CNRT dissent; and Portugal and Australia were united in ensuring that every advantage of this window of opportunity remained open. In any case, the ballot was the brainchild of President Habibie, who remained determined to have the issue resolved during his presidency.[36] Nonetheless, the UN's involvement was highly supported by the majority of the population. During the twenty-four years of Indonesia's occupation, the UN remained the only realistic hope for achieving self-determination. The East Timorese political leaders were conscious of this reality and were committed to working with the UN, despite differences of opinion on certain issues.

Immediately following the ballot, however, the international community's worst fears were realized when widespread violence erupted as pro-integration militias, organized and supported by elements from the TNI, embarked on a systematic campaign of destruction and terror.[37] The exact number of deaths and other human rights violations remains uncertain, but it has been estimated that the number killed was "greatly in excess of 1,000 persons."[38] Most buildings and utilities were completely destroyed. The Oecussi enclave was razed. The entire population was displaced, and more than 250,000 people were transported under Indonesian and militia control to West Timor, many against their will. Most UNAMET personnel were evacuated to Darwin in two stages, but the chief MLO, Brigadier Rezaqul Haider from Bangladesh, and a small group of UNAMET personnel stoically retained a UN presence in Dili.[39] Considerable disappointment and criticism was leveled at the UN following UNAMET's evacuation, mainly because UNAMET had encouraged the East Timorese to register and vote on the understanding that they would not be "abandoned" by the UN.[40] However, the effective reestablishment of UNAMET coincident with INTERFET's arrival alleviated much of the distress felt by the people, who greatly appreciated the UN's return.

INTERFET AND THE RESTORATION OF SECURITY

The Mandate

Reacting quickly to the violence and total breakdown of law and order, and in response to the outcry of international condemnation, the UN Security Council acted decisively and unanimously to authorize a peace enforcement force under Resolution 1264 of 15 September. The mandate was under Chapter VII of the UN Charter and provided the MNF with "all necessary measures" to restore security and deal forcefully with the militias and other threats. Prudently, it was based on a worst-case threat assessment, and it unambiguously allowed for security to be restored and maintained using all necessary and legitimate force, including the use of deadly force. This was one of the most strongly worded mandates ever given by the Security Council, exceeding the mandate for the establishment of the NATO-led international force in Kosovo, which had preceded it in June. It specified three tasks for the MNF: "to restore peace and security in East Timor, to protect and support UNAMET in carrying out its tasks[41] and, within force capabilities, to facilitate humanitarian assistance operations."

Ultimately, this mandate was feasible and achievable, and its implementation was swift and highly successful. The structure of the MNF was based on preparatory planning that had been completed by the UN Secretariat's DPKO. The 5 May Agreements had required the orderly handover of security from Indonesia to the UN in the case of rejection of the autonomy proposal. DPKO had, therefore, already derived a force structure and commenced discussions with member states for possible contributions. This information was readily shared with Australia and became the start-state for INTERFET's planning, particularly since the MNF was mandated as an interim force and would subsequently transition to a UN PKF.

Force Structure and Operations

As already noted, INTERFET was capably led by Major General Peter Cosgrove, an experienced and highly decorated infantry officer from Australia. Australia was the logical country to lead this force, having for many years maintained ready deployable forces for a range of short-notice contingencies throughout the region. But Australia's willingness to lead the coalition was conditional on Indonesian consent, which the UN eventually acquired.[42] Both Indonesia and Australia were keen, in fact, to ensure that INTERFET's deployment was successful and that military action to restore security would not inadvertently lead to conflict between INTERFET and the Indonesian security forces still deployed in East Timor. From 14 to 16 September, high-level military discussions were conducted at the UN Secretariat in New York between Indonesia and Australia to ensure that procedures were in place and that the two field commanders, Major General Cosgrove and Major General Kiki Syahnakri, were in agreement and committed to the success of the operation.[43]

INTERFET began its deployment in Dili on 20 September. By the end of September, the force headquarters was fully operational in the burnt-out public library in Dili, and more than 4,000 troops had been deployed. In the first six weeks of its deployment, INTERFET progressively restored security in all districts, assuming de facto responsibility for governance and the rule of law until the UN's presence could be effectively reestablished. By 1 November, a force of over 8,200 was operating throughout the entire country (including the Oecussi enclave), and security had been totally restored. As the coalition strengthened and more forces arrived, INTERFET continued to maintain security, countered militia activity, and maintained liaison with the TNI to manage the border following the TNI's final withdrawal from East Timor on 1 November. Twenty-two countries contributed to INTERFET, which at its zenith numbered around 11,000 troops. As the lead nation, Australia provided the core element of the force headquarters, much of the aviation and logistics support, and approximately 5,000 troops.

In the initial stages of deployment, INTERFET's combat power came mainly from Australia's 3rd Brigade and the Special Air Services Regiment, both of which had trained together since the early 1980s for a range of short-notice contingencies. Since World War I, the Australian and New Zealand armies had established and maintained a strong relationship, and during recent years the New Zealand army had regularly provided a battalion for combined exercises with 3rd Brigade.[44] Accordingly, a "Kiwi" battalion was quickly added to the force. Additional infantry troops included a British Gurkha company from Brunei and a Canadian company. There was also the added advantage that these countries, along with the United States, which provided logistics support and intelligence capabilities, had worked closely together over many years as part of the combined armies "ABCA" interoperability program.[45] To this core were added capable forces from France, Italy, Korea, Thailand, and the Philippines, all of which greatly strengthened the coalition and sent a potent political, as well as military, message to the militias and their supporters. Toward the end of

INTERFET's operation, a company group from Kenya, a battalion from Jordan, and medical staff from Egypt were successfully deployed in preparation for transition to the PKF.

INTERFET was well provided with combat support and combat service support capabilities. Australia took the lead in these areas, giving high priority to logistics and emphasizing the importance of CMA and public relations. The speed and success of INTERFET's tactical operations was largely due to the capable air and maritime assets that were deployed quickly to East Timor. Helicopters and landing craft proved invaluable in executing and sustaining tactical operations. Logistics support was provided by strategic air and sea lift, principally from Darwin, by a number of coalition partners but principally by Australia and the United States. Having been requested not to deploy ground forces at this stage, Portugal made a significant contribution with the positioning of a Hercules C130 aircraft and a naval surface combatant in Darwin. As the operation continued, INTERFET progressively replaced military support capabilities with civil contracts in preparation for the transition to the PKF, including in the sensitive area of communications.

INTERFET's operational concept, referred to as an "oil spot" strategy, was based on the principle of methodically reinforcing success in a step-by-step approach commensurate with the buildup of forces. Dili was secured first, and then the regional centers, with troops continually expanding from the various oil spots until the entire territory had been pacified. The Oecussi enclave was the final district to be occupied, on 22 October 1999, after which INTERFET could claim to have restored security throughout the entire territory. The eastern districts remained free of militia activity, but sporadic incidents continued for some time in the western districts and in Oecussi. The Australian military analyst and historian Alan Ryan notes that initially General Cosgrove's oil spot strategy "was criticised in the media and even from within the coalition for what was seen as an overly cautious approach, but the strategy was later fully justified."[46] There is little doubt that with the limited forces at his disposal, Cosgrove moving more quickly would have been too risky, both for his own forces and for the confidence of the coalition that was still being formed. The proof of the effectiveness of INTERFET's operations is that no battle fatalities were sustained and only two nonbattle fatalities occurred during the force's five-month deployment. At the same time, INTERFET fully restored security and earned high respect from their East Timorese hosts. The reasons for these outcomes are to be found in the professional standards of all the elements of the multinational operation.

These same standards ensured the development of a constructive relationship between all parties involved in restoring security throughout the territory and assisting a shattered population. Throughout its deployment,

INTERFET established and maintained close relations with UNAMET and the East Timorese leaders—and subsequently with UNTAET as it became established. In addition, Cosgrove and Syahnakri expended considerable effort to ensure the maintenance of professional military relations between INTERFET and the TNI. Until Indonesia's final withdrawal on 1 November, these efforts were focused on preventing inadvertent conflict between the two forces. Priority was later given to establishing border modalities aimed at countering militia infiltration from West Timor and avoiding conflict between the Indonesian and INTERFET forces deployed along the border. Cosgrove's task was aided by the operational flexibility within the theater granted to him by Defence Headquarters in Canberra, which kept him regularly informed of higher strategic developments. He was greatly assisted, however, by the close personal relations he quickly established with all coalition commanders, particularly with his deputy, Major General Songkitti Jaggabattara from Thailand. In return for acknowledging and respecting the conditions imposed by coalition partners regarding the conduct of operations, the INTERFET commander received, and could rely on, their loyalty and support in fulfilling the mission's objectives.

As an example of peace intervention, INTERFET's deployment was rapid and highly successful. INTERFET's speed of action marks a significant milestone in the history of peace enforcement operations, all the more remarkable because of the limited port and airfield infrastructure available for the buildup of the force.[47] The speed and success of the operation was greatly assisted, however, by the INTERFET Trust Fund. The major contribution to this fund came from Japan's pledge of U.S.$100 million, but taking the lead and responding as quickly as it did, Australia accepted the financial risk that reimbursement for its expenditure would have to be justified later against the conditions of the fund. Notwithstanding all the external factors that contributed to the restoration of security in East Timor, a number of conditions existed on the ground that contrived to facilitate INTERFET's task.

Falintil

A major factor that contributed to alleviating the burden on the MNF to restore and maintain security was the behavior of Falintil. This was exemplary throughout the period of violence in the lead-up to, and following, the ballot. In preparation for the ballot, and as a mark of good faith in the peace process, the resistance force cantoned itself in four locations[48] and agreed not to conduct military operations or carry weapons outside these cantonments. But fearing both TNI and militia action, Falintil refused requests to disarm and surrender its weapons, and as the militia rampage gained momentum, force numbers increased rapidly to around 1,500–2,000. Nonetheless, led impressively by Taur Matan Ruak, Falintil kept to its agreement and its actions quickly won the respect of UNAMET. In an amazing act of restraint and strategic vision, Ruak resisted calls from some of his field commanders to fight the militias. Backing the wishes of his commander in chief, Xanana Gusmão, and further requests from José Ramos-Horta, Ruak ordered his commanders to remain cantoned and to ensure their own security in readiness for the next phase of operations.

This strategy of disengagement was a most difficult decision, particularly given that Falintil's support came from the civilian population that was being so cruelly treated by the militias. Ruak's decision was predicated on the belief that the militia violence was being orchestrated by TNI elements, partly for reasons of deniability but primarily to force Falintil to engage the militias in order to give the appearance of a "civil war," similar to what had occurred in 1975. As difficult as it was for Falintil to remain disengaged, Ruak never lost sight of the crucial fact that the Indonesian army was in the process of leaving East Timor, and he assessed that to take action would further escalate the violence and jeopardize future prospects for international support. Following INTERFET's arrival, Falintil centralized and relocated to a single cantonment at Aileu (50 kilometers south of Dili), where its members displayed admirable discipline and endured considerable hardship, initially living in extremely poor conditions until humanitarian assistance and funding could be authorized by UNTAET. Falintil showed itself to be a disciplined and compliant force—a factor unusual in postconflict situations—and its disengagement from the postballot violence and its cooperation with the MNF can only be described as invaluable to the maintenance of a secure environment.

Disarmament and Separation of Combatants

The success or failure of UN interventions to achieve and maintain a secure environment often rests on two important requirements: effective disarmament and separation of combatants. The main military threat in East Timor came from the two opposing sides at the time of the ballot: the pro-integration militias that had been created and supported by the TNI, and the Falintil resistance fighters with their twenty-four-year history of fighting the TNI.

Unlike most postconflict situations, disarmament did not present a huge problem in East Timor. During the postballot violence, most armaments were held by the militias. These were a mix of small arms, grenades, and homemade weapons. Falintil was also armed with a modest number of light weapons and grenades. Neither the militias nor Falintil possessed heavy weapons, nor was there evidence of landmines. The militias took most of their arsenal to West Timor, and INTERFET quickly confiscated all other weapons but permitted Falintil to remain armed within specified cantonments. There were occasional incidents of handguns being used by criminal elements, but this practice was not widespread. In this sense, East Timor quickly became a less lethal society than many "peaceful" and developed countries. There were several reasons for this situation: first, East Timor's physical remoteness and isolation mitigated against an arms buildup; second, apart from their own forces, Indonesia had prevented the widespread circulation of weapons during its occupation; and, third, Falintil was never able to establish an external pipeline for the provision of armaments and was forced to rely on old Portuguese weapons and what it could capture from the TNI. In summary, an arms race between combatants never eventuated in East Timor.

The separation of combatants was simplified by the militias' response to the deployment of the MNF in the wake of the widespread and systematic violence and destruction perpetrated by the pro-integration forces following the ballot. With the arrival of INTERFET, the militias quickly fled East Timor and reestablished themselves in the refugee camps in West Timor. Therefore, compared with many postconflict environments, the desired separation was quickly achieved and the possibility of renewed conflict was reduced. The problem of militia infiltration, however, remained for the UN forces. Because INTERFET and UNTAET had no mandate to operate across the border, the control of the militia there relied totally on action taken by the Indonesian authorities. Such action was slow to occur, and militia infiltration and sporadic attacks continued well into the UNTAET period (see Chapter 3).

HUMANITARIAN ASSISTANCE AND DISPLACED PEOPLE

In the burnt-out ruins of East Timor in September 1999, the need for coordinated humanitarian assistance was real. More than sixty humanitarian organizations (including some twenty-three UN agencies) became active in providing humanitarian assistance, and coordination between these groups was critical. This priority was clearly stated by the Security Council in Article 2 of Resolution 1264, which emphasized "the urgent need for coordinated humanitarian assistance and the importance of allowing full, safe and unimpeded access by humanitarian organisations." The resolution also called upon "all parties to cooperate with such organisations so as to ensure the protection of civilians at risk, the safe return of refugees and displaced persons and the effective delivery of humanitarian aid."

Working as part of UNAMET initially, the lead in this was taken by the UN's Office for the Coordination of Humanitarian Affairs (OCHA), which quickly established a UN Humanitarian Operations Centre (UNHOC). Key among the humanitarian assistance organizations was the World Food Programme (WFP), which assumed responsibility for the delivery of much-needed emergency food relief. Due to security implications, close collaboration was also established with the MNF. INTERFET's mission was to restore peace and security, but the UN mandate also required the MNF "to facilitate humanitarian assistance operations within force capabilities." Australia had only limited expertise in this area, but General Cosgrove was well aware of the problems that had occurred in Somalia and the need for close cooperation with humanitarian agencies. Realizing the importance of CMA, he made provision for a small Civil-Military Operations Centre (CMOC) to prioritize requests for MNF assistance. To enhance its effectiveness, the CMOC was augmented by an experienced U.S. Army civil affairs detachment. Cosgrove was also careful not to take control from UNAMET and OCHA and was keen to provide humanitarian organizations with as much latitude and independence as the security situation would permit. The INTERFET commander never lost sight of his primary security mission, and he was careful to ensure that the provision of humanitarian assistance by an interim force did not overstretch his resources or create dependencies that could not be replicated when the MNF departed.

A major problem in East Timor following the ballot in 1999 was the dislocation of around 70 percent of the total population (well over 500,000 people). Although this figure was numerically lower than those for many other countries facing a similar plight, proportionate to total population it was higher than most. Despite the major difficulties presented by the total devastation of East Timor and its rudimentary infrastructure, overall the resettlement of people was handled very professionally by a variety of agencies. The successful outcome of their efforts was aided by and largely due to the discipline and cooperation of the East Timorese people. UNHCR demonstrated positive leadership in resettling the displaced population, which included internally displaced persons (IDPs), refugees, and returnees. Although a range of security and personnel problems arose, the close coordination forged between UNHCR and INTERFET, and later UNTAET, ensured that these were quickly and satisfactorily resolved.[49] The absence of subsequent difficulties within the East Timorese community is tribute to the willingness of the East Timorese people to assist in the reconciliation and rehabilitation process.

Two particular issues faced the people of East Timor and the international community. The first was the resettlement of the large number of displaced people (both internally displaced and returnees) within East Timor. In terms of numbers this was the major task, but with the restoration of security by INTERFET, the people began to return to their areas and rebuild their shattered lives. INTERFET, and also later the PKF, demon-

strated that if military forces maintained a visible presence, then the traumatized population would slowly gain confidence and gradually return to
their home locations.[50] Due to the widespread devastation, however, Dili
attracted many people in search of protection, food, and shelter.[51] The second problem was the return of refugees from West Timor. This was a more
difficult task that became a major undertaking for UNTAET from the time
it took over from UNAMET in November 1999. UNTAET's role is discussed in more detail in Chapter 3.

CONCLUSION

East Timor's journey to freedom was complex, long, and arduous. It is a
story of a stoic and courageous people who refused to give in. It is also a
sad story, replete with violence, death, and enormous suffering. At time of
writing, this journey is yet to be completed, and the future longevity of a
stable and secure environment cannot be guaranteed. Much of East Timor's
tragedy was the result of foreign rule and international power politics.
Ironically, its ultimate triumph will largely depend on strong international
recognition and assistance. A number of unpredicted external events shaped
the path to independence: rapid decolonization after World War II, the
Portuguese revolution of 1974, the end of the Cold War, the Asian economic crisis of 1997, and finally the decision by a caretaker Indonesian president in 1999 to offer autonomy or independence.

Throughout the twenty-four years of Indonesian rule, the UN provided
a forum for the East Timorese to keep their dream for self-determination
before the international community. Although no action was taken to support this quest during this period, the UN moved quickly to provide the
means by which self-determination could be realized once the first step was
offered by Indonesia. UNAMET was an outstanding achievement, particularly considering the short preparation period, the underdeveloped and
harsh physical environment, and the unpredictable security situation. Good
planning and speed of action enabled a complex operation to be successfully conducted in three months from time of arrival in country. Yet the final
success of the ballot rested with the courage of the East Timorese who
voted for their freedom in the knowledge that their security could not be
guaranteed. INTERFET's success in assembling and deploying to restore
security quickly was equally impressive. Aided by the separation of combatants and the cooperation of the TNI, the speed and professionalism with
which the MNF brought order and stability to a chaotic situation provides a
useful model for future interventions. INTERFET's achievement provided
the necessary platform for the work of UNTAET, which is discussed in
detail in Chapter 3.

NOTES

1. José Ramos-Horta, "Democracy and Diplomacy in the Asia–Pacific Region," address to the Nobel Peace Laureates Conference on Human Rights, Conflict and Reconciliation, University of Virginia, Charlottesville, 5–6 November 1998, in Jeffrey Hopkins, ed., *The Art of Peace* (New York: Snow Line, 2000), p. 34.

2. An excellent overview of East Timor's history and culture is contained in James Dunn, *Timor: A People Betrayed* (Sydney: ABC Books, 1996).

3. See James J. Fox, "Tracing the Path, Recounting the Past: Historical Perspectives on Timor," in James J. Fox and Dionisio Babo Soares, eds., *Out of the Ashes: Destruction and Reconstruction of East Timor* (Adelaide: Crawford House, 2000), p. 16.

4. East Timor's districts, islands, and borders are shown on the map on p. 15.

5. Dunn, *People Betrayed,* p. 15.

6. For accounts of Portuguese and Dutch conquests and rivalry in Timor and adjacent islands, see ibid., pp. 13–14; and Fox, "Tracing the Path," pp. 6–18. The Topasses were the offspring of Portuguese soldiers, sailors, and traders who inter-married with local Timorese women. They were also known as the "Black Portuguese" and often referred to generally as *mestiços.*

7. The Timor Sea Arrangement between Australia and East Timor was initialed in Dili on 5 July 2001 giving East Timor 90 percent of the revenues from oil and gas reserves. On 21 December 2001, the East Timor Transitional Government and Phillips Petroleum reached an understanding on allowing gas development in the Timor Sea to proceed. It has been estimated that revenues from the Bayu–Udun area in particular will be U.S.$2.5–3 billion over the life of the field.

8. UNTAET reaffirmed its commitment that all social, religious, and ethnic groups would enjoy exactly the same rights and benefits, including protection by the authorities, following acts of violence and harassment against the Muslim community living in the Anur mosque in Dili on 1–2 January 2001. In addition to UNTAET's efforts to bring an end to the intimidation suffered by this community, Bishop Belo, Xanana Gusmão, and José Ramos-Horta have all repeatedly urged that the well-being and safety of the mosque's residents be respected. UNTAET daily press release, 3 January 2001. Available online at http://www.un.org/peace/etimor (accessed 17 December 2001).

9. Except for the UNTAET communications system and mobile phone access in a limited number of locations, there is no telecommunications coverage outside Dili.

10. In 2000, the Asian Development Bank assessed that road damage caused by INTERFET and PKF forces would require an additional U.S.$25 million to restore.

11. Privately owned buses and taxis ply the streets of Dili and the rural roads.

12. Fox, "Tracing the Path," p. 23.

13. See Geoffrey C. Gunn, "The Five-Hundred-Year Timorese *Funu,*" in Richard Tanter, Mark Selden, and Stephen R. Shalom, eds., *Bitter Flowers, Sweet Flowers: East Timor, Indonesia and the Word Community* (Sydney: Rowman & Littlefield, 2001), pp. 3–14; and Dunn, *People Betrayed*, pp. 16–17, 28–29.

14. Annex to the Report of the Special Committee with regard to the Implementation of the Declaration on the Granting of Independence to Colonial

Countries and Peoples: Chapter VIII Territories Under Portuguese Administration, A/10023/Add. 1, 20 November 1975-A/AC.109/L.1015.

15. In February 1941, Australia agreed with Dutch and British officials that Allied troops would be needed to reinforce Timor should Japan enter the war, given the island's proximity to Australia and the fact that Japanese and Australian forces would by then be fighting each other in other locations. (Sparrow Force, as the allied presence on Timor was known, was part of a strategy of defending forward airfields, which also involved deploying Lark Force at Rabaul and Gull Force at Ambon.) Portugal protested vigorously against the Dutch/Australian intervention in December 1941 as a violation of its neutrality. Albeit reluctantly on both sides, Portugal and Britain subsequently agreed that the troops could remain, but only until a contingent of Portuguese forces arrived from Mozambique. The allied intervention, nonetheless, made Japanese invasion of Portuguese Timor more likely.

16. Force numbers were approximately 400 Australians and 200 Dutch.

17. Australian commandos from Z Special Unit and Australian-trained Timorese continued to land and operate in Timor but, unknown to Australian authorities, the operations were soon compromised. Successive landing groups were quickly captured. The Australian operations in Timor throughout 1942 had little positive strategic value, but they demonstrated the effectiveness of guerrilla tactics against the Japanese. See Bernard (later Sir Bernard) Callinan, *Independent Company: The 2/2 and 2/4 Australian Independent Companies in Portuguese Timor, 1941–1943* (Melbourne: Heinemann, 1953); and Benjamin Evans, "Australian Operations in Timor 1942–1943," *Wartime*, no. 10, (autumn 2000): 28–29.

18. See Dunn, *People Betrayed,* pp. 78–89, 99–107.

19. Historical research indicates fairly conclusively that Australia and the United States were aware of Indonesia's plans to invade East Timor and took no firm steps to prevent it. See James Cotton, "'Part of the Indonesian World'": Lessons in East Timor Policy-Making, 1974–76," *Australian Journal of International Affairs* 55, no. 1 (2001): 119–131; Dunn, *People Betrayed,* chaps. 7, 9; "East Timor Revisited: Ford, Kissinger and the Indonesian Invasion, 1975–76," in William Burr and Michael L. Evans, *National Security Archive Electronic Briefing Book No. 62,* December 2001. Available online at http://www.gwu.edu/~nsarchiv (accessed 8 January 2002); and DFAT, *Australia and the Indonesian Incorporation of Portuguese Timor 1974–1976* (Melbourne: Melbourne University Press, 2000).

20. Peter Carey and G. Carter Bentley, eds., *East Timor at the Crossroads: The Forging of a Nation* (London: Cassell, 1995); and Dunn, *People Betrayed*, chap. 10.

21. For a detailed account, see Desmond Ball and Hamish McDonald, *Death in Balibo, Lies in Canberra* (Sydney: Allen and Unwin, 2000).

22. James Dunn, *The East Timor Situation: Report on Talks with Timorese Refugees in Portugal* (Canberra: Legislative Research Service, Australian Parliament, 1977). See also Carmel Budiardjo and Liem Soei Liong, *The War Against East Timor* (London: Zed Books, 1984); and John Taylor, *Indonesia's Forgotten War: The Hidden History of East Timor* (London: Zed Books, 1991).

23. For a succinct summary of this incident, see DFAT, *East Timor in Transition*, pp. 7–8.

24. Australia was the only country to give formal recognition, but it can be argued that thirty-one other countries gave implied recognition. For a discussion on this, see ibid., pp. 12–13.

25. The organizations of internal opposition working with Falintil were usually referred to as the Rede Clandestina (Clandestine Network), but also as Frente

Clandestina (Clandestine Front) or Resistência Clandestina (Clandestine Resistance).

26. Indonesian control was confined to the main towns and villages, and although Indonesian military casualties remain unknown, some estimates place them as high as 10,000 for the period 1976–1980. Estimates for East Timorese deaths from military action, famine, and disease range 10–20 percent higher for the same period. See Adam Schwarz, *A Nation in Waiting: Indonesia in the 1990s* (Sydney: Allen and Unwin, 1994).

27. Region I covered the districts of Lautem and Viqueque and was commanded by Lere Anan Timor. Region II was commanded by Taur Matan Ruak, covering Dili, Baucau, and Manatuto. Region III was commanded by Falur Rate Laek with responsibility for Manufahi, Ainaro, and part of Cova Lima. Region IV was commanded by Ular Rihik with responsibility for Liquiça, Ermera, Bobonaro, and part of Cova Lima. See Dionisio Babo Soares, "Political Developments Leading to the Referendum," in Fox and Babo Soares, *Out of the Ashes*, p. 62.

28. Howard's letter had not specifically advocated autonomy or independence but rather a process similar to the Matignon Accords in New Caledonia. Habibie reacted adversely to this proposal. For a summary, see DFAT, *East Timor in Transition*, pp. 29–33.

29. Ibid., p. 38. The announcement was made by the information minister, Yunus Yosfiah, who had served as a junior military commander in East Timor and had been implicated in the death of five Australian-based journalists at Balibo in October 1975.

30. See John B. Haseman, "East Timor: The Misuse of Military Power and Misplaced Military Pride," in Fox and Babo Soares , *Out of the Ashes*, pp. 180–191.

31. An excellent account of this period is covered in Ian Martin, *Self-Determination in East Timor: The United Nations, the Ballot, and International Intervention* (Boulder, CO: Lynne Rienner, 2001).

32. The complete 5 May Agreements are contained in DFAT, *East Timor in Transition*, pp. 191–209; and Martin, *Self-Determination in East Timor*, pp. 141–148.

33. The delay with the mandate was caused by the U.S. requirement to consult Congress. This delay, however, did not affect proceedings because concurrent planning and deployment were already well advanced. The spokesperson and head of public information, David Wimhurst, was in place before Martin's arrival, and other key staff (police commissioner [Álan Mills], chief electoral officer [Jeff Fischer], chief military liaison office [Brigadier Rezaqul Haider], political officer [Beng Yong Chew], and chief administrative officer [Johannes Wortel]) gradually followed.

34. The DPA had an excellent team of political analysts who, under the leadership of Under-Secretary-General Sir Kieran Prendergast and the director for Asia and the Pacific, Francesc Vendrell, had worked closely over a long period with PRSG Jamsheed Marker.

35. The electoral staff in East Timor comprised seventeen core professionals and over 400 UN volunteers, supported by 600 local staff whose numbers expanded to 4,000 on ballot day.

36. No doubt historians and political scientists will analyze for many years the timing of the ballot and the prevailing security situation in August 1999 as further information about this period gradually becomes available.

37. See Parliament of the Commonwealth of Australia, *Final Report of the Senate Foreign Affairs, Defence and Trade References Committee: East Timor,*

December 2000, pp. 92–95; Martinkus, *A Dirty Little War* (Sidney: Random House, 2001); Peter Bartu, "The Militia, the Military, and the People of Bobonaro District," *Bulletin of Concerned Asian Scholars* 32, nos. 1–2 (2000): 35–42; and James Dunn, "Crimes Against Humanity in East Timor, January to October 1999: Their Nature and Causes," unpublished UN Report, 2001. Available online at http://www. etan.org/news/2001a/dunn1.htm (accessed 9 January 2002).

38. Dunn, "Crimes Against Humanity," p. 20.

39. Eighty personnel stayed on after the first withdrawal on 10 September, but all, with the exception of Haider and his group, were evacuated four days later. Martin, *Self-Determination in East Timor*, p. 100–101.

40. A small UNAMET presence was maintained throughout, but in the minds of the people, the UN had evacuated—and deserted them in their hour of need.

41. This protection was extended to UNTAET when it took over from UNAMET on 25 October 1999, until the MNF's transition to the PKF on 23 February 2000.

42. The United States and the International Monetary Fund (IMF) provided heavyweight support for the UN in acquiring Indonesian consent. The United States warned of the fiscal consequences to Indonesia of noncompliance with the Security Council resolution, and the IMF linked Indonesian access to funding to compliance. See Bill Hayden, "Defence After Timor," *Quadrant* 44, no. 78 (2000): 18–23.

43. The key Indonesian delegates were Lieutenant General Soesilo Bambang Yudhoyono and Rear Admiral Yoost Mengko. Australia's key delegates were Martin Brady and the author.

44. From troops fighting together as part of the Australian and New Zealand Army Corps in Turkey in World War I, an ANZAC legend was born that has been sustained over many generations. In remembrance of all those who have served, died, and suffered in war, ANZAC Day is commemorated by both nations annually on 25 April.

45. The ABCA armies interoperability program is comprised of the United States, Great Britain, Canada, and Australia. New Zealand has observer status.

46. Ryan, *Primary Responsibilities and Primary Risks: Australian Defence Force Participation in the International Force East Timor,* Study Paper No. 304 (Duntroon: Land Warfare Studies Centre, 2000), p. 73.

47. Dili provided the only port facilities for lodgment and buildup. These facilities were rudimentary and allowed only two ships at any one time. Only two airfields existed for lodgment: Dili and Baucau. The Dili airfield could not take military aircraft above C130 Hercules. Baucau airfield was more capable but was isolated at several kilometers from Baucau township. The roads from Dili and Baucau to the districts were subject to frequent closure, particularly after rain. No land corridor existed to the Oecussi enclave, which had to be supported by helicopter, small fixed-wing aircraft, and landing craft.

48. Region I cantoned at Atelari in Baucua district; Falintil Headquarters and Regions II and III at Waimori in the northern area of Viqueque district; and Region IV at two locations, Ermera and Suai.

49. UNHCR chief of mission for UNTAET was Nellie Chan (Singapore). She was preceded and ably assisted by her chief of operations, Bernard Kerblat (France), who subsequently succeeded her as chief of mission. Kerblat's personal commitment and involvement with INTERFET and the PKF on refugee and returnee issues was outstanding.

50. Many East Timorese would return to their destroyed villages only if a mil-

itary presence was visible, which required INTERFET, and later the PKF, to deploy military detachments in deserted villages.

51. Cedric de Coning, "The UN Transitional Administration in East Timor (UNTAET): Lessons Learned from the First 100 Days," *International Peacekeeping* 6, no. 2 (2000): 85, maintains that the "September 1999 violence disrupted the agricultural cycle, destroyed most of the agricultural tools, including tractors and trained animals, and destroyed the seed stock and food reserves."

3

UNTAET and the Path to Independence

The mandate given by the Security Council . . . to establish a national civil administration, assist in the development of civil and social services and support capacity-building for self-government was unprecedented .
—Kofi Annan, 2001[1]

The declaration of the results of the ballot was followed by a wave of violence and destruction that rendered the political and military situation in East Timor volatile and unstable. UN intervention was now needed to alleviate the plight of the East Timorese people and to guide the territory to independence. The previous chapter provided an overview of the major events in East Timor's modern history, including the UNAMET and INTERFET missions. This chapter now considers the UNTAET period as the transitional administration.

ESTABLISHING THE MISSION

On 25 October 1999, the Security Council authorized the establishment of UNTAET under Resolution 1272 (see Annex B), and the Secretary-General appointed the highly regarded Sergio Vieira de Mello from Brazil as SRSG. UNTAET's purpose, in partnership with the East Timorese, was to administer the non-self-governing territory and prepare it for independence. But it was also mandated to conduct a number of specific tasks, including the provision of security and the maintenance of law and order. Although this was not the first occasion on which the UN had acted in a transitional capacity, the depth and breadth of its responsibilities in East Timor surpassed previous missions. Here, in addition to an uncertain security situation, the infrastructure was almost totally destroyed and the population dislocated. To all intent, UNTAET was to be the de jure government of a broken country.

UNTAET assumed responsibility from UNAMET in November 1999, inheriting a small number of experienced UNAMET personnel and what remained of its equipment. INTERFET continued to guarantee security until arrangements for a UN PKF could be finalized, but they remained separate from UNTAET with General Cosgrove and Vieira de Mello working in close collaboration. However, in contrast to UNAMET and INTER-FET, UNTAET was slow to get started. The UN Secretariat's resources had been fully committed to the ballot and then to authorizing the MNF. From the signing of the 5 May Agreements (where it was predicated) to the ballot on 30 August, little detailed planning was undertaken to establish a transitional administration. Most of the planning had focused on the military component, with some being undertaken on the requirements for CIVPOL. Virtually no planning occurred regarding the composition and responsibilities of the civil administration and the manner in which UNTAET would work in partnership with the East Timorese. This inadequate situation arose, and was compounded, within the Secretariat, where uncertainty remained for some time as to whether it was the DPA or the DPKO that would take the lead.[2] The DPKO was not confirmed in this role until September. From that point intensive planning did take place, but it took time to identify and select key personnel and staff.

The deployment and speed of action by UNTAET therefore fell short of the swift implementation of the UNAMET and MNF mandates. SRSG Vieira de Mello arrived in Dili on 16 November, but many of his key staff and much of the logistic support did not arrive until the early months of 2000. This slow deployment directly reflected the lack of detailed planning by the Secretariat during the previous months and served to compound the initial difficulties experienced in establishing the mission. Although fewer imperatives for speed applied to UNTAET, the slowness in assembling and resourcing the mission did not help in building confidence with the East Timorese. UNTAET soon began to attract criticism from them as well as from some members of the mission itself and the international media.[3]

THE INDONESIAN POSITION

Before addressing the UNTAET period, it is important to understand the critical role Indonesia played as the former governing power. In a practical sense, UNTAET's task was made more difficult because of Indonesia's inability, or unwillingness, to prevent the postballot violence and destruction. On the other hand, Indonesia's acceptance of the ballot outcome removed the major political obstacle to UNTAET achieving its mission.

Most analyses of the East Timor crisis see Indonesia—and more particularly the TNI—as the unwelcome invader and perpetrator of significant human rights violations. While there is evidence to support this view,[4] consideration should also be given to the fact that it was President Habibie who proposed and then agreed to the UN-sponsored ballot at a time of real political change taking place in Indonesia following the fall of the Suharto regime. This readjustment of the Indonesian government's policies on East Timor in 1999 provided legitimacy for the UN's intervention—even if these policies were not always properly implemented, and were even undermined, by Indonesian security forces and East Timorese pro-integrationists. In the wake of the postballot violence, whatever the degree of international or bilateral pressure brought to bear, Indonesia agreed to the deployment of the MNF to restore security. Further, although the Indonesian government indicated a preference for an Asian nation to lead the force, it did not attempt to impose conditions on the force's makeup or to stonewall Australia's leadership when this was announced.

Since that time, successive Indonesian presidents—Habibie, Wahid, and Megawati Sukarnoputri—consistently acknowledged East Timor's independence and the legitimate role of the UN as transitional administrators. The TNI, once INTERFET was deployed, also cooperated in a joint effort to prevent the escalation of hostilities. The relationship established between the TNI and INTERFET/PKF leadership greatly assisted the containment of the militia problem, even if it did not succeed in fully resolving it. This cooperation enabled joint border control mechanisms to be put in place to reduce the possibility of border clashes. Three important areas in which Indonesia was slow to act, however, were in resolving the refugee/militia problem in West Timor; bringing to trial those Indonesians accused of human rights violations; and demarcating the land and maritime borders.

Nevertheless, in terms of international dispute resolution, and considering Indonesia's pressing domestic political and economic problems, the situation facing UNTAET could have been far worse had Indonesia embarked on a deliberate campaign to fully support the militia and/or to destabilize East Timor. Indonesia's efforts to resolve the militia and refugee problems in West Timor and to bring to justice the Indonesian authorities and militia leaders implicated in human rights violations failed to meet UN requests, but overall UNTAET's task was assisted by Indonesia's policies and actions. Acknowledging this support, the international community needs to remain positive when dealing with the Indonesian government, which must be encouraged to develop its relationship with its newly independent neighbor. This is, and will continue to be, a demanding and difficult process, but in comparison with many other international disputes, it is proceeding reasonably well to date. Much will depend on the capability of the Indonesian government to handle its many domestic political, economic, and social problems, not least of which are the disaffected separatist movements throughout the archipelago. Neither the future political stability of Indonesia nor its relations with East Timor can be predicted with any certainty.

MANDATE, STRUCTURE, AND DEVELOPMENT

The Security Council clearly established the parameters of UNTAET's responsibilities to prepare East Timor for independence. The mandate provided a structure for UNTAET and endorsed the Secretary-General's report of 4 October 1999. Part IV of this report identified the critical importance of maintaining a secure environment; specified fourteen objectives to be achieved; and required UNTAET "to perform its duties in close consultation and cooperation with the people of East Timor."[5] The mandate was decisive in what needed to be done, although many of the tasks were broadly defined (e.g., "to establish an effective administration"; "to support capacity building for self-government").[6] The SRSG, however, was allowed considerable freedom of action. The difficulties UNTAET experienced did not so much reflect the mandate as it did the enormity of the task and the lack of prior planning and resource attribution. It must be pointed out that UNTAET faced a situation in East Timor in which there were few qualified indigenous officials and no infrastructure. The mandate therefore started quite literally from ground zero.

UNTAET was initially organized into three distinct pillars, all working through the SRSG to the UN Secretariat in New York. By far the largest was the military pillar (of around 8,000 personnel), which replaced INTERFET in February 2000 and continued to maintain security. The military pillar and the transition from INTERFET are covered in more detail later.

The second component was known as the Humanitarian Assistance and Emergency Rehabilitation (HAER) pillar, under the leadership of Akira Takahashi from Japan. The initial work of this pillar began with the coordinating role of OCHA and the establishment of UNHOC to bring emergency relief to the devastated territory, as mentioned in Chapter 2. As its name implies, the HAER pillar was instrumental in coordinating a range of relief and humanitarian organizations and working with the East Timorese to determine relief assistance priorities. With INTERFET looking after security, the first important task for UNTAET was to ensure that emergency relief was effective. This often proved difficult due to elements beyond UNTAET control: bad weather conditions, poor communications, misdirected air drops and delivery failure, and inadequate supply of essential commodities. Cedric de Coning notes that the food relief stage "established the first relationships" between UN personnel and the East Timorese, and breakdowns in the food distribution system "heavily influenced the early perceptions towards UNTAET" and its ability to deliver.[7] Nonetheless, by late 2000, the emergency phase was over and the HAER pillar was dismantled, having accomplished its task. Akira Takahashi moved to become Special Adviser on Development and Humanitarian Affairs to the SRSG.[8]

The third, and most difficult, pillar was known as Governance and Public Administration (GPA), led stoically by the experienced French prefect Jean-Christian Cady, who was also appointed as deputy SRSG.[9] This pillar was responsible for reestablishing governance at the central and district levels, for regenerating public and social utilities, for establishing the rule of law, and for encouraging and regulating investment in the private sector. This was an enormous task, and more so given the total destruction of the territory's infrastructure and the failure of the UN to provide an overarching strategic (corporate) plan. Political and foreign policy issues were nominally part of GPA also, but in reality these were handled directly by the SRSG and his Head of Political Affairs, Peter Galbraith, former U.S. ambassador to Croatia. Unlike the situation in some other UN missions, however, the CIVPOL component, which by February 2000 still numbered only 480 of its mandated strength of 1,640 international staff,[10] was not a pillar in its own right.[11] The police commissioner was subordinated to Cady and, unlike the force commander, did not have a major role in the decision-making process.

GPA faced three particular challenges: creating a sustainable budget, developing a larger and more experienced staff, and winning the confidence of the East Timorese. Budget and funding arrangements were complicated. The distinction between the use of assessed and trust fund contributions often seemed blurred, and the flexibility of the SRSG to utilize funds in the best way seemed often to be constrained by UN fiduciary procedures. Bureaucratic constraints in the use of the assessed and trust fund budgets also impeded efficiency. The SRSG was often limited in the assistance he could provide to reconstruction activities because these could not be authorized under extant regulations for the assessed budget. From the military perspective, this meant that engineer units, which had specifically been included in the force to assist with reconstruction, were often underutilized because materiel could not be procured quickly under assessed budget arrangements.

Recruitment and funding for the civil service were major difficulties that required immediate attention. Replication of the large Indonesian civil service would have been economically unsustainable under UNTAET, or later by the newly independent country. Additionally, many civil servants had departed following the ballot and there were few trained personnel available for selection. Again, the UN Secretariat's failure to plan adequately for a civil administration caused problems due to shortages in international civil staff; and these problems were compounded by the appointment of underqualified or unsuitable personnel for some of the important positions. UNTAET proved to be an "unattractive" mission for many UN civil servants, and consequently it suffered from high vacancy and separation rates.

In February 2000, UNTAET itself made a concerted effort to produce a strategic plan. It was intended that this plan would enhance unity of effort by providing clearer direction, setting milestones, determining priorities, and deriving measures of effectiveness. One suggestion was to use the objectives and tasks in the Secretary-General's Report of 4 October 1999 and apply appropriate timelines. This was relatively easy for the military and HAER pillars, but it proved too difficult a task for GPA and other peripheral organizations. Consequently, the much-needed strategic plan for UNTAET was never produced, and the mission continued to feel its way in a rather uncoordinated manner.[12] In hindsight it is easy to see how daunting the tasks were for the transitional civil administration and to appreciate its inability to produce such a plan in an environment where "today's survival" sapped all its energies and resources. Nevertheless, strategic plans for complex enterprises are essential, and more could have been done by the Secretariat to assist in this regard.

"TIMORIZATION"

As the months progressed, the slow pace of reconstruction and other aspects of UNTAET's presence were subject to increased local and international criticism. The UN was accused of saturating Dili with vehicles and personnel, creating an artificial and unsustainable local economy—a situation that did little for the East Timorese. The GPA was seen to be too Dili-centric in its attention, evoking criticism from district administrators, nongovernmental organizations (NGOs), and East Timorese leaders. District administrators found themselves allocated paltry resources and left too much to their own devices to implement governance and enhance development. The initiative some of these officials displayed was admirable, but their efforts suffered from the lack of an overall working plan. Locally engaged UN workers became discontent with perceived inequities in the UN salary system and with their working conditions.[13] A particularly long wet season in 2000 caused severe degradation to the already fragile road network, testing the ability of UNTAET and the Bretton Woods financial institutions to proceed with reconstruction efforts and increasing the difficulty of bringing governance to remote communities. Unemployment was high, particularly in Dili where the population had grown quickly in the wake of the postballot destruction and rural dislocation. Crime was on the increase in Dili and Baucau, and the effectiveness of CIVPOL and the

Border Service was being questioned.[14] Power supply in Dili became less reliable, and much of the hinterland remained without electricity for many months.

UNTAET had difficulty in explaining its proposals to remedy these situations to the population largely because, like in so many other areas, its branch of the UN's Office of Communications and Public Information (OCPI) remained poorly resourced for many months.[15] Consequently, a coordinated information program was not implemented throughout the mission until early 2001. The SRSG's intention to establish nationwide radio coverage as quickly as possible, as the most sensible means of communicating with the East Timorese people, was also not finally realized until April 2001.[16] In this difficult environment, tough decisions were required. Some of these decisions were criticized by East Timorese leaders and interest groups, who were particularly critical of what was seen as a lack of proper consultation in the decisionmaking process and a reluctance to fully utilize qualified East Timorese.[17] Impatient and frustrated now that the end of the East Timorese struggle for independence was in sight, these parties were also quick to blame the UN for what they perceived to be the slow pace of recovery.

Fully appreciating these problems and recognizing the essential need for the UN and the East Timorese to work more closely in partnership, Vieira de Mello progressively implemented changes. In July 2000, GPA was replaced by the East Timor Transitional Administration (ETTA).[18] This was a major change in the transitional process, reversing the philosophy on how the transition should be managed. GPA had started by addressing "Timorization" at the administrative level, with political transformation to come nearer the proposed national elections. ETTA was structured to begin the political transition earlier, the rationale being that a state cannot be prepared for self-government without giving the national leadership direct experience of government. In accordance with the mandate, the SRSG remained in charge (with Cady as his deputy), but a transitional cabinet that comprised nine de facto ministries was created. Five were headed by East Timorese and four by international staff.[19] The transition from GPA to ETTA was an important step on the path to independence, but it did not come without tension. Some of the East Timorese heads of departments felt underresourced with the staff and facilities they had been provided, and some of the UN personnel resented taking instructions from non-UN supervisors. Within the cabinet, the views of East Timorese members were sometimes contradictory and discussions sometimes inconclusive, but the meetings were well controlled under the SRSG's chairmanship. UNTAET, in fact, faced a significant constraint in effecting a constructive working relationship with East Timorese appointees who themselves had not yet received democratic legitimacy through the ballot box. Despite these difficulties, the creation of ETTA was a positive step in improving the partnership between the UN and the East Timorese.

From the outset, Vieira de Mello himself took the initiative in efforts to break down perceived barriers and institute a productive dialogue process mutually beneficial and supportive to all parties. On his arrival, he moved quickly to establish close personal relations with the key party leaders and eminent East Timorese and insisted on the same approach from his senior staff. To assist in this process, the CNRT, as the umbrella organization for all the pro-independence parties, undertook to negotiate with UNTAET on the members' behalf. The National Consultative Council (NCC) was soon established with representation from most political parties, the Catholic Church, and special interest groups. With the formation of ETTA, this was further refined into the National Council (NC). For most East Timorese, moral leadership rested with Xanana Gusmão, who was president of both CNRT and the NCC/NC. Not surprisingly, Vieira de Mello and Gusmão worked closely together. On important social matters, the bishops were also consulted. José Ramos-Horta became increasingly involved in sensitive foreign policy issues and was subsequently appointed the de facto minister for foreign affairs with the formation of ETTA. In order to establish the rule of law to address the increased crime rate, greater attention was given to the judicial sector and the introduction of corrective services. CIVPOL was provided additional resources and was thus able to extend its presence by opening stations in most subdistricts.

True to its word, and in preparation for the "all Timorese" Constituent Assembly elections on 30 August 2001 (the second anniversary of the ballot), the CNRT was dissolved on 9 June 2001 to allow parties to contest the elections. The CNRT had provided unity and focus throughout a long and difficult period, but its task was complete with the decision to hold elections. The Constituent Assembly election was peaceful and well planned,[20] resulting in the swearing-in of the eighty-eight members of the assembly on 15 September, fifty-five of whom came from the dominant Fretilin party. After dealing with its own rules and procedures, the assembly commenced drafting the constitution. On 20 September, the all Timorese Second Transitional Government was confirmed, made up of twenty ministers, vice-ministers, and secretaries of state. A Council of Ministers, led by Chief Minister Mari Alkatiri, presided over this transitional government and supervised the East Timor Public Administration, which replaced ETTA and by mid–September had recruited 90 percent of its 10,500 civil servants.[21] Although still under the overall authority of the SRSG, the Timorization process progressed a long way, with East Timor under the effective control of its own people.[22] The date for East Timor's independence was set for 20 May 2002.

TRANSITION FROM INTERFET TO PKF

The transition from INTERFET to the PKF was set to take place during February 2000. To maintain a secure environment for the process of nation building, it was important that this transition be handled well and that the PKF then prove itself capable of continuing the high standard set by the MNF. Overall, the transition progressed smoothly, aided by the fact that 70 percent of the deployed forces remained in location and changed to UN blue headdress. Australia also deployed the Egyptian, Kenyan, and Jordanian contingents during the last weeks of INTERFET in order to have them ready for transition. The major non-INTERFET units to join the PKF included a Portuguese battalion, two engineer battalions (Pakistan and Bangladesh), a force communications unit (Pakistan), an infantry company (Nepal), and military aviation elements (Chile, Peru, and Portugal). In particular, the East Timorese greatly appreciated the arrival of the Portuguese contingent, which had for many months been prepared to deploy.[23]

For the East Timorese, the transition appeared seamless, but some risks and gaps emerged in force capability. Although the DPKO had begun planning for a PKF many months before—subsequently the basis for the INTERFET deployment—by necessity the DPKO focused its efforts from September on establishing the civil administration. The PKF force commander, Lieutenant General Jaime de los Santos from the Philippines, was not appointed until 30 December. In these circumstances it was largely left to Australia and General Cosgrove to determine and dictate the transition strategy and timetable. Australia also agreed to bridge the gap in logistics support until the UN administrative system was fully functional. After conducting reconnaissance, de los Santos deployed to Dili on 25 January 2000, which provided him with little opportunity to meld his team or make adjustments to INTERFET's timetable. The transition began one week later and was conducted progressively by sectors from 1 to 28 February. De los Santos formally accepted full command from Cosgrove on 23 February. Although the transition went smoothly, there was a loss of capability in the critical areas of engineering and aviation for a number of weeks. The greatest weakness, however, rested with the new force headquarters. This had been inadequately prepared for the task and had to commence operations with only seventy-five of its 200 personnel, drawn from fifteen nations, few of whom had previously worked together. INTERFET provided some support for the new headquarters, and a small number of staff transferred to the PKF. Nonetheless, the PKF headquarters was initially somewhat dysfunctional, and it took several months before it matured to a level of proficiency necessary to run peace enforcement operations effectively. Although some of the billets that had been authorized by the DPKO were never filled, the headquarters eventually performed to a high standard.

THE PKF AND THE MAINTENANCE OF SECURITY

INTERFET restored security. The PKF's task was to maintain it and to hand over responsibilities progressively to the civil administration.[24] The main difference between the two forces was that INTERFET was an independent UN-mandated operation, while the PKF was an integral part of UNTAET and responsible to the SRSG. INTERFET had performed the tasks of a de facto military government until UNTAET was established, but it was important that the PKF quickly demonstrate its subordination to civil authority. It was also clear from the outset that the new nation at independence would be unable to replicate the PKF and that it would be necessary, therefore, to gradually disengage the PKF from all but essential military security tasks. Accordingly, the PKF began to focus on preventing militia infiltration, managing the border with the TNI, and helping CIVPOL maintain law and order when required.

PKF Organization and Disposition

More than thirty countries contributed to the PKF, with the main combat forces coming from ten countries.[25] There were two components: an unarmed UN Military Observer Group (UNMOG), which was progressively reduced from 200 to 120 officers by mid–2000; and the armed PKF, which had been mandated at 8,950 but which hovered for most of the time around 8,000.[26] Each component maintained its identity and performed different tasks, but they were generically referred to as the PKF. The force commander was given unity of command over both components, providing a single and clear focus for military operations. The combat force was organized into four sectors—East, Central, West, and Oecussi—with sector boundaries conforming to district boundaries. During the INTERFET period, UNMOG deployed on a district basis, but with the transition to the PKF the observers progressively worked more closely with the combat force and adjusted its dispositions to conform to the sector boundaries. With the improvement in security, the PKF was to reduce in strength "to some 5,000 troops by independence,"[27] progressively handing over responsibility to the East Timor Defence Force (ETDF), commencing in the eastern districts.

PKF Operations

Soon after transition, the PKF was tested with militia infiltration and attacks. The Oecussi enclave, Sector East, and most of Sector Central remained peaceful, but the militias remained active in the western border districts of Bobonaro and Cova Lima where the Australian and New Zealand (composite) battalions were deployed.[28] In March, the militias infiltrated into the adjoining district of Ermera and targeted the isolated town of Atsabe, the home of the original pro-integration Apodeti in 1974–1975, where neither INTERFET nor the PKF had established a permanent presence. UNTAET's response was strong and effective. The SRSG dispatched the force commander and the director of the Office of Political Affairs to Jakarta to meet with Indonesia's foreign and defense ministers, the chief of the Defence Force, and other senior officers to seek Indonesian action in stopping the incursions. At the tactical level, PKF patrolling was increased in the border region, force protection measures were enhanced, and the Kenyans were redeployed to Ermera, where they captured some militia members and quickly won the trust and confidence of the people. Force headquarters, which was still being established, conducted after-action reviews and progressively reassessed and improved its procedures.

With fewer and less capable aviation assets dedicated solely to military operations, the PKF's mobility was never as effective as INTERFET's.[29] To offset this limitation, the PKF extended its permanent presence in the countryside, establishing a number of new positions and increasing local foot and vehicle patrols. With greater permanence, some of the contingents became proficient in the language, further gaining the confidence of the population and enhancing situational awareness. In most units, however, there was a lack of language assistants. Patrolling was normally conducted in a visible manner to acquire information and reassure the population, but in high threat areas, combat patrols were conducted to counter militia infiltration. In these instances, warfighting skills were fully tested with enemy "contact" demanding a quick and professional response. Relations between the PKF commanders and district administrators were also strengthened. Without jeopardizing security, efforts were quickly made to change the face of Dili from a garrison town of barbed wire and machine gun posts to that of a more peaceful city recovering from devastation. At the same time, the PKF gave high priority to force protection issues, not only against militia action but also against sickness and accident. Learning from INTERFET's experience, malaria and dengue rates declined, but deteriorating road conditions continued to take a heavy toll on vehicles and personnel.

Despite the PKF's active patrolling program, mobility and maneuver remained one of its weakest links. Except for the battalions in Sector West, UNTAET air assets provided limited ability to redeploy reserves quickly. A night-capable helicopter remained on standby for aeromedical evacuation, but across the force there was no ability to move troops at night by helicopter (except for the Australians who, under national restrictions, were not normally permitted to deploy outside their area of operations). Mobility deteriorated further during the wet season when weather conditions restricted air and vehicle movement. During the wet season, landslides made road conditions hazardous, causing a number of PKF fatalities and forcing the PKF to remain more static. A number of units had only limited equipment to operate effectively at night, further restricting mobility.

From late July through September, significant militia infiltration occurred into the southern Sector Central districts of Ainaro and Manufahi, where the Portuguese battalion had only small footprints. The militias timed this infiltration to coincide with the Portuguese battalion's rotation and the important CNRT congress in Dili (to which much of the Portuguese battalion had been heavily committed). Infiltrating in small groups, totaling around 150, the militias took considerable care to avoid PKF forces deployed along the border. They were well armed and trained to a high standard. Using handheld radios, they were able to communicate with their leaders in West Timor. On arrival in their home districts of Ainaro and Manufahi, these militias attempted to win over the population, claiming repentance for their former brutality, which they blamed on a corrupt UN ballot. The infiltration was well planned and executed and deliberately targeted isolated areas where the PKF patrolled infrequently and where there was no CIVPOL or other permanent UNTAET presence. The purpose of this militia infiltration was not confirmed, and although some reports suggested they were exploring the possibility for the peaceful return of their families, it is more probable that they were intending to lay the foundations for an insurgency campaign designed to discredit UNTAET.

The reaction from the people was immediate, with almost 3,000 quickly evacuating their villages in panic and heading for the district capitals. Using the support of the people, and with increased assistance from Falintil, the newly arrived Portuguese battalion quickly increased its presence to counter the threat, with no loss of civilian life. Operation Cobra was launched in Manufahi, led by the PKF but closely coordinated with the district administration and CIVPOL. In a parallel operation, coordinated by UNHCR with PKF support, the population was resettled and the militia discredited. Following the success of Cobra, Operation Crocodilo was launched in Ainaro yielding similar success.[30] Throughout this period, Sector West and the Kenyans intensified their operations, keeping the militia off guard and further restricting their ability to maneuver. The New Zealand (composite) battalion in Cova Lima was particularly active at this time, performing to a high standard and losing two of its soldiers in separate actions against the militias—Private Leonard Manning from New Zealand and Private Devi Ram Jaisi from Nepal.[31] All these operations proved the need for CIVPOL to establish a permanent policing presence at the subdistrict level, and this was quickly authorized by the SRSG and then progressively implemented throughout the territory. The PKF's greater use of Falintil for information gathering and as liaison officers and guides proved invaluable in helping retain the trust of the people. It also helped reinforce respect between the PKF and Falintil. By October, the militias, certain that UNTAET would prevent them establishing permanent bases in East Timor, had totally withdrawn to West Timor with their credibility as a fighting force seriously impaired. Throughout 2001, militia infiltration and incidents decreased, but security concerns persisted along the border where illegal markets and armed groups continued to operate.[32]

Rules of Engagement

A key issue was the PKF's rules of engagement (ROE). The UN mandate for INTERFET provided for robust ROE, and General Cosgrove ensured this was so. Because 70 percent of INTERFET transitioned to the PKF and because the role of the PKF was a continuation of INTERFET's fine achievements, it was essential that the ROE for the PKF be equally robust. This was ultimately achieved but not without some rancor. In October 1999, an Australian military liaison team in New York assisted the Military Planning Service in drafting the ROE and requested that these be cleared with the Office of Legal Affairs and with troop-contributing nations before transition. The UN format was used, but considerable care was taken to ensure that there was no major change from INTERFET for the soldiers on the ground. Unfortunately, the draft ROE were not received in Dili until the eve of the change of command. These ROE showed little resemblance to those that had been drafted in New York, reflecting the name of another UN mission and being inappropriate for conditions in East Timor. Following a hectic period of amendment, the DPKO provided the PKF with acceptable ROE.

In some areas, the PKF's ROE were even more robust than INTERFET's, but as the months passed and with increased militia activity, there was a need to amplify the ROE so as to regain the initiative and better protect PKF troops. Following considerable discussion, the UN responded positively to requests from the SRSG to approve a theater-specific amplification to the ROE regarding the concept of self-defense, which better enabled PKF troops to act with certainty when compelled to use force. In effect, this amplification permitted PKF soldiers to engage the militias without warning if they were under threat. It also had the additional benefits of being a positive influence on PKF morale, reassuring the local community and further restricting the militias' freedom of movement. The situation on the ground was further aided by the UN responding favorably to requests from the SRSG to augment the force with additional capabilities.[33]

Command

The first force commander, Lieutenant General de los Santos, worked hard to establish the PKF, but he decided not to renew his contract and in July was replaced at short notice by Lieutenant General Boonsrang Niumpradit from Thailand.[34] A strategist of keen intellect, with an infectious sense of humor and impressive people skills, Boonsrang quickly made his presence felt. Under his leadership the force became more closely knit, and the concept of operations underwent a subtle but important adjustment. Reflecting his understanding of guerrilla operations, Boonsrang appreciated that the militias' success would be directly related to their ability to intimidate and win over support from the local population, particularly in remote areas. As with INTERFET, the PKF's center of gravity had been focused on directly countering militia activity, but now it changed to maintaining the support of the local population. This change had little effect on the PKF's presence and active patrolling program, but it intensified PKF efforts to become closer to the people and required a psychological shift in thinking by field commanders. Units became more conscious of the need to work more closely with district administrations, to maintain a more active presence, to give more emphasis to constabulary-CMA activities, to enhance partnership with CIVPOL, to utilize the knowledge and skills of Falintil, and most important to establish closer relations with community leaders. The application of this concept throughout the entire PKF assisted in further unifying the force with a common cause. Its success was clearly demonstrated in Operations Cobra and Crocodilo. Importantly, the PKF was perceived by a still traumatized population to be an honest, professional, and friendly military force free from major human rights violations and intent on maintaining their security and support.[35]

The contribution of the military observers was also significant. As mentioned, MLOs had deployed as part of UNAMET under the command of Brigadier Rezaqul Haider. Following the postballot violence and the arrival of INTERFET, they were renamed UNMOG. Initially tasked with maintaining a useful UN presence in each district and reporting on the security situation, Haider and the longer-serving observers gained considerable knowledge during the UNAMET and INTERFET periods. They were thus able to assist the PKF as it became established. Under UNTAET, however, the observers were asked to do much more, particularly in relation to Falintil and border monitoring. As already discussed, soon after INTERFET's arrival, Taur Matan Ruak had relocated the four cantonments of Falintil to a single location at Aileu, where its members lived in atrocious and overcrowded conditions with no assurances as to their future. In these circumstances, it was essential that close relations be maintained between UNTAET and the armed resistance fighters to prevent, and deal with, potential security situations. Extending the good work begun by INTERFET, the observers took the lead in this difficult assignment and forged a great deal of trust with the Falintil commanders.

The other major task for UNMOG was to assist in managing the border and the sensitive relationship with the TNI. To achieve this, the number of observers deployed to the border was increased and a closer relationship developed with the PKF and the TNI commanders. Along the border, the observers lived and performed well in difficult conditions. Haider, who had commanded so well during UNAMET, was replaced in July by Brigadier Louis Gardiner from New Zealand. Gardiner quickly established a close personal working relationship with the new force commander and with key UNTAET and East Timorese representatives. He provided clear guidance, visited his officers regularly, and proved to be a strong and forthright leader.[36]

Civil-Military Affairs

The PKF's structure and modus operandi largely reflected INTERFET's. This included a CMA branch as part of the force headquarters and a CMOC to plan and process requests for assistance from the civil authorities. Two multirole engineer battalions were included in the force to provide military engineering and to contribute to national reconstruction. Medical and dental capabilities were designed to meet the requirements of the force, with excess capacity being utilized to assist the civil authorities. Aviation and maritime assets were provided for operational tasking but were used for CMA on a case-by-case basis depending on other mission priorities.

So long as security prevailed, the PKF was keen to remain in a supporting role to HAER, the civil administration, NGOs, and aid agencies. The PKF developed a CMA plan to prioritize its efforts and assist the key agencies, but this plan was not based on an overarching UNTAET concept. The PKF's highest priority was given to IDPs and returnees, but considerable assistance was also provided in areas of transportation, medical support, food distribution, engineering, shelter relief, agriculture, education and language training, family reunion visits, physical education, and sporting events. Many PKF units sponsored orphanages or local hospitals, but care was taken not to duplicate the work of civilian agencies or create dependencies that could not later be transitioned to the civil sector. Generally, the PKF provided humanitarian support in those areas where civil agencies had most difficulty establishing themselves.

Much of the PKF's effort was decentralized. All units liaised with local authorities and implemented CMA within their resources. Initially, however, most units had no specialist CMA staff, and those that based their force structure on the standard UN organizations had limited CMA capacity. As the mission continued, the PKF learned a great deal about CMA and made a number of adjustments. With knowledge gained through experience, CMA training courses were implemented and contingents enhanced their capabilities in successive force rotations. There was more than altruism in this approach: the PKF learned that effective CMA brought them closer to the people, which in turn provided them greater situational awareness, thereby helping them maintain security and accomplish their mission.

In retrospect, it is fair to assess that the importance of CMA was underrated in initial planning by the Secretariat, reflecting a lack of experience in the DPKO and by most of the contributing nations. Few defense forces have this capability embedded permanently within their force structures or have well-developed doctrine. Hopes of having the United States run the CMA branch within the PKF failed to materialize when the U.S. contribution to UNTAET was limited to military observers and CIVPOL. As a backstop measure, the United States agreed to provide a small military humanitarian support team known as the U.S. (Military) Support Group East Timor (USGET). USGET was a separate military force to the PKF, but its efforts were coordinated through the CMOC, and close cooperation and joint planning were ensured. USGET performed outstanding work and was a value-adding component.

CIVPOL AND THE MAINTENANCE OF LAW AND ORDER

With the transition to UNTAET, CIVPOL was one element of the mission that did not function as well as it might have, or as was required. During UNAMET, CIVPOL assisted with the ballot and provided liaison and advice to POLRI. These were important but nonetheless simple tasks in comparison to the difficult requirement of maintaining law and order in a postconflict environment under UNTAET. CIVPOL comprised many fine police officers, but from the outset there was considerable criticism of CIVPOL's overall performance. In the main, this criticism came from the East Timorese, but the SRSG and senior UNTAET officials were also less than satisfied with the implementation of this aspect of the mission's mandate. It was obvious that insufficient planning had occurred prior to deployment and that, in contrast to the PKF, CIVPOL operations lacked focus and commitment. For many months the police commissioner was reluctant to take policing to the people and to establish permanent police stations at the subdistrict level. To be fair, during this period CIVPOL was inadequately resourced, and there was disagreement as to whether or not its members should be armed. From February 2000, with increasing civil unrest in Dili, some CIVPOL carried sidearms. But following a violent disturbance involving civilian youth gangs in late April, the SRSG, on 1 May, declared a policy of zero tolerance to the carrying of handheld weapons of any kind and authorized all CIVPOL in Dili to carry sidearms. This practice was gradually extended throughout all districts.[37]

Additionally, and unlike the PKF, CIVPOL worked individually and in small groups. Some were well trained in negotiation and conflict resolution techniques, but success in these areas—as well as in general policing duties—required good language and translation skills, which were difficult to acquire in East Timor. The riot control unit from Portugal did not deploy (in Dili) until March 2000, and the Jordanian unit (in Baucau) not until mid-June. By the last quarter of 2001, the mandated maritime police unit had still not arrived in East Timor. Although UN procedures for CIVPOL required compulsory predeployment training and testing, it was obvious that some were inadequately prepared and that the caliber of some police was below standard. This lack of preparation caused many CIVPOL to have difficulty in establishing rapport with and in winning the trust and confidence of the East Timorese.

In an effort to improve CIVPOL's effectiveness, the SRSG sought not only additional resources, but also improvements to the UN selection and vetting processes. Aware of the importance of CIVPOL in postconflict situations, Vieira de Mello requested that only member states possessing properly qualified police be approached to provide personnel. The SRSG also proposed that CIVPOL stations be manned by national (rather than multinational) contingents, along similar lines to the PKF, and he instituted a trial to validate this proposition.

CIVPOL-PKF Coordination

In the early days of UNTAET, the SRSG decided to separate the military and the police and to make a clear distinction between military security matters and those of law enforcement. From the outset, therefore, the PKF and CIVPOL remained distinct entities, with a conscious decision being taken not to replicate the military predominance that had existed under the Indonesians. Much of TNI's prime real estate was allocated to CIVPOL, with the PKF occupying more temporary facilities. This was sensible inasmuch as it emphasized to the people the separation of power from the military and the importance of the police as a permanent force. But this separation also caused difficulty in the two forces fully coordinating their activities, not least because of the unequal status of the respective commanders. The force commander was a component head and had full access to the SRSG. In comparison, the police commissioner reported to the deputy SRSG (and police minister) and was rarely included in higher-level discussions.

CIVPOL-PKF relations were generally good, but the lack of police-military coordination reflected both inadequate preparation by the Secretariat and the fact that CIVPOL began its deployment in advance of the PKF and operated totally independently of INTERFET. Before UNTAET began, the DPKO had not conducted any serious police-military planning, and no joint doctrine or concept for joint operations was prepared. Nor did this occur in Dili, with respective commanders being fully occupied with the numerous challenges they encountered in establishing their own forces. The Joint Operations Centre (JOC) inherited from UNAMET, which had proved invaluable up to and during the withdrawal, had not been planned for by either CIVPOL or the PKF. Under UNAMET it was staffed by CIVPOL and MLOs, but it quickly proved dysfunctional for the conduct of national military and police operations and was discontinued. Instead, military-police planning groups were assigned as required for specific joint operations, and a permanent CIVPOL liaison officer was attached to the PKF headquarters. Such planning worked reasonably well, but it was far from an optimum solution. Had joint planning occurred before deployment, a better system could have been instituted.

A particular area that demanded early coordination was PKF support to CIVPOL in the event of internal unrest. This task was assigned to the PKF in the mandate, but not until the prospect of elections in early 2001 did serious joint planning get under way. Some emergency planning was done for earlier potential crises, such as security for important visitors and at political rallies, but there was no permanent coordination. Most PKF units were not properly trained and equipped to assist in riot-control duties, and the concept for employment of CIVPOL's two riot-control units and their coordination with PKF units remained inchoate for many months.

In an effort to improve security coordination between various agencies and to inform various interest groups on security issues, a weekly interagency meeting was jointly initiated in mid-2000 by the PKF and CIVPOL, under the chairmanship of the deputy police commissioner (operations). However, not until the establishment of the Council for National Security (CNS) in September 2000 were significant security issues discussed at a senior level in a coordinated manner.

NATIONAL SECURITY FRAMEWORK

By mid-2000, it was clear that mechanisms needed to be put in place for a sustainable security system at independence, integrating the various elements of national security. Accordingly, a proposal to establish an enduring national security framework, initially developed by the PKF, was agreed to by the SRSG. After consultation with the East Timorese, this proposal was implemented and the CNS was established at the central government level and held its first meeting on 28 September. Chaired by the SRSG or

DSRSG, CNS membership included ministers, the force commander, and the police commissioner. With approval to create the ETDF, membership was extended to the head of the Office of Defence Force Development (ODFD), Roque Rodrigues, and the chief of Defence Force (and former Falintil commander), Brigadier General Taur Matan Ruak.[38] The CNS met monthly (or as required) to discuss important security policy issues. Provision was made to appoint a national security adviser (NSA) and a small secretarial staff to oversee security matters and prepare agendas and minutes. The NSA appointment was filled in April 2001.[39]

The security framework also identified the need for a National Operations Centre (NOC) to coordinate security information from the PKF, police, and other agencies and to manage security crises if they occurred. Rather than create an additional operations center, it was agreed that the NOC collocate with Headquarters CIVPOL, working in close coordination with the NSA. An option to collocate the NOC with Headquarters PKF was rejected on the basis that this might prove unsustainable following independence. The PKF and ETDF were also reluctant to take primacy for civil security issues.

The strength of the security framework also depended on the effective passage of information between the NOC and the districts. Because many security incidents occurred in remote rural communities, it was essential that information be passed quickly and accurately to and from the districts. Accordingly, District Operations Centres (DOC) were established, normally working from existing CIVPOL stations but incorporating information from the PKF and other sources within each district. Independent from the DOCs, each district administrator was responsible for establishing a District Security Council to ensure security coordination and the primacy of the civil authority in that area.

It is too early to judge the effectiveness of the national security framework, although early indications are positive. The East Timorese may well make adjustments after independence. It is important, however, that with the agreement of the East Timorese leaders a sustainable system was in place and trialed well before independence. The establishment of a national security framework provided the East Timorese with an example of civilian control. It demonstrated the subordination of the military to civilian authority, and it assisted in relieving the PKF of security responsibilities in anticipation of its eventual downsizing and withdrawal.

BORDER CONTROL MECHANISMS

In many postconflict environments an important step in maintaining security is to establish effective border control mechanisms—land, air, and maritime. In East Timor this was quickly accomplished for land and air boundaries between military forces, but agreement on maritime boundaries and the establishment of sustainable political mechanisms proved more difficult.

On 12 January 2000, INTERFET and the TNI reached agreement on a memorandum of (technical) understanding (MOU) to control the border and minimize the risks of unintended conflict between the two sides. In the absence of an approved international border, a tactical coordination line (TCL) was agreed, based on the old Dutch-Portuguese borders. Both sides set about improving the delineation of the TCL, which was porous and poorly marked. Each party agreed to respect the TCL and to discourage retaliatory militia violence. Eleven junction points were established along the line to enable coordination between local commanders and to assist in refugee movement, family reunion visits, and limited trade. On 11 April, this MOU was reviewed by the PKF and the TNI to include an additional junction point, provide more accurate definition of the TCL, and confirm the role of unarmed military observers. A Tactical Coordination Working Group, established between the commander of Sector West and his Indonesian counterpart under INTERFET, now took greater form and substance. Meetings were held every two weeks (or as required) on alternate sides of the border; and as a mark of good faith, the visiting delegation went unarmed, entrusting security to the hosting party. At a higher level, the force commander and his Indonesian counterpart established communications between their respective headquarters and met when required.

All these mechanisms helped to create a clearer delineation between East and West Timor and to resolve disputes related to cross-border violations. On 28 August 2001, the MOU was updated by a new Military Technical Agreement designed to further "improve the practical understandings between the UNTAET military component and the TNI on information-sharing and the coordination of military activity in the vicinity of the TCL."[40] Border violations were infrequent but not uncommon. Most of the PKF's border violations resulted from overflights, normally caused by bad weather or pilot error; but occasional coastal or land infringements occurred as a result of poor navigation. On the TNI side, most violations were from lost patrols or individual soldiers, often on hunting expeditions. Along the border, the military observers monitored the situation, using their good offices to help resolve disputes and pass information between UNTAET and Indonesian authorities.

Although meetings between the PKF and the TNI were professional, they also reflected differences of emphasis between UNTAET and the Indonesian authorities. Indonesia's focus for many months centered on preventing a clash between the TNI and the PKF along the border, and they distanced themselves from having any responsibility for militias operating within East Timor. The PKF was equally committed to avoiding conflict with Indonesian forces, but its main focus was directed toward encouraging the TNI to prevent militia infiltration from sanctuaries in West Timor and for the Indonesian security forces to disarm militia elements that continued to operate with impunity and spread propaganda in the refugee camps. Sadly, it took the killings of Privates Manning and Jaisi in East Timor; the tragic murder of three UNHCR workers at Atambua in West Timor on 6 September 2000; and a resolution from the Security Council[41] before the Indonesian authorities began serious action to control the militias. From October 2000, the TNI and POLRI commenced operations to minimize militia activity and improve the security situation in West Timor. As a result, the incidence of cross-border infiltration by the militia diminished significantly throughout 2001. Considerable credit for this improved situation rested with Major General Willem da Costa, who replaced General Kiki Syahnakri as the regional commander in November 2000.

Agreement on the use of air space was achieved quickly. At the strategic level, agreement was reached between INTERFET/UNTAET and Indonesia based on international protocols. At the tactical level, air boundaries conformed to the TCL. Overflights were permitted with prior clearance, and both sides investigated violations promptly. In contrast to the management of air and land borders, the maritime boundaries were less clear. Neither the PKF nor CIVPOL possessed capabilities for maritime patrol and interdiction, reducing the risk of armed maritime incidents between Indonesia and UNTAET and lowering the priority for early resolution on maritime boundaries. Nevertheless, the East Timorese remained concerned about the possibility of maritime threats, particularly given the number of nearby Indonesian islands.

To address border issues at a higher political level, a Joint Border Committee was established between UNTAET and Indonesia in September 2000. This committee was intended to oversee the workings of a number of subcommittees designed to normalize border activities in areas of demarcation, security, maritime boundaries, policing, trade, resource management, and the movement of people. Progress in these areas proved slow, as did efforts to open the agreed road corridor to the Oecussi enclave. The implementation of effective border control mechanisms will be an important consideration in the postindependence environment.

EAST TIMOR SECURITY FORCES

The requirement for an East Timor Police Service (ETPS) was recognized in the mandate. With the establishment of UNTAET, the creation of this service was a high priority. CIVPOL was given the task and had to overcome two major difficulties before the training process could begin. First, in the ruins of Dili following the postballot violence, it took time to locate and refurbish a suitable training center. Second, initial planning in New York failed to consider recommendations that the UNAMET police commissioner, Alan Mills, made to select and segregate specialist trainers as part of the UNTAET CIVPOL contingent. It took some time, therefore, for appropriate trainers to be identified from within the force. (This oversight was corrected for subsequent rotations.) Training began in early 2000 and was highly successful, with more than 1,000 graduates by September 2001.[42] The young East Timorese police cadets, male and female, impressed everyone, and CIVPOL deserves considerable credit for its achievement in this area. The police graduates were then assigned on probation to CIVPOL stations for a six months of additional training.

As more East Timorese police filled the ranks, their affinity and familiarity with the population, and their obvious language proficiency, enhanced CIVPOL's image and credibility. The throughput, however, was not large, and the force was not estimated to reach maturity until 2003, well after independence. Efforts to shorten this timeline proved difficult due to funding restrictions. The creation of the ETPS was a success story for UNTAET, but the new force will require ongoing and specialist training if it is to develop as a professional institution.

The formation of the ETDF was a very different story. UNTAET's mandate had not made provision for a military force, partly because it was outside the UN's area of expertise but more so because it was expected that Falintil would disarm and demobilize. Before the ballot, the East Timorese leadership had also indicated that it had no intention of having an army, just a heavy police brigade. Early thinking by the Secretariat, therefore, was that an affordable police force, augmented by a small paramilitary component for riot control, would be sufficient to meet East Timor's security needs. During UNAMET, Ian Martin was alerted to the difficulties in demobilizing Falintil, and in the wake of the postballot violence he advised that prospects for this happening had evaporated. Falintil had earned the respect and support of the majority of the population, and they had survived against incredible odds because of this support. Indeed, it was largely because of Falintil's efforts that freedom had been achieved. Consequently, with the militia movement still alive in West Timor, and with disturbing memories of Japanese and Indonesian occupation, all the major political leaders agreed that a defense force would be required.

The sensitivities surrounding the future of Falintil were clearly visible with the triumphant return from house arrest in October 1999 of Xanana Gusmão, Falintil's commander in chief, in full military uniform. The difficulty in resolving Falintil's status was further evident when, on 19 November, Gusmão attended a meeting in Dili with the newly arrived SRSG accompanied by a group of heavily armed bodyguards in clear breach of the cantonment agreement. General Cosgrove and Vieira de Mello were able to defuse a tense situation, with Gusmão agreeing to disarm his protection party and again allow INTERFET to provide for his safety. Subsequently, there were two further incidents, in May and June 2000, when elements of Falintil again broke cantonment, further highlighting the need to settle the future status for the popular freedom fighters.[43]

Falintil's frustration with its circumstances was understandable but not easily resolved. Having fought so gallantly for East Timor's freedom for twenty-four years, and having behaved with such restraint and discipline during the violence, its troops now had no guaranteed future and were living in deplorable conditions. Conscious of the need to resolve this dilemma, and with considerable pressure to do so from John Bevan, the district administrator in Aileu, the SRSG authorized measures to improve Falintil's living conditions, while at the same time exploring options for Falintil's future. After considerable negotiation, including an independent international study by a team from King's College London,[44] it was agreed that East Timor should have a modest light infantry force of two battalions, comprising 1,500 regulars and 1,500 volunteer reservists. (A small naval component of fifty personnel and two patrol craft was later added with provisioning from Portugal.)[45] The UN was given responsibility to commence preparation of the ETDF before independence. Six hundred and fifty Falintil members were selected for the first battalion, and those not selected were reintegrated into society under the Falintil Reinsertion Assistance Programme, funded by the World Bank and the U.S. Agency for International Development (USAID) and implemented by the International Organization for Migration (IOM). With this closure of its cantonment, Falintil surrendered most of its weapons to UNTAET, retaining some small arms for training purposes under ETDF security arrangements.

The King's College study emphasized certain preconditions for the establishment of the ETDF, including its subordination to the state, its separation from politics, and its economic sustainability.[46] Falintil quickly demonstrated its separation from politics when Xanana Gusmão relinquished command to his loyal deputy, Taur Matan Ruak, at the force's twenty-fifth anniversary celebrations on 20 August 2000. Then, in a moving ceremony at Aileu on 1 February 2001, Falintil was officially disbanded and the ETDF was raised under the command of Brigadier General Taur Matan Ruak. The mission of the force is to provide for the military defense of East Timor—its people and territory—by stopping militia incursions and deterring aggressors; and to provide assistance during natural disasters and other emergencies. To plan the development of the ETDF, an ODFD was established as a quasi–defense ministry under Roque Rodrigues, reporting to the SRSG. The ODFD was provided with professional staff from a number of nations, and Australia and Portugal jointly agreed to take the lead in funding and training the ETDF. Donor conferences were held in November 2000 and June 2001 to confirm international assistance.[47] Training of the first battalion commenced in Aileu in February 2001 and relocated the following July to a new training facility at Metinaro (30 kilometers east of Dili), constructed by Australia.[48] By December 2001, the first battalion had completed basic training, recruitment for the second battalion (open to all East Timorese over the age of eighteen, including women) had begun, and a code of military discipline had been developed. The force was expected to reach maturity by late 2003.[49]

The establishment of the ETDF enhanced the prospects for security within East Timor in two particular ways. First, it helped in a programmed and orderly manner to facilitate PKF downsizing (and eventual withdrawal) as the ETDF came on line. Second, it avoided having an armed and disaffected group within East Timorese society. The longer Falintil remained cantoned and armed without a clear purpose, the greater the prospects of security incidents occurring. The psychological and physical tensions within cantoned and armed forces are real. This was clearly demonstrated by the need to send on leave large numbers of unarmed Falintil soldiers for protracted periods and by the instances (albeit infrequent) of armed Falintil members illegally leaving the cantonment.

In retrospect, the creation of the ETDF and its transition from Falintil was a difficult exercise, but one that helped cement an effective partnership between the UN and the East Timorese. In UNTAET's difficult first year, a seemingly intractable problem had been resolved. In the process, the UN broke new ground in conflict resolution and gained valuable experience. The key to the success rested upon the commitment and discipline of Falintil, the watchful assistance and advice of the PKF, the UN's flexibility, and the diplomatic and financial support from Australia and Portugal.

JUSTICE AND THE RULE OF LAW

One of the greatest challenges facing UNTAET was to restore an effective judicial system quickly and thereby establish the rule of law. Indonesian law, with which the East Timorese were familiar, was quickly reinstituted as the norm, with necessary modification to ensure UN conventions on human rights.[50] It was not the law that was the major problem but rather the ability of the transitional administration to implement it effectively. The justice sector was slow to get started, and it progressed incrementally under difficult circumstances and with limited resources. UNTAET's slowness reflected the enormity of the task and the difficulty in finding and training qualified judicial and correctional (penal) staff and in securing sufficient resources. But the slow progress in establishing the rule of law was also caused by the lack of preparatory planning by the Secretariat in the months following the 5 May Agreements. The Dili District Court did not begin public proceedings until 11 May 2000, and the correctional system did not begin to function adequately until later that year. It was early 2001 before the judicial system for serious crimes started to operate effectively.[51] By October 2001, the justice system was still in a nascent state, with only twenty-five East Timorese judges and thirteen prosecutors, most of whom "had only secondary education and less than two years of training and experience."[52]

The slow implementation of the rule of law also impacted on CIVPOL and PKF operations. Much of the criticism of CIVPOL's inaction to prevent petty crime could have been averted had UNTAET been able to implement the rule of law more quickly. For many months there was a backlog in the courts, due in part to a lack of judges, and the single detention center established by INTERFET was overflowing. CIVPOL's credibility to arrest offenders was for many months undermined by this lack of detention facilities and an effective judicial system. Likewise, the PKF sought continuously to reconcile its powers under its ROE with the burgeoning volume of UNTAET legal regulations. This was particularly the case with the procedural rights of persons within East Timor (especially in relation to surrendered militia and the handing over to civil authorities within twenty-four hours of any person detained in accordance with ROE).

HUMAN RIGHTS AND CRIMES AGAINST HUMANITY

An important consideration for UNTAET in reestablishing the rule of law was the requirement to ensure that human rights issues were fully incorporated. This necessitated implementation throughout all areas of government and within society. But it also required handling crimes against humanity, particularly those that had occurred throughout 1999 in connection with the UNAMET ballot. These two separate issues were somewhat entwined in the early days of UNTAET and took time to disentangle. In practical terms, the general human rights issues for the emerging nation were appropriately handled on a case-by-case basis, although, here again, a lack of mission planning soon became evident. The human rights coordinator arrived in the mission without a budget or adequate staff. There was no human rights concept of operations or a detailed plan, and liaison with other elements of UNTAET remained haphazard. After some months, the first coordinator, who had worked with great diligence and commitment, resigned in frustration.[53] More work is required to prepare human rights staff for such missions, and the role and responsibilities of the Office of the High Commissioner for Human Rights (OHCHR) requires greater fidelity.

Efforts to address the more sensitive human rights issues relating to crimes against humanity proved more problematic. "Addressing the past" in such circumstances is always difficult and often takes considerable time. This was the dilemma in East Timor. Both the UN and Indonesia conducted some notable work to identify possible war criminals, but progress to bring to account those identified was slow. This was not surprising considering the stature and influence still exerted in Indonesia by some senior military officers and militia leaders who had been implicated. At the same time, however, while eventual justice was seen to be important by some East Timorese leaders, there was also a sense that this should not impede reconciliation for the majority of displaced people languishing in refugee camps in West Timor. The issue of reconciliation was important and difficult to delineate, as the East Timorese remained divided on the subject. In an effort to encourage the refugees to return from West Timor, Xanana Gusmão, supported by Taur Matan Ruak and Bishop Nascimento, advocated clemency, even amnesty, to returning militia leaders. UNTAET's position remained that all refugees were welcome to return but that there would be no amnesty for crimes committed in 1999 and that suspects would face the East Timor justice system.

Regardless of the final outcome in such circumstances, the necessity for the UN to effectively gather and preserve evidence is a fundamental requirement, and there has been criticism that the UN has been underresourced and slow to act. A Serious Crimes Investigation Unit was created, but it was described by staff members as suffering from "mismanagement, weak leadership, and inadequate resources"[54] and, according to one of the unit's former prosecutors, "the criminal justice system has become the black mark on the UN Mission's record in East Timor."[55] Nevertheless, by December 2001, thirty-three indictments, charging eighty-two individuals with crimes against humanity committed between 1 January and 25 October 1999, had been filed with the Office of the East Timor General Prosecutor. Fourteen cases had also been tried before the Special Panel for Serious Crimes of the Dili District Court (established by UNTAET on 6 June 2000), with twenty-one convictions handed down.[56] Judgment on the major trial for crimes against humanity in connection with the postballot violence in the Los Palos area was handed down on 11 December 2001.[57] In early 2001, a UN report analyzing human rights violations during the ballot period was compiled, identifying senior Indonesian military and police commanders.[58] At time of writing the Indonesia government had taken little action against the main perpetrators named in this report.[59] To assist further in the healing process, a Reception, Truth and Reconciliation Commission, along the lines of the one in South Africa, was being established to deal with those implicated in lesser crimes.[60] It was to be staffed predominantly by East Timorese, assisted by an international technical assistance unit.

HUMANITARIAN ASSISTANCE AND DISPLACED PEOPLE

The difficulties encountered in dealing with the large numbers of IDPs within East Timor following the postballot violence were discussed in Chapter 2. The second and more taxing problem was the return of refugees from West Timor. UNTAET had no mandate to operate in West Timor, and the Indonesian authorities initially proved lukewarm in their efforts to see the problem resolved quickly. The responsibility fell to the UNHCR, which received excellent cooperation from IOM and various NGOs in its efforts to implement an effective system to resettle the refugees. In this, however, UNHCR was more successful once the refugees were across the border in East Timor than it was in West Timor. There it faced a major challenge: not only did the people have to be freed from the militia-controlled refugee camps, but they also had to be convinced that retribution would not be taken against them. To make matters worse, within the refugee camps the militias activated a malicious propaganda campaign fabricating stories of murder and rape against those returning, often resorting to actual intimidation.

The militias' activities hindered UNHCR's efforts to implement its resettlement program, but a comprehensive plan was activated nonetheless, which included the establishment of refugee holding centers, "look and see" visits, and family reunion meetings. UNHCR's program was more successful in the special arrangements made for the reception and reintegration of returnees within their communities. Occasional problems occurred, but generally the resettlement went smoothly.[61] The East Timorese themselves made a clear distinction between key militia personalities and the vast majority of the population they accepted as bystanders. Most of the credit for this peaceful reintegration goes to the people and to the positive role played by the church and the CNRT, who actively campaigned for peace and forgiveness. Xanana Gusmão's leadership in advocating assistance and forgiveness to those returning was generally heeded by the people.

A sensitive issue requiring careful handling was the balance to be achieved between quickly resettling refugees and maintaining security. To this end, military forces and UNHCR can have different outlooks, and without close cooperation tensions and misunderstandings are bound to arise. UNHCR's focus is on vacating refugee camps and resettling the population as quickly as possible. The military's focus is on maintaining security and avoiding situations that might cause instability. INTERFET and the

PKF worked very closely with UNHCR to ensure that this balance was achieved. To handle the possibility of a mass return of refugees, an SRSG directive was issued to ensure proper coordination between all agencies. UNHCR established a crisis center that was jointly manned with the PKF, and rehearsals were conducted in the border region to ensure that procedures were in place. These rehearsals ensured cooperation and commitment at the working level and enabled initial plans to be amended in accordance with the wishes of both UNHCR and the PKF. CIVPOL and the Border Service played important roles in refugee processing and were fully included in the development of resettlement plans. The human rights coordinator was kept well informed and, working with the church and various East Timorese groups, made provision for the more sensitive cases. On occasion, Falintil assisted with the resettlement program to prevent acts of retribution.

By July 2000, approximately 170,000 refugees had been returned successfully and resettled with few difficulties. But following the peak of 9,845 returnees in March, the regular flow of returnees slowed significantly, and by February 2001, only an additional 6,000 had returned.[62] This reflected the continued uncertainty of the hardcore pro-integration elements about returning and the impact of the militias' propaganda campaign throughout the camps. This reduction caused the cessation of the family reunion meetings at the border, which were becoming increasingly insecure and yielding few dividends. With Xanana Gusmão's agreement, the SRSG intensified efforts to liaise directly with militia leaders, appointing his Malaysian chief of staff, Nagalingam Parameswaran,[63] to explore all possible options. At the same time, the bishops maintained close contact with their counterparts in West Timor and did all they could to encourage the refugees to return. Occasional meetings occurred between militia and Falintil leaders, but the latter showed little enthusiasm, perhaps understandably, for enhancing the militias' credibility by becoming politically involved in efforts to resolve old disputes. While fully supporting reconciliation, and even assisting in resettling some of the more sensitive returnee cases, the Falintil leaders were not inclined to involve themselves with, or empower, their old adversaries.

A major setback occurred with the murder in September 2000 of the three UNHCR workers in Atambua, which resulted in the immediate closure of the UNTAET office in Kupang and withdrawal of all UN personnel from West Timor. Intense negotiations between UNTAET and Indonesian authorities quickly began in a combined effort to stabilize the security situation in line with the Security Council's resolution of 8 September.[64] However, a visit by representatives of the Security Council to Indonesia and East Timor on 12–17 November failed to reassure the UN that security in West Timor had sufficiently improved to justify the return of UN personnel. Additionally, UNHCR remained reluctant to endanger its personnel and reestablish a permanent presence. Agreement to reposition UNHCR workers was not reached until September 2001, one year after the murders and only after Indonesia had taken steps to improve security by deploying an additional battalion from Java to the Atambua district.

Before his promotion and handover to General da Costa, General Syahnakri initiated a proposal to return the milsas to East Timor.[65] Syahnakri considered that if ex-military East Timorese, and their estimated 20,000–30,000 family members, could be resettled successfully, this might convince others to return. This prospect was quickly embraced by UNTAET, but little action was taken by the Indonesian authorities for several months until pension entitlements could be resolved. Following the Atambua incident, this proposal was revisited, and in November 2000 around fifty ex-milsas and their families (400 total) were resettled without incident in the eastern districts. Following this success, modest refugee movement resumed. By late October 2001, UNHCR in partnership with IOM and UNTAET had helped some 188,646 refugees return to East Timor, but an estimated 60,000 to 80,000 still remained in Indonesia.[66] It had seemed unlikely that the hardline pro-integrationists would return, partly because of their strong convictions but also because of their involvement in the postballot devastation and their unwillingness to face criminal proceedings. However, a major breakthrough occurred on 17 October when a key ex-militia figure, Nemésio Lopes de Carvalho, and more than 370 refugees returned from camps in West Timor in a process facilitated by Gusmão and Parameswaran.[67] In all, 3,233 East Timorese returned during October 2001, making it the highest number to do so in a single month since March 2000. This increase may be attributed to a growing confidence in the situation in East Timor, particularly since the successful elections on 30 August. But Indonesia has also strengthened its resolve to assist with the refugee issue in setting an end-date of 1 January 2002 for continued support to East Timor refugees. (At time of writing, final resolution of the refugee problem was still to be achieved.)

Overall, the efforts to resettle the displaced population and to resolve the refugee problem were extremely successful. This was a complex problem, but it was actioned with professionalism and commitment by all concerned. The role the East Timorese leadership played and the conduct of the people deserve special mention. There are many valuable lessons to be learned from the East Timorese experience, and the UN should be encouraged to examine these in more detail.

UNTAET AND THE
INTERNATIONAL FINANCIAL INSTITUTIONS

The important role of the Bretton Woods financial institutions deserves brief consideration. In general terms, the critical linkage between poverty reduction and postconflict reconstruction gained prominence in the World Bank with the end of the Cold War, and in 1997, the Bank established a Post-Conflict and Reconstruction Unit and created a separate Post-Conflict Fund. East Timor was identified early by the World Bank as a possible location where assistance might be appropriate. In 1998, the Bank conducted a detailed assessment mission and started formulating a strategy for early involvement. Following the ballot and violence, agreement was reached in September 1999 with the UN for a Joint Assessment Mission (JAM) to visit East Timor and to include Bretton Woods representatives. The JAM arrived in Dili on 29 October and, through discussions and field visits, confirmed the need for early representation in East Timor by the financial institutions and for their close cooperation with the transitional administration.[68] Although a full assessment is required, the World Bank deserves great credit for its assistance to East Timor. Led by its energetic and competent coordinator, Sarah Cliffe, it quickly established close relations with the East Timorese and, from the outset, engaged them fully in development planning and in the decisionmaking process.[69] As early as 21 February 2000, World Bank president James Wolfensohn, Xanana Gusmão, and the SRSG signed a grant agreement for the disbursement of U.S.$21.5 million over two-and-one-half years for community empowerment and local government projects. Funds were provided through the Trust Fund for East Timor (TFET), with grants for economic reconstruction and development activities prepared and supervised by the World Bank and the Asian Development Bank.[70] In January 2002, international pledges to the fund amounted to U.S.$167.5 million. Acting as trustee for the TFET, the World Bank played a key role in helping maintain international support for East Timor. It also worked closely with UNTAET's professional Donor Coordination Unit in preparing the background papers for the regular international donor conferences. The early involvement and role of Bretton Woods institutions in the planning and execution of future postconflict missions requires further examination, and the lessons from East Timor will be particularly instructive.

CONCLUSION

The UN's intervention in East Timor reflected one of partnership with the East Timorese and overall cooperation by Indonesia. The coalescence of these two factors, so essential for successful intervention, is rare in postconflict situations.

As with most partnerships, there were differences of opinion and tense situations, particularly during the first six months of UNTAET. But UN intervention was ultimately successful because of the common goals underpinning the relationship. Much of the credit for this goes to the East Timorese, who after enduring so much under Indonesian rule, were still prepared to forgive the mistakes and inadequacies of an international transitional administration that had not been specifically trained or prepared for the task.

Throughout the UNTAET interregnum, the critical importance of maintaining a secure environment stands out as an obvious, but essential, precondition for success. INTERFET and the PKF deserve great credit for their performance in East Timor, but as demonstrated, the demands for national security go beyond the competency of military forces and embrace all aspects of governance and development. The effective establishment of the rule of law is fundamental to success, and East Timor provides useful lessons for the UN in the judicial, penal, and police sectors.

In analyzing the UN's intervention in East Timor, it is essential to highlight the lessons to be learned both from its successes and from its mistakes and disappointments. This is the subject of Chapters 4 and 5.

NOTES

1. Kofi Annan, *Report of the Secretary-General on the United Nations Transitional Administration in East Timor*, S/2001/983, 18 October 2001, par. 83, p. 11.

2. Ian Martin, *Self-Determination in East Timor: The United Nations, the Ballot, and International Intervention* (Boulder, CO: Lynne Rienner, 2001), p. 126. See Astri Suhrke "Peacekeepers as Nation-Builders," *International Peacekeeping* 8, no. 4 (2001): 6, who contends that "the planning of UNTAET took place in the context of a fierce bureaucratic power struggle between DPA and DPKO" that was finally resolved by the Secretary-General in mid-September 1999.

3. Jarat Chopra, "The UN's Kingdom of East Timor," *Survival* 42, no. 3 (2000): 32–34.

4. See Parliament of the Commonwealth of Australia, *Final Report of the Senate Foreign Affairs, East Timor,* pp. 79–95; and James Dunn, "Crimes Against Humanity in East Timor, January to October 1999," unpublished UN Report, 2001. Available online at http://www.etan.org/news/2001a/dunn1.htm (accessed 9 January 2002).

5. Kofi Annan, S/1999/1024, Part IV, pars. 25–31, pp. 7–9.

6. See Annex B for a copy of the mandate—Resolution 1272(1999)—and objectives.

7. Cedric de Coning, "The UN Transitional Administration in East Timor: Lessons Learned from the First 100 Days," *International Peacekeeping* 6, no. 2 (2000): p. 85. De Coning served as a civil affairs officer with UNTAET from December 1999 until the end of February 2000 and acknowledges that most of the officers were relatively young, with little prior experience or local knowledge, and lacked local language skills. They nonetheless, "had to understand, grasp and make decisions that would affect the food security situation of thousands of people" (pp. 85–86).

8. Shin-ichi Suzuki, also from Japan, replaced Takahashi in August 2001.

9. On 5 July 2001, Cady was replaced by Dennis McNamara (New Zealand). Before assuming this appointment, McNamara was the UN Special Coordinator on Internal Displacement. With twenty-five years of experience with the UNHCR, he had also served previously as Deputy SRSG in Kosovo, heading the humanitarian pillar.

10. De Coning, "UN Transitional Administration in East Timor," p. 87. Kofi Annan advised the Security Council on 18 October 2001 that CIVPOL numbered 1,485 personnel. Annan, S/2001/983, par. 23, p. 3.

11. UNSC Resolution 1272 had authorized a total strength of 1,640 CIVPOL, but this figure was never realized.

12. De Coning, "UN Transitional Administration in East Timor," pp. 88–89, also notes the need to improve "the overall coordination and cooperation" and that "it should be an overarching initiative." He further argues that this will not happen "until mission co-ordination is recognised as a specific specialised function with its own resources and until this task is seen as a crucial mission management tool."

13. In late April 2000, more than 100 Timorese staff hired by UNTAET went on strike to demand salary increases and better working conditions. UNTAET daily press release, 25 April 2000. Available online at http://www.un.org/peace/etimor (accessed 23 January 2002).

14. The Border Service was responsible for customs and immigration.

15. The first director of UNTAET OCPI was Manoel de Almeida é Silva. He made a significant contribution but was soon recalled for higher duties in New York. The office then progressed slowly until the appointment of Anne-Margrete Wachtmeister in December 2000.

16. By April 2001 also, the reconstruction program was approaching the halfway mark: 47 percent of the more than 67,000 houses in East Timor made unlivable during the 1999 violence had been rehabilitated; and 20 percent of the 2,329 villages had electricity restored, which was 10 percent lower than before 1999. UNTAET daily press release, 4 May 2001. Available online at http://www. un.org/peace/etimor (accessed 20 January 2002).

17. Initially, the interim health authority was the only UN agency to appoint an East Timorese in a dual leadership role. This contrasted with the World Bank's approach of including East Timorese personnel in decisionmaking from the outset. See Suhrke, "Peacekeepers As Nation-Builders," p. 15.

18. The need to reorganize UNTAET and empower the East Timorese was first announced in a speech by Peter Galbraith at the Conference on Reconstruction of East Timor, in Liquiça in May 2000.

19. First Transitional Cabinet ministries: Police and Emergency Services, J. C. Cady; Justice, Gita Welch; Political, Constitutional and Electoral Affairs, Peter Galbraith; Finance, Michael Francino; Foreign Affairs, José Ramos-Horta; Internal Administration, Ana Pessoa; Infrastructure, João Carrascalão; Economic Affairs, Mari Alkatiri; Social Affairs, Fr. Filomeno Jacob.

20. Particular credit goes to the dedicated staff of the Electoral Office, led by Carlos Valenzuela.

21. Annan, S/2001/983, par. 10, p. 2.

22. For further detail on these political developments, see ibid., pars. 4–8, pp. 1–2.

23. The Portuguese battalion had in fact been ready to join the MNF from the outset, together with other ground and air forces, but Portugal acceded to the Secretary-General's request not to send ground troops until the transition to PKF.

During INTERFET, however, Portugal still provided a frigate and Hercules aircraft.

24. The military component's mission was periodically adjusted to reflect changes in UNTAET and mandate update. As at December 2001, the mission of the PKF and UNMOG was "to help maintain a secure environment in East Timor in accordance with UN Security Council Resolutions 1272 and 1338; to assist UNTAET in the conduct of safe and democratic elections; and to assist the East Timor Public Administration, within its capabilities, in the development of sustainable East Timorese organizations and infrastructure."

25. The number of troop-contributing nations varied as the mission continued. A summary is in Annex C and the organization of the force headquarters is in Annex D.

26. Some of the logistics and aviation support was provided by civilians, thereby reducing military numbers.

27. Annan, S/2001/983, par. 56, p. 8.

28. The New Zealand (composite) battalion included infantry companies from Fiji and Nepal and an infantry platoon from Ireland (and later Singapore).

29. Whereas INTERFET's aviation concentrated on military operations and assisted the civil administration and humanitarian agencies when able to do so, UNTAET's aviation serviced the entire mission. Many of UNTAET's helicopters were also less capable for combat operations than INTERFET's Blackhawks.

30. Operations Cobra and Crocodilo were mounted in September by Sector Central, commanded by Colonel José Alberto Martins Ferreira, who had returned from leave in Portugal in time for the CNRT Congress. Ferreira had for the previous six months served as head of the Military Information cell in Headquarters PKF, where he had developed a deep understanding of the militia. His leadership was fully tested during this difficult time, and he gained the full confidence and respect of the East Timorese.

31. Private Manning was killed on 24 July and Private Jaisi on 10 August 2000.

32. A major incident occurred on 29 May 2001 in which five civilians were killed and up to forty wounded, when hand grenades were thrown among a group of Timorese attending a market on the border 7 kilometers southeast of Balibo.

33. Additional force capabilities, totaling 500 troops and including an electronic warfare capability, were requested on 31 August. These force enhancements were quickly approved by the Secretary-General, and the PKF was progressively reinforced over the next six months.

34. Lieutenant General Winai Phattiyakul, also from Thailand, replaced General Boonsrang Niumpradit on 31 August 2001.

35. There were very few allegations and instances of human rights violations by the PKF. Overall, the PKF maintained considerable respect from the East Timorese because of its professionalism.

36. Brigadier Gardiner was replaced by Major General Sergio Rosario from Brazil in July 2001.

37. To enhance public safety, UNTAET promulgated a regulation, dated 23 April 2001, restricting the possession, sale, and use of weapons (UNTAET/REG/2001/5).

38. The Transitional Cabinet approved the establishment of an ETDF on 12 September 2000. The ODFD commenced operations on 23 November.

39. This position was filled by Nici Dahrendorf (UK), who had led the King's College study on security force options for East Timor in July 2000.

40. Annan, S/2001/983, par. 30, p. 4.

41. Resolution 1319(2000) of 8 September 2000 called on the Indonesian government to take immediate additional steps, in fulfillment of its responsibilities, to disarm and disband the militia immediately, restore law and order in the affected areas in West Timor, ensure safety and security in the refugee camps and for humanitarian workers, and prevent cross-border incursions into East Timor.

42. Annan, S/2001/983, par. 24, p. 3. By 30 September 2001, the ETPS comprised 1,068 officers (of a maximum projected force of 3,000), including 126 placed at command-level positions.

43. On 30 May 2000, Company 5 rebelled under the leadership of its former commander, Ele Sette, as a result of Faltintil's internal restructuring. The insurrection was quickly resolved, with Ele Sette and a number of followers leaving the cantonment peacefully. The second incident occurred on 16 June, when sixty Falintil departed the cantonment for Dili to intervene in a security dispute between rival gangs. They were intercepted by the PKF and CIVPOL on the outskirts of Dili and persuaded to return peacefully to Aileu.

44. Centre for Defence Studies, King's College London, "Independent Study on Security Force Options and Security Sector Reform for East Timor," 8 August 2000.

45. The fifty ETDF Marine officers began training with Portuguese specialists in February 2001. Two modified Albatross (now termed Oecussi class) patrol boats were delivered by the Portuguese government on 11 December 2001, as part of a $U.S.2.2 million Portuguese aid package to the ETDF navy. Named Oecussi and Atauro, they were formally offered to the ETDF naval component on 12 January 2002.

46. For the duration of UNTAET'S mandate, the transitional administrator has command and control of the ETDF and the authority to appoint and dismiss the chief of the Defence Force and to appoint its officers. UNTAET Regulation 2001/1, Section 4, 31 January 2001. Available online at http://www.un.org/peace/etimor (accessed 11 January 2002).

47. At the June 2001 conference, representatives of Australia, Brazil, Japan, Malaysia, Mozambique, New Zealand, the Philippines, Portugal, the Republic of Korea, Singapore, Thailand, Great Britain, and the United States indicated they would provide continued matériel and technical support to the ETDF. The support is expected to continue until the Defence Force becomes fully functional. UNTAET daily press release, 26 June 2001. Available online at http://www.un.org/peace/etimor (accessed 15 January 2002).

48. Basic training for ETDF recruits was conducted by Portugal and specialist training by Australia.

49. Annan, S/2001/983, par. 65, p. 9. The PKF will be responsible for East Timor's defense and security until independence, after which arrangements will be made by the new government and the UN for safeguarding the country's security until the ETDF is in a position to do so.

50. UNTAET/REG/1999/1, 27 November 1999, "On the Authority of the Transitional Administration in East Timor," stated that the laws applied in East Timor prior to 25 October 1999 would apply except where they conflicted with internationally recognized human rights standards, the fulfillment of UNTAET's mandate under Resolution 1272(1999), or any other regulation or directive issued by the transitional administrator. Particular laws that no longer applied were those on antisubversion; social organizations; national security; national protection and defense; mobilization and demobilization; and defense and security. Capital punishment was also abolished.

51. Dili and Baucau district courts were fully functional by the end of 2000 and had jurisdiction over 90 percent of the criminal cases being investigated at that time. The Special Panel for Serious Crimes, a three-judge panel set up by UNTAET, began hearings in January 2001. The Dili district court had jurisdiction over pretrial matters prior to this date, pending the establishment of the Special Panel.

52. Annan, S/2001/983, par. 20, p. 3.

53. The first coordinator was Sidney Jones from Human Rights Watch.

54. Elizabeth Neuffer, "Slaughter Suspects Elude UN's Reach," *Boston Globe,* 9 February 2001, p. A6.

55. Ibid.

56. In the eleven cases not connected to the Los Palos trial, the sentences ranged from seven to fifteen years. One of these convictions was under appeal as of December 2001. Annan, S/2001/983, par. 33, p. 5.

57. Ten members of the pro-Indonesia Team Alpha militia were convicted of the 25 September 1999 killing of two nuns, three priests, and an Indonesian journalist, as well as a number of other people in the Los Palos subdistrict (Lautem district); they received jail terms of up to thirty-three years. An eleventh suspect—Indonesian Syaful Anwar, second in-command of Indonesian Kopassus special forces, Lautem district—was indicted but is currently at large.

58. See Dunn, "Crimes Against Humanity," pp. 40–52.

59. Some progress may be under way with the announcement (Reuters, 26 November 2001) that Indonesia would set up a special court to try suspects accused of human rights abuses over the past few decades, including those responsible for the killings in East Timor following the 30 August 1999 ballot.

60. UNTAET/REG/2001/10 of 13 July 2001 authorized the commission, which will have a two-year mandate and be empowered to hold hearings and seek evidence to establish the truth about all relevant events that occurred in East Timor 25 April 1974–25 October 1999. Annan, S/2001/983, par. 40, p. 6.

61. The ultimate success of the refugee resettlement program must await future evaluation. Radical factions may have infiltrated as part of the process and may resume their political activities once the PKF departs East Timor.

62. UNTAET daily press release, 29 October 2001. Available online at http://www.un.org/peace/etimor (accessed 20 January 2002).

63. Parameswaran was a former Malaysian ambassador to Vietnam and, prior to joining UNTAET, served as director-general of the ASEAN secretariat in the Malaysian Ministry of Foreign Affairs.

64. The meeting took place in Denpasar on 14 September 2000. The UNTAET delegation was led by the SRSG and Xanana Gusmão, and the Indonesian delegation was led by Indonesia's coordinating minister for political, social, and security affairs, General Susilo Bambang Yudhyono, who had ensured that additional TNI reinforcements were sent to Atambua immediately after the murders.

65. "Milsas" was the name given to East Timorese armed auxiliaries that formed part of the TNI.

66. Annan, S/2001/983, par. 36, p. 5.

67. Nemésio Lopes de Carvalho was deputy commander of the Mahidi militia group. He was brought by staff from UNTAET's Serious Crimes Unit to Dili, where he appeared before a judge working to ascertain the degree of his involvement in the violence surrounding the 1999 popular consultation. He was later conditionally released.

68. For an account of the mission, see Sarah Cliffe, "The Joint Assessment Mission and Reconstruction in East Timor," in James J. Fox and Dionisio Babo

Soares, eds., *Out of the Ashes: Destruction and Reconstruction of East Timor* (Adelaide: Crawford House, 2000), pp. 252–261.

69. Initially, as Suhrke, "Peacekeepers As Nation-Builders," p. 16, asserts, UNTAET "opposed [this] scheme, arguing that local participation must await formal, UN-held elections."

70. TFET receives funds from Australia, Finland, Ireland, Italy, Japan, New Zealand, Norway, Portugal, Great Britain, the United States, the European Community, and the World Bank. *Trust Fund for East Timor, Update No. 14*, 15 January 2002, p. 1. Available online at http://www.worldbank.org/eap (accessed 19 January 2002).

4

Lessons for Successful UN Intervention

But when the United Nations does send its forces to uphold the peace, they must be prepared to confront the lingering forces of war and violence, with the ability and determination to defeat them. . . . But force alone cannot create peace; it can only create the space in which peace may be built.

—Brahimi report, 21 August 2000[1]

This chapter identifies the main lessons from the UN's intervention in East Timor, with particular emphasis on UNTAET, and provides a checklist for future UN complex peace operations. The conditions for UNTAET's success are considered on the broader level, with emphasis on the issues that optimize prospects for lasting peace and East Timor's viability as a new state. Specific military lessons are covered in Chapter 5.

DEFINING "SUCCESSFUL INTERVENTION"

Defining "success" in peacekeeping missions is not easy. On the one hand, the result of a mission can be judged against its mandate. Clearly, if a mission achieves its authorized tasks, it must be successful. On the other hand, it is possible to consider success in a broader context. The litmus test for successful interventions might arguably be the extent to which they contribute to lasting peace and to the development of democratic and viable states. But UN missions often have limiting mandates. Intervention may be restricted to facilitating a democratic election, to monitoring an agreed cease-fire, to relieving or preventing unnecessary human suffering, to reducing unacceptable casualty levels, or simply to stabilizing a situation by enforcing a cease-fire and maintaining the separation of combatants. There are examples where UN missions, such as UNMOGIP (Kashmir) and

UNFICYP (Cyprus), have existed for years successfully meeting their mandate but having limited influence on the prospects for long-term peace and resolution. UNTAET, on the other hand, was provided with a strong mandate, one that was feasible and achievable and one, therefore, that provided every opportunity to produce the desired longer-term objectives.

A. B. Fetherston, in her analysis of the literature on traditional and modern peacekeeping, has noted some contradictions between commentators and identified more than twenty main factors that impact on the success or failure of peacekeeping missions.[2] Some of these factors were within the control of the UN and others were not. Fetherston suggested that "the potential negative impact of factors over which the UN has more or less direct control can be minimised, while factors over which the UN has little or no control can cause great difficulties."[3] She concluded, "There are obvious problems with our current level of understanding about which elements of peacekeeping (and other interventions) contribute most to success or failure. Indeed, definitions of success vary widely. And findings are by no means congruous."[4]

A more recent study of five "successful" missions—Namibia, El Salvador, Cambodia (mixed success), Mozambique, and Croatia—argues that "a permissive 'situation,' consensual interests of the Security Council," and, importantly, "the UN's ability to 'learn' *during* the process of implementing its mandates" are each "necessary for success, and jointly they are sufficient." The study specifically contends that a mission will be unable to implement its mandate if its ability to learn in the field is inhibited. It further points out that the Secretariat needs to implement changes that enable it to learn *between* missions.[5]

It is unlikely that a template can be contrived to guarantee UN success in complex peace missions, not least because many factors interact to determine an operation's success or failure. No two missions are ever the same, and each mission reflects the specific conditions prevailing on the ground at a particular time. Sometimes there is genuine commitment by the conflicting parties for the UN to bring lasting peace, but sometimes UN intervention may be only reluctantly accepted as politically expedient. On other occasions, UN intervention might not be invited but imposed—normally in situations where there has been a total breakdown in governance and massive human rights violations. To complicate matters further, circumstances may change throughout a mission's tenure, thereby requiring frequent review by the Security Council and often causing reassessment of and changes to the mandate.

Nonetheless, UNTAET provides an example of successful UN intervention and raises the question as to whether the conditions of implementation can be replicated, and the lessons learned applied, in future peacekeeping missions. For example, Sergio Vieira de Mello has indicated similarities between the situations in East Timor and Afghanistan, noting that East Timor could be used as a model and stating that "the experiences we [UNTAET] had, the mistakes we made, can be learnt from and applied in Afghanistan."[6] By using East Timor as a case study, it is possible to construct a checklist against which the prospects for lasting peace in other circumstances can be assessed. This does not mean that future UN interventions will or will not occur, or that they will succeed or fail, but rather that the Security Council might be better able to realistically assess the prospects for meaningful and long-term resolution if intervention is to be authorized. Clearly, if the Security Council were to assess that all or most of the factors in the checklist were unlikely to result in success, then serious questions should be asked about the justification for intervention in the first place. In such circumstances it might be better not to intervene at all rather than to intervene with the likely prospect of failure.

THE PEACEKEEPING BAKER'S DOZEN

While acknowledging the dissimilarity of missions, and having explained the unique circumstances surrounding the East Timor operation, this study identifies thirteen factors that impacted on the success of the UN's intervention in the devastated territory. These "conditions for success" provide a suggested checklist—referred to as the Peacekeeping Baker's Dozen—against which future UN interventions might be assessed. Depending on the specific circumstances of each mission, some of these factors, listed below, will be more important than others, but they are all likely to impact on success or failure in multidimensional peacekeeping operations.

1. Legitimate intervention.
2. Sustained international commitment.
3. Achievable political objectives and exit strategy.
4. Host-country support.
5. Feasible and achievable mandate.
6. Thorough and timely preparation and planning.
7. Restoration and maintenance of a secure environment.
8. Effective governance.
9. Capable leadership and effective partnership.
10. Sustainable economic and social development.
11. Implementing human rights and addressing the past.
12. Managing displaced people.
13. Effective emergency relief.

Legitimate Intervention

The most important condition for successful intervention is legitimacy, which influences the other factors and significantly affects the final success or failure of a mission. Legitimacy can be legal, moral, and political. The legal legitimacy for intervention is that it accords with international law, whereas the moral legitimacy relates more to the humanitarian justification for the intervention and the level of force deemed acceptable. The question of moral legitimacy as a sole basis for intervention, particularly in relation to humanitarian intervention, is a controversial concept in international law. The UN can work to win wider support for an operation, enhancing its political legitimacy. It might also argue the moral and legal cases for a given intervention. When legality and morality coincide, considerable international political support for intervention is likely to exist, improving the prospects for success. This was the case in East Timor, where a strong regional and broader international commitment was evident. Also, the action taken by Indonesia as the governing power to initiate the ballot, and Indonesia's agreement (following the violence) to honor the ballot results, further ensured the UN's legitimacy to intervene.

UN intervention in other trouble spots has rarely experienced the same level of international support as was the case in East Timor. This was largely because of the clear requirements and obligations contained in the 5 May Agreements and Indonesia's failure to guarantee security following the ballot. In such circumstances, and particularly in light of the widespread and systematic violence and destruction, the international community and Indonesia confirmed the need for MNF intervention to restore security, followed by a transitional administration. Moreover, the people of East Timor demanded no less and fully supported the UN's intervention.

The importance of legitimacy to mission success is an obvious lesson from East Timor. It provides the UN with authority and largely shapes the strength of the mandate under which the mission will work. Also, member states are less likely to seek diplomatic compromise in situations where legitimacy is so apparent, thereby increasing the likelihood of mission success.

Sustained International Commitment

Closely aligned with legitimacy is the degree and longevity of international support for intervention. Sustained international commitment is the strategic center of gravity for UN success because it represents the collective will of member states to act. International support is further strengthened if it has the political support of the P-5 nations in the Security Council and, particularly, support from the United States as the world's superpower. These circumstances applied in East Timor. A key lesson that emerges from the UN's intervention in East Timor is that its success derived from this solid and unwavering international support. The degree of commitment was a key factor in enabling the Security Council to provide the mandates required by the successive UN missions and to sustaining UNTAET in its long and difficult task. Such strong international resolve has seldom been achieved, or sustained, in international politics. East Timor clearly demonstrates, however, the benefits that can result and the positive changes that can be made when such an approach is taken.

International support can be political and materiél, and East Timor attracted both despite its minor strategic significance to most of the contributing countries. Unlike in many other trouble spots, it is probable that East Timor's strategic insignificance actually assisted in galvanizing the international response. To the member states, East Timor represented the core values of the UN. Consequently, not only could international support be legitimized, but following other less successful UN operations, East Timor offered good prospects for a successful outcome. The strong international backing for the UN effort in East Timor, therefore, was based primarily on the legitimacy of each mandate, but it was also sustained by the constructive progress achieved by each of the missions. In this sense, "donor fatigue" did not materialize as quickly and as easily as it had with some other missions. Clearly, there is a strong relationship between the degree of international commitment and the level of progress achieved. With security restored and reconstruction begun within a relatively benign environment, the international community was prepared to continue support to East Timor. Another factor influencing this outcome was the perception of the manageable size of East Timor, with a population of under 1 million people rather than tens of millions. An obvious lesson is that most countries find it more palatable to reinforce success than to continue to invest in failure.

The degree of international commitment was particularly demonstrated in the military and CIVPOL contingents. Military contributions for Chapter VII peace enforcement operations are sensitive, mainly because member states are fearful of sustaining casualties and of risking adverse public criticism at home. Yet for a relatively small military force, INTERFET comprised twenty-two nations and the PKF more than thirty nations.[7] Having a lead state was probably also beneficial in maintaining international support. Member states know that the lead state will carry the heaviest burden and (usually) continue to the end of the mission. The force composition of the MNF and the PKF provided an impressive mix from regional countries and from every continent. The willingness of member states to contribute civilian police and military contingents was matched in the fields of governance, human rights, rehabilitation, reconstruction, and development. As well, numerous nations contributed to the two trust funds for East Timor and/or provided bilateral assistance. The commitment and longevity of international support for East Timor may not be so easily replicated in other interventions. Yet sustained international support is critical for success.

Achievable Political Objectives and Exit Strategy

A significant lesson from East Timor is that the prospect for successful UN intervention is enhanced considerably when there are clear and achievable political objectives. The 5 May Agreements and the UNTAET mandate provided for such an outcome. UNTAET was predicated on the transition of authority to the East Timorese in an environment of lasting peace and coincident with the establishment of a democratic and viable nation-state. Successful intervention, therefore, should always be considered in a political context, with a final "endstate" and "exit strategy." Care must be taken not to confuse endstate and end-date. There is an understandable temptation for member states to declare victory early and to confuse initial with sustainable success. The endstate and exit strategy should be clear from the start of the mission, but the end-date may require continual readjustment based on mission progress and the ability of the local authorities to assume the responsibilities of nationhood. It may take some time, therefore, before an end-date can be confirmed, and too great a focus on an early end-date may increase the prospect of a failed state.

Additionally, the role of the military in achieving political objectives must always be clear. Clausewitz understood this well in advocating that military action was an extension of politics by other means rather than an end in itself. It is instructive to compare UN intervention in Somalia and East Timor. The former lacked an achievable political endstate, with the center of gravity of military operations being on food distribution and the maintenance of its own security.[8] By comparison, military action in East Timor always supported the central political objective of transferring authority to a legitimate government in a secure environment.

In reaching a suitable endstate and exit strategy, a national strategic plan should be developed by the incoming government with assistance from the transitional UN administration and in partnership with the Bretton Woods financial institutions. This plan needs to cover the essentials of governance, security, and sustainable economic and social development, all interlaced with acceptable human rights protocols and practices. A lesson from UNTAET is that more work could have been done to construct a strategic plan from the outset of the mission.

Host-Country Support

An essential condition for success in UN interventions is the degree of acceptance and support provided by the host country. It is extremely difficult for UN missions to be effective in situations where influential sections of the host country's population do not support the UN's presence.

In East Timor, the UN's involvement was highly supported by the majority of the population. During the twenty-four years of Indonesia's occupation, the UN remained the only realistic hope for the territory's achieving self-determination. The East Timorese political leaders were conscious of this reality and were committed to working with the UN, despite differences of opinion on certain issues. UNAMET and INTERFET were welcomed by most of the population. Although the initial euphoria of UNTAET's presence waned as the months passed, no sensible alternative was ever seriously contemplated. Effective partnership between UNTAET and the East Timorese, although slow to develop, generally progressed well from mid-2000. The separation of combatants—Falintil and the militias—in the lead-up to the ballot, and the departure of the militias following the post-ballot violence, made it easier for host-country support to develop. A number of small groups of "spoilers" did exist, but none had any political impact.

East Timor's domestic political situation was unique in another way. None of the major political leaders wanted the UN to withdraw too quickly—nor were they keen to have independence declared too early. Above all, they wanted the UN to continue to help support the country following independence. Although the political leaders sometimes criticized UNTAET and UN procedures and capabilities, they did not want East Timor to be abandoned by the UN. The basis of the East Timorese complaints about the UN arose not from any wish to be freed from UN involvement, but rather from the desire to have the UN work more closely with them and be more sensitive to the needs of the people they were supporting. All the political leaders understood the difficulties to be faced in the postindependence environment and clearly recognized the need for international assistance to continue. This view was not based on a "cargo-cult" mentality, but rather on the practical understanding that East Timor's viability and freedom would be jeopardized if it were to be abandoned too quickly by the international community. In a fledgling country with no resilient public institutions, limited economic prospects, and insufficient experience in governance and bureaucracy, the East Timorese political leaders maintained a steadiness of purpose. Their determination in advocating a measured approach to ensuring the sustainability of independence for this tiny new state demonstrated considerable political maturity.

There are two important and related lessons that emerge here for future

UN transitional administrations: first, mission success depends largely on the degree of support provided by the local population; and, second, the partnership between the UN and the local population must be effective and sincere. These circumstances may seldom exist in postconflict environments, but every effort must be directed toward achieving a modicum of resemblance to them, for without them success will be difficult to achieve. The favorable domestic circumstances that applied in East Timor may prove the exception rather than the rule, but they stand as indisputable evidence of the benefits to be had if they can be aspired to. The degree of host-country support for the UN's intervention in East Timor was greater than in many other UN interventions and is unlikely to be so easily replicated in future missions. But the importance of host-country support in achieving a lasting peace is a critical issue that should never be underestimated.

Feasible and Achievable Mandate

The existence of a UN Security Council mandate provides legal, moral, and political legitimacy to international intervention, but the success of UN missions is often more directly related to the appropriateness of the provisions of that mandate. In general terms, these provisions should be based on a worst-case threat assessment and reflect political reality. In short, mandates should be feasible and achievable. A feasible mandate is one whose provisions reflect a worst-case threat assessment; unambiguously state the purpose of the mission; provide the SRSG with clear direction; clearly establish the mission's tasks; authorize a mission organization capable of fulfilling assigned tasks; specify the conditions under which force may be used (including the use of deadly force if necessary); and instruct the SRSG to regularly report on progress and to take all necessary legitimate action to achieve success.

For a mandate to be achievable it must be compatible with the political realities of the situation, reflecting commitment from all the major stakeholders and the allocation of appropriate resources to fulfill the mandate. Key stakeholders include the immediate parties to the dispute as well as other states and institutions whose interests are most affected. The position of the United States, as the sole superpower, will always be important. The mission must also be properly organized and resourced. Additionally, the timing of the mandate may be a significant factor in achieving mission success.

Thus, the need for feasible and achievable UN mandates is an essential condition for success in UN interventions. Mandates based on realistic worst-case planning are more likely to save lives and achieve a secure environment for all—host-country populace, peacekeepers, and other international personnel. It is essential that military and police forces have the necessary freedom of action to ensure security for themselves and those they protect. The deployment of UN personnel and military peacekeepers into insecure environments, without achievable mandates, jeopardizes prospects for success, undercuts international commitment, and is morally irresponsible. In the case of East Timor, successive mandates from the UN Security Council were well constructed, timely, feasible, and achievable.

There are two additional outcomes of feasible UN mandates that add more weight to the Security Council's need to be diligent in ensuring that UN missions are so equipped. First, such mandates enable missions to develop and implement appropriate codes of conduct for UN international staff, as well as for the military and police components. These codes of conduct provide clear guidance on acceptable behavior relevant to the culture and society in which the mission operates. Under the guidance of the SRSG, UNTAET established such a code, which was further developed by the PKF and incorporated into contingent training. Second, strong mandates provide for the requirement in peace enforcement for robust ROE to ensure the necessary application and level of force.[9]

Thorough and Timely Preparation and Planning

A mission's task is to work toward achieving solutions, and it must be provided with the basic tools necessary to begin its undertaking as quickly and as efficiently as possible. The importance of mission preparation and planning was highlighted in all areas of the implementation of UNTAET's mandate. Overall, the Secretariat's planning process for the mission was slow and inchoate. Considerable planning was done in advance for the PKF, and detailed planning was conducted by the Electoral Division for the UNAMET ballot and later for the Constituent Assembly elections. But this planning was not mirrored in other areas within the Secretariat. Little early planning was conducted that recognized the complexities of forming a civil administration and its need for necessary partnership arrangements with the East Timorese, the capability to implement a human rights program, an effective CIVPOL, and the ability to establish the rule of law effectively. To this end, such factors as effective speed of action, logistics, and the provision of public information were essential. As discussed in Chapter 3, UNTAET came under increasing criticism as it became established for being slow to act; this criticism was fueled in part by the visible failure of the Secretariat to have a responsive logistics system in place.

The reason for much of this criticism can be traced to the lack of detailed preparation and planning by the Secretariat. Unfortunately, UNTAET was assembled in advance of the far-reaching recommendations contained in the Brahimi report. Many of the problems encountered in the UNTAET planning process could have been averted had the Brahimi recommendations for the early formation of an IMTF and for timely and worst-case planning been applied for East Timor. As noted in the Brahimi report, the Secretariat is significantly understaffed and lacks integrated planning.[10] In 1999, stovepipes existed not only within the DPKO, but also between the DPKO and the other departments.[11] Bureaucratic difficulties were compounded by the parlous state of DPKO staffing levels, and planning for UNTAET was conducted on the run. There was little integration between departments and UN agencies, only infrequent liaison between the UN and the Bretton Woods institutions, and little provision for including the East Timorese in the planning process. This situation prevented holistic planning and resulted in the SRSG and his key staff having to undertake much of the strategic decisionmaking in a reactive manner from Dili. It also meant that UNTAET was unable to commence operations with a coherent strategic (corporate) business plan. The situation was compounded by the fact that the UN personnel also brought with them many different organizational paradigms, and once deployed, the difficulties in addressing day-to-day problems further hindered UNTAET's ability to construct such a plan. The success or failure of all enterprises rests largely on the fidelity of their planning processes. UN missions are no different, and a fundamental lesson from the UNTAET experience is that UN planning procedures need to be honed.

Speed of action. An important reason for the Secretariat to improve mission planning is to enhance the speed with which missions can deploy. The trend in complex peace operations is for decisive action to be taken on short notice. The UNAMET operation was mounted quickly and implemented decisively because of thorough planning. INTERFET was also mounted speedily with outstanding success, but this was beyond the capability of the UN and relied on Australia quickly forming a "coalition of the willing." There was ample time for UNTAET to have been planned in much greater detail, and the prospects existed for it to deploy and reach maturity more quickly than it did. Although the postballot destruction significantly complicated UNTAET's tasks, the central purpose of the mission had been predicated on the 5 May Agreements. Had more preliminary planning been done and UNTAET's buildup been more professional, it is probable that it would have attracted far less criticism. Notwithstanding the enormous challenges facing UN transitional administrations, it should be possible for the UN to act more quickly and decisively than was the case for UNTAET. This is an important lesson for the UN to consider and act upon.

Logistics. The need to review current UN logistics practice and implement changes are among the recommendations in the Brahimi report,[12] and East Timor provides additional evidence for this. Most of the logistics problems

UNTAET experienced could be traced to poor planning and preparation within the Secretariat, hampered by archaic and unresponsive procurement and financial regulations. The impact of a poor logistics system on military operations is discussed in Chapter 5, but logistics reform is one of the major hurdles to be overcome by the UN if it is to meet the requirements of modern peacekeeping. In particular, greater emphasis needs to be given to the thorough preparation of a mission support plan well in advance of deployment. Consideration should also be given to devolving greater authority to the mission and to outsourcing many of the logistics functions currently undertaken by the UN. The Brahimi report notes the importance of effective logistics support and asserts that without such support "missions cannot function effectively."[13]

Public information. A significant lesson relearned by UNTAET was the importance of public information, both within the mission area and to the broader international audience. As mentioned in Chapter 3, UNTAET's public information program was ineffective for many months. A major lesson is that transitional administrations must quickly implement an effective public information program and be adequately resourced to do so.

Restoration and Maintenance of a Secure Environment

A secure environment is pivotal to success in peace operations. In its absence, nothing will flourish except crime and poverty. A secure environment provides time and hope, allowing democracy and social and economic reconstruction to take root. In East Timor, the establishment and maintenance of security was central to everything. This applies to most interventions. Moreover, security cannot be based on fear, nor should it be founded on an overwhelming and dominating military and police presence. The international military and police presence should be temporary, working to a clear exit strategy while building rapport with and providing reassurance to the population it is there to support. The pursuit of peace and security is the main purpose of the UN, so it should be axiomatic that the UN gives priority to this matter. The UN will not always be responsible for providing security—as was the case with UNAMET—but the absence of a secure environment will result in the breakdown of governance and society, as was demonstrated during East Timor's postballot violence and destruction.

A major lesson from the UN's intervention in East Timor is that security must be considered in a holistic manner. To be sustainable, security involves much more than effective military and police forces, as important as these are. Security is dependent on good governance (which includes the establishment of the rule of law), on sustainable economic and social development, and on the agreement and cooperation of the majority of the local population. The importance of host-country support has already been discussed, and the importance of governance and of development is covered below. Additionally, however, sustainable security requires highly professional security forces, the effective separation of combatants, disarmament and demobilization mechanisms, border management, the preparation of the indigenous forces, and the establishment of a national security framework. As shown in Chapters 2 and 3, and with the exception of a professional CIVPOL, these requirements were satisfied in East Timor, and overall the maintenance of a secure environment by INTERFET and UNTAET was an outstanding success.

Military forces. The deployment of multinational military forces to restore and maintain security represents the greatest visible presence of intervention and the highest cost of a mission. When such forces are deployed under the blue helmet (as opposed to an MNF), they also represent the most substantial drain on assessed contributions. It is therefore important that these forces are highly professional and that the UN delivers good value for the money expended by the member states. Detailed military lessons are covered in Chapter 5, but it is appropriate here to briefly consider the military requirements in relation to the threat environment.

While the operational tempo in East Timor was high, neither INTERFET nor the PKF encountered sustained or protracted combat. It is instructive to compare the failure of UNOSOM II in Somalia—also a Chapter VII enforcement action—with the military success in East Timor. A clear difference was the intensity of combat the peace enforcers faced. An important deduction is that coalition forces must be capable of dealing with the threat and that worst-case planning must always determine the composition and capability of the force. A related deduction is that the higher the likelihood of sustained combat, the more critical the robustness of the command and control arrangements. Such situations call for all coalition partners to commit their troops unreservedly for peace enforcement operations and for these forces to be trained and equipped to carry out the required tasks. Peace enforcement is not traditional peacekeeping, and to deploy coalition forces under unrealistic national caveats is to court defeat. This problem thwarted the success of UNISOM II and had similar potential in the early days of INTERFET when some contingents were initially unwilling to prosecute full peace enforcement operations.[14] A key factor in the military's success in East Timor seems to be that the militias were actually deterred from pursuing hostilities out of fear of an effective military response. The low level of violence might not have occurred had militia numbers been larger and the UN forces less combat-ready. In summary, the INTERFET/

UNTAET military model worked in East Timor, but it is likely to require modification for future operations in more hostile environments.

A further lesson relates to the continuing need for MNFs to restore order. The UN was unable to deploy a PKF quickly to restore security in East Timor. Notwithstanding the Brahimi report's recommendation for member states to provide standby forces,[15] it seems unlikely in the foreseeable future that the UN would be capable of assembling, deploying, commanding, and sustaining a coalition force rapidly, particularly for complex peace operations. There is likely to be an ongoing requirement, therefore, for lead nations and coalitions of the willing.[16] This is largely because of the practical necessity to have an established and well-practiced force headquarters and a significant combat component that has worked with that headquarters. Both these elements provide the core around which a coalition force can be built. The imperatives of time are against assembling an effective fighting force from completely disparate units on arrival in theater. In some cases, coalitions will be based on existing alliance or coalition arrangements, but on other occasions (such as INTERFET), it will be required that ad hoc coalitions be arranged quickly for specific missions. The reality is that there is a political dimension to most states' decisions as to which operations they are prepared to commit their forces. There is also the possibility that specific trust funds will have to be established if the MNFs are to be financially viable.

CIVPOL. The high standard of performance achieved by the military forces in East Timor was not matched by CIVPOL. The UNTAET experience has shown that CIVPOL planning, recruitment, training, and provisioning require significant improvement. There are many reasons for this situation, and Eirin Mobekk's study of CIVPOL operations in East Timor highlights in particular the difficulties international police experience in community policing and in establishing an indigenous police force.[17] Police forces in most countries represent a scarce asset: they are generally in high demand and are overtasked and underresourced.[18] In some countries, they have been associated with criminal activities and human rights violations. There is also less international consistency in the caliber of the various national police forces than is evident in national defense forces, largely because greater international training and commonality in doctrine exists within the military arena. An obvious example is that in some countries the police are armed, while in others they are unarmed. All these factors contribute to the difficulties to be overcome in creating an effective international policing system.

Yet, if the UN is to continue to be involved in the important role of "policekeeping,"[19] CIVPOL's performance must be improved. The implementation of recommendations contained in the Brahimi report will help,[20] but overcoming the critical deficiency in CIVPOL numbers and ensuring proper selection and training are a priority. As they stand, these areas are likely to remain a weak link in postconflict management for many years. All practitioner and academic commentary concludes that such a prospect must be remedied. Supporting the findings of the Brahimi report, John McFarlane and William Maley note that "international order will require greater priority to be given to the requirements and delivery of CIVPOL peace operations in broken states so that those states can be rebuilt . . . without having to rely on military or other coercive means to survive."[21] The presence of an effective police force in postconflict situations is, and will remain, a critical aspect in maintaining security and establishing the rule of law.

It is imperative, therefore, for the UN to enhance its training and selection criteria, given the likelihood that UN CIVPOL will continue to be based on national contributions. In addition to the recommendations contained in the Brahimi report, acceptable benchmarks need to be established and CIVPOL members tested both before departure from home country and on arrival in the mission area. There also exists the tendency for most countries to prepare their personnel for peace operations in an ad hoc fashion, with few countries having specific training establishments for UN police contingents. The UN should encourage specialized training for UN operations, develop better doctrine, and set the common benchmarks to be achieved by all nations. Associated with this model, and in accordance with the findings of the Brahimi report, is the requirement for member states to identify an element of their national forces for UN service at short notice. Other, and more radical, approaches currently receiving attention include the possibility of outsourcing police functions to commercial enterprises and creating a permanent UN police force.[22]

A solution to the current dilemma of policekeeping will not be easy to achieve, but if the UN is to be effective in complex peace operations, it must improve on its performance in East Timor.

Military-CIVPOL coordination. The experience of East Timor has also shown that better coordination is required to enhance joint PKF-CIVPOL operations. There are advantages in establishing an efficient JOC to coordinate military and police operations and to share information. To be effective, however, such a system must be planned in advance of the mission and be based on agreed doctrine. It also requires the promulgation of an SRSG Joint Directive (to the force commander and police commissioner) and agreed standard operating procedures (SOPs). In the hectic atmosphere of Dili in February 2000, the reality was that the PKF and CIVPOL found themselves fully occupied in getting their own forces up and running.

Improved coordination was incremental rather than systematic. The lessons from East Timor are that military-CIVPOL coordination is a critical area warranting examination and development by the DPKO, and that joint procedures should be agreed on before deployment and should be mirrored in each of the force's operations orders.

National security framework. As outlined in Chapter 3, UNTAET recognized the need to create a national security framework, based on civil authority and supported by the military, that could be sustained after independence. The example of East Timor provides a useful model for further development by the UN and for use in future postconflict environments. The earliest possible implementation of such a framework assists in reaching endstate and in UN withdrawal.

Effective Governance

Although a secure environment provides the conditions for mission success, it is not the benchmark against which transitional administrations are judged. The fundamental task of a transitional administration is to govern effectively and to prepare for a smooth transition to a sustainable nationally elected government. UNTAET is an ideal case study of the skills required by an interim administration to perform the duties of a government until replaced by local authorities. The UN has limited experience in the business of government administration, and one of the most important lessons from UNTAET is that the UN was ill prepared for this difficult task. Nor is it feasible to expect a mission to develop this expertise as it goes. Transitional administrations must be able to rely on much greater practical assistance from the Secretariat, particularly in relation to prior planning and preparation and the provision of startup packages at inception. As previously discussed, perception was reality to the East Timorese and other observers, and UNTAET's performance was often perceived to be inefficient and ineffective. An important lesson for transitional administrations is that the UN's reputation is jeopardized by perceptions of poor performance. In turn, the efforts (often quite extraordinary) of its people on the ground are less appreciated, and the much-needed support and cooperation of the host country and other organizations can either fail or be difficult to maintain. Such factors have a significant impact on mission morale and the achievement of long-term peace.

Rule of law. An important aspect of good governance is the effective implementation of the rule of law. This is a difficult task in postconflict situations but an essential one for the UN if it is to assume the role of an interim administration. In mature societies, the rule of law is demonstrated by how effectively order and security are maintained in concert with democratic principles and the assurance of human rights. Seldom, to date, has the UN been solely responsible for establishing the rule of law in postconflict situations, yet the success of many UN interventions is often related to the effectiveness of the legal systems and procedures established. The UNTAC mission in Cambodia, in particular, was criticized (fairly or unfairly) because it failed to enforce the rule of law. There was therefore considerable pressure on UNTAET in this area, particularly given that the mission's mandate provided far greater responsibilities than had applied to UNTAC.

Establishing the rule of law entails much more than setting in place professional police and security forces. The process has at its core the establishment of sustainable judicial and penal systems that reflect cultural imperatives and that have the confidence and trust of the population. The assurance of international human rights standards is important, but previous judicial regimes and local customs must also be accommodated. As shown in Chapter 3, UNTAET was unable to establish the rule of law within an acceptable time frame. The resultant loss of security, and of confidence in the UN's capability to deliver, have shown that transitional administrations must be able to commence operations quickly to establish the rule of law and progressively enhance it as the mission continues. It is therefore essential that considerable planning and preparation be undertaken by the UN to develop judicial packages for implementation at the beginning of a mission. Obviously the final product will need to accord with local customs and have the agreement of the local leaders, but the basic implementation plan must be in place before the mission arrives. The requirements for establishing the rule of law will be similar in most postconflict situations, and a study of the lessons that emerge from each mission cannot be neglected if the UN is to undertake the role of transitional administrations in the future.

UN competency, training, and procedures. Other lessons from UNTAET's governance relate to the competency of mission staff, their level of training, and the flexible application of UN budgets and regulations. A general observation is that UNTAET did not have the necessary assets or expertise to perform many of the tasks required of a transitional administration. Public administration is very different from political and/or human rights monitoring and electoral management. In addition to good technical knowledge and, ideally, expertise in developing countries, proven public management skills are essential. Such skills are vital when setting up government departments from ground zero (as was the case in East Timor) if an accountable and transparent bureaucratic structure is to be handed over to the host country.

The UN must therefore reconsider its personnel and fiduciary arrangements if it is to enhance its governance and nation-building role more effectively. The UN's lack of expertise in providing effective governance is hardly surprising and should not be considered an inherent failure, given that the organization was not created to run governments. That being said, the UN now faces a dilemma if it is to become involved in future transitional administrations of a similar magnitude to UNTAET. It would appear that if it is to do so, the UN will be reliant on the goodwill of member states to provide quality people, or it will need to subcontract much of this work to the commercial sector. In both instances, the acceptability of the key civil staff to the host country is of prime importance. Mechanisms must be in place to ensure that key positions are acceptable to the local leaders and that cultural acceptability is considered in the selection process. It would seem sensible, therefore, to implement the recommendation of the Brahimi report to establish a standby list of qualified key personnel.[23] Another important aspect is longevity of tenure. It takes time for international staff to develop the trust of the host population and to gain situational awareness. It is therefore essential that it be prepared to accept a long appointment.

As part of assigning suitably qualified people, the UN must ensure that its personnel receive the necessary additional training required for each particular mission. While the need to raise the performance level of CIVPOL has already been discussed, and training issues for the military component are addressed in Chapter 5, the training requirement is no less true for the civilian elements of UN missions. This area continues to suffer from serious neglect at the organizational level, despite the deficiency being highlighted in academic research. The large gap between "the day-to-day reality of peacekeeping and the concepts and training through which it is implemented" was noted by Fetherston in her 1994 study. She concluded that "in general, specific training for civilian peacekeepers is significantly less adequate than military training, and for many civilian peacekeepers it is non-existent."[24]

The UNTAET experience also suggests that the UN lacks flexibility in its personnel practices and financial regulations. These were developed for the earlier concept of traditional peacekeeping, and they warrant overhaul for complex multidimensional missions. As it stands, there are considerable constraints in locating the right number of suitable civilian personnel from within the UN system and in binding a nation-building mission to fiduciary procedures developed for other purposes. Two particular criticisms of the UNTAET administration were the slow system of provisioning and the constraints placed on the use of the assessed budget. One option would be to outsource the running of such missions to commercial enterprises, which would be funded through specific trust funds, with assessed contributions being applied only to the personnel costs of military and police contingents. Trust funds are useful to help kick-start and sustain missions, and outsourcing can provide flexibility in helping overcome the bottlenecks often encountered through standard UN procurement procedures. Avoiding the latter is important, and Ian Martin noted for UNAMET that "the use of a trust fund that received immediate voluntary contributions meant that financial commitments did not have to await the authorisation of assessed contributions."[25] The UN, therefore, needs to explore options to improve fiduciary and procurement practices for complex peace missions. In particular, valuable time can be saved, available resources utilized, and potential political and social problems averted if the SRSG is authorized more flexibility in using the assessed budget. These are important issues of governance that require urgent review by the Secretariat and member states.

Language assistants. An important aspect of governance for transitional administrations is to ensure that effective communication is maintained throughout the community. This responsibility falls primarily within the ambit of public information, but it also includes the requirement for the mission to have sufficient numbers of capable language assistants drawn from the local community.[26] This need was particularly relevant in East Timor, where the absence of a common language, coupled with a lack of suitably trained personnel, complicated the mission staff's ability to gain proper situational awareness. Overall, sufficient language assistants were found for higher-profile political and administrative functions, but this generally was not the case for the PKF and CIVPOL deployed throughout the territory. Because maintaining security is pivotal to mission success, this is a totally unsatisfactory situation. The incoming transitional administration must take measures quickly to ensure the necessary numbers of indigenous language speakers and, where necessary, set up a language training school at the outset of the mission. The potential for language difficulties and the possible funding that might be required to alleviate the situation need to be considered during mission planning, with a view to incorporating this aspect of the mission's task within the strategy for nation building. In East Timor, considerable effort was taken to establish a Civil Service Academy to train East Timorese personnel to assist with the transitional administration and to prepare for independence.[27] But many more deployed mission personnel would have been equally well served by having more language assistants to help compile information and establish closer contact within the local communities. Effective communication at all levels throughout a mission greatly helps develop trust and understanding between mission staff and the people they are supporting. Cooperative partnerships and committed teamwork can be the only acceptable result.

Capable Leadership and Effective Partnership

In determining the success of the UN's intervention in East Timor, the importance of leadership and partnership stand out as major lessons. As noted in the Brahimi report, "Effective, dynamic leadership can make the difference between a cohesive mission with high morale and effectiveness despite adverse circumstances, and one that struggles to maintain any of those attributes. . . . The tenor of an entire mission can be heavily influenced by the character and ability of those who lead it."[28] The leadership displayed in successive East Timor missions was of a high quality. Ian Martin, Major General Peter Cosgrove, and Sergio Vieira de Mello all demonstrated sound leadership qualities under difficult circumstances. In comparison to UNTAET, however, the other missions were more limiting in scope and of relatively short duration—each was five months. UNTAET's tenure was uncertain but estimated to be two to three years. It was important, therefore, that competence and continuity of leadership be established between UNTAET and the East Timorese leadership, and Vieira de Mello performed outstandingly in this regard. There is no doubt that the sustained personal commitment of Sergio Vieira de Mello as SRSG is one of the key factors in the overall success of UNTAET. While East Timorese leaders were sometimes critical of the UN and UNTAET, they all recognized and solidly supported the efforts and commitment of the SRSG.

Within UNTAET's major components, however, the same continuity and level of leadership was not always demonstrated. The first force commander and police commissioner were replaced for different reasons after only six months. The human rights coordinator resigned in frustration, and a number of experienced district administrators and senior civil servants elected not to renew their contracts. This turnover in high-level appointments suggested that insufficient planning underpinned the selection and preparation of these personnel. A significant lesson from UNTAET is that intramission teamwork is an important element of mission success and that team building should start in the preparatory phase, with personnel being encouraged to stay for as long as possible. This lesson is endorsed in the Brahimi report, which clearly identifies "the need to assemble the leadership of a mission as early as possible, so that they can jointly help to shape a mission's concept of operations, its support plan, its budget and its staffing arrangements."[29]

The caliber of leadership within the host country is no less important than that within the UN mission. In East Timor, the leadership displayed by Xanana Gusmão and other East Timorese leaders was competent and mature, particularly considering East Timor's fractious political history and given the physical conditions and emotional trauma being endured by the population. Differences between East Timorese political factions were generally managed well and resulted in few cases of violence. The two bishops (Belo and Nascimento) and José Ramos-Horta played important moderating roles. Importantly, close personal relations were established between the East Timorese leadership and the three UN missions. Although at times there were differences of opinion, these were generally managed in a mature and professional way. The East Timorese respected the authority under which the UN operated, even if they were not always in agreement with the implementation of UN policy.

The need to establish effective partnerships is also confirmed from the UN's intervention in East Timor. Although this lesson applies equally to UNAMET and INTERFET, it has particular relevance to UNTAET and future transitional administrations. In complex missions it is not feasible for the UN authority to make decisions and conduct business unilaterally. At the same time, partnership, or teamwork, is important within the UN administration itself, enabling all mission personnel to work in concert to achieve common objectives. But it is even more necessary between the key stakeholders. These include the host population, donor countries, important NGOs, and the Bretton Woods institutions. In particular, the UN needs to establish closer linkages with the World Bank's Post-Conflict and Reconstruction Unit and to ensure that the United Nations Development Programme (UNDP) and other UN development agencies work in close collaboration with the Bretton Woods institutions. An observation from the UNTAET period is that partnership between the UN and the East Timorese was slow to develop, and that partnership between the transitional administration and the Bretton Woods institutions was not adequately promoted. An obvious lesson from this is that partnerships between all the key stakeholders must start during the initial planning period and be strengthened progressively throughout the mission's duration. The IMTF—assembled to plan the mission—is the place where full partnership should begin and where mutual respect and commitment first needs to be established. Failure to establish and cement workable partnerships causes resentment toward the UN and lessens the chances of success.

Sustainable Economic and Social Development

Successful intervention in insecure and/or postconflict situations depends on more than restoring and maintaining a secure environment. Security is the first and ongoing requirement for successful intervention, but in addition to good governance, it must be accompanied by economic and social development. War and conflict are spawned in the shadows of poverty, where human suffering and indignation provide fertile ground for crime and violence. An important responsibility for transitional administrations is to ensure that economic and social mechanisms are progressively in place to sustain the new country at independence. The resilience of the new state at the time of transition is the ultimate benchmark against which the UN is judged. To claim success, UN transitional administrations must be more than caretaker governments; they must prepare the new country for survival and avert possibilities for future reintervention. This is a complex undertaking. It is a task for which the UN was not specifically created or structured, a task for which it has limited expertise, but a task that is now more commonplace.

East Timor provides a good case study to examine the development of viable social and economic structures, often referred to as capacity building or, more generally, nation building. Consideration of the UNTAET experience reveals a number of associated lessons. The first lesson is that partnership with the East Timorese was fundamental to success, but UNTAET lagged behind the World Bank in this critical area. A second lesson is that development priorities needed to be established and methodically implemented. These priorities were slow to emerge, however, giving rise to false expectations by the East Timorese and wasting valuable time. Early involvement of UNDP in the planning stage appears a sensible option in enhancing economic and social development. The UNDP office in Dili was not opened until March 2000, and an East Timor National Planning and Development Agency was not established until 27 October, three months after the formation of ETTA. It was mid-2001 before a National Planning Commission was created to set and coordinate development priorities. A third lesson is that better coordination between a large number of development stakeholders could have been achieved. Although the Donor Coordination cell within UNTAET did an admirable job, there was a lack of coordination between the major development agencies—the ETTA ministries, UNDP, World Bank, and bilateral donors. Regular international donor conferences were productive in maintaining financial support for East Timor's development, but coordination and efficiency on the ground in East Timor was less impressive. A fourth lesson is that development priorities tended to focus on developing economic sustainability after independence rather than on balancing the requirements for national security. This was particularly so with the critical lines of communications (road, air, sea, and telecommunications), where little thought was initially given to the security requirements in the sensitive border districts necessary to maintain essential government control and avert the rise of insurgency. A final lesson is the lack of flexibility in using the assessed budget for basic development needs, thereby preventing, for example, the optimization of military engineering units at a time when they should have been fully utilized in the reconstruction program (see Chapter 5).

There can be no doubt that sustainable economic and social institutions were developed in East Timor during UNTAET's interregnum, for which the mission deserves great credit. This does not alter the fact that further examination of the difficulties that arose is required if improvements are to be in place to benefit future missions.

Implementing Human Rights and Addressing the Past

Separate from the rule of law, but allied to it, is the need to establish sustainable mechanisms to promote human rights and to effectively manage war crimes and crimes against humanity.[30] These are different but related issues. Human rights is concerned primarily with establishing norms and practices that ensure the dignity and security of the individual and the society. This is an important aspect of nation building, and it focuses on the present and the future. In comparison, managing war crimes and crimes against humanity is about addressing past atrocities that have breached basic human rights in specific context. In postconflict environments, the management of war crimes and/or crimes against humanity is one of the most difficult issues facing OHCHR and the broader human rights community. Due to the sensitivities involved, it also requires incredible perseverance and diplomacy. History suggests that the winning side in a conflict has had greatest success in bringing such criminals to justice, but the road has seldom been easy and often takes many years. This is largely because war crimes and crimes against humanity are rarely confined to one side, or to one specific point in time, and are most often symptomatic of a long period of retribution by protagonists on both sides. Too great an emphasis on this issue may cause reversal on other fronts, thereby retarding reconciliation and jeopardizing the normalization of relations. Too little emphasis may result in severe domestic dissatisfaction and the possible rise of vigilante groups to dispense justice. This was the dilemma faced by UNTAET. A significant lesson learned by UNTAET, however, was the need to focus not on how to resolve this issue, but rather on having proper systems in place to collect and record evidence. As indicated in Chapter 3, UNTAET was criticized for the lack of resources allocated to the Serious Crimes Unit. In the shadow of UNTAET, the Secretariat should ensure that better procedures are prepared for future interventions.

The implementation by UNTAET of more mainstream human rights programs in East Timor reveals other lessons. Human rights is the basis of good governance and is a multidimensional issue that cuts across all facets of rebuilding and maintaining stable societies, including addressing gender inequities. Many of the tasks involved can be difficult in a society that is not familiar with human rights and that must be made to accept them. Accordingly, the first lesson is that human rights considerations need to be integrated across the mission and included in premission planning. To this end, the UN should review the role of the OHCHR in Geneva, as advocated in the Brahimi report.[31] The OHCHR is concerned with policy issues but currently has little impact on field operations. Moreover, it is divorced from the Secretariat, where mission planning takes place. The OHCHR should emulate the practices of UNHCR, where staff deployed to the field are fully prepared and supported to achieve meaningful results. Second, UNTAET Regulation 1999/1, of 27 November 1999, clarified much about the mission's mandate and, in particular, noted seven human rights conventions on which the mission was based. But the human rights program in East Timor was not properly prioritized or, as in many other areas, adequately resourced. Human rights coordinators must quickly promulgate the human rights program and work with the various mission components to ensure its effective implementation. The third and obvious lesson is that human rights must be implemented with the agreement of, and in partnership with, the hosting community. To this end, international human rights workers must be familiar with the history and culture of the society in which they are working and have appropriate communications skills.

A particular issue is the emphasis that UN human rights workers should give to implementing agreed policies and the degree to which they should monitor and report on human rights performance. The boundaries will never be clear, but it would be more appropriate for transitional administrations to focus predominantly on implementing procedures rather than on monitoring performance within the society. A final lesson to be learned from UNTAET in this area relates to human rights training and monitoring within the mission. Human rights violations by UNTAET personnel were infrequent, but such violations risked damaging the reputation of the mission and alienating it from the East Timorese people it was there to assist. In complex peace operations, it is recommended that human rights liaison officers be assigned to each of the components and that they regularly conduct training and provide advice. The desired outcome is to prevent human rights violations by mission personnel and to take swift remedial action where such offences occur. Associated with this is the need to ensure that human rights issues are included in predeployment and induction training for all mission personnel, and particularly for military and police contingents.

Managing of Displaced People

A significant factor affecting the success of UN interventions is the manner in which displaced people are handled and resettled. As explained in Chapters 2 and 3, this was a complex operation for the UN in East Timor over a protracted period of time, but it was actioned with professionalism and commitment by all concerned. The performance of UNHCR and IOM workers in East and West Timor deserve great credit, but resettlement operations also required the full support of other components of the mission, including the PKF, CIVPOL, Border Service, and Human Rights. The personal involvement of the INTERFET commander, and then the SRSG, helped maintain focus on this critical issue. The role played by the East Timorese leadership and by village and district elders also deserves special mention. The people displayed considerable patience, restraint, and tolerance, with few cases of retribution or revenge. Many valuable resettlement lessons were learned during the INTERFET and UNTAET periods, and the UN should be encouraged to examine these in more detail for application in future missions. Continued but modest UN support in this sensitive area is likely to be required following independence.

Effective Emergency Relief

A significant problem in most postconflict environments is the provision of humanitarian and emergency assistance. The degree of UN responsibility may vary depending on the circumstances, but in situations of adversity it is important for coordination to be established between a variety of agencies. In some situations, providing humanitarian assistance is the central purpose of the mission. In Somalia, for example, controlling food distribution became the main focus for security operations.

Given the widespread and systematic violence and destruction following the Popular Consultation of 30 August 1999, and the difficult terrain and poor infrastructure, East Timor provides a good case study for emergency relief operations on a wider scale. In examining this period carefully, the UN can confirm relevant lessons for future implementation in other missions. Overall, emergency relief operations were conducted efficiently, coordinated by OCHA until UNTAET established its HAER pillar. An important lesson, however, is the need to coordinate NGO activities, particularly in the early stages of humanitarian assistance. Another lesson is in the supporting role played by INTERFET and the PKF to assist in relief operations, which remained within their force capabilities and was not to the detriment of their primary security mission. As a general rule, East Timor confirmed the preference for the military to provide support for rather than manage relief operations, but obviously this depends on the degree of security and freedom of movement of the relief organizations. (Additional military comments on this matter are included in Chapter 5.)

CONCLUSION

The conditions for successful UN intervention in East Timor were favorable, and each of the UN missions achieved its mandate and greatly assisted East Timor in becoming an independent state and the newest member of the UN. As has been demonstrated, however, East Timor does not provide a template for future UN interventions. The circumstances prevailing in East Timor were specific and are unlikely to be replicated in many other trouble spots. In particular, the security situation was more benign and the degree of host-country support was greater than in many other UN interventions. The importance of these factors in achieving a lasting peace is a critical issue that should not be underestimated. Nonetheless, the magnitude of UNTAET's mandate and its achievements while working in difficult conditions should not be underestimated. The success of the UN's intervention was also aided by Indonesian compliance and by the major East Timorese political factions that remained committed to democratic solutions and averse to the use of violence. The lessons learned in East Timor generally support the recommendations of the Brahimi report and warrant further examination and action. Consideration of the Peacekeeping Baker's Dozen may prove useful both by the Security Council in determining the likely success of future interventions, and by member states in considering their degree of commitment for future transitional administrations.

NOTES

1. *Report of the Panel on United Nations Peace Operations* (Brahimi report), UN General Assembly Security Council, A/55/305-S/2000/809, 21 August 2000, p. viii.

2. A. B. Fetherston, *Towards a Theory of United Nations Peacekeeping* (London: Macmillan, 1994), pp. 40–42.

3. Ibid., p. 41.

4. Ibid., p. 42.

5. Lise Morje Howard, "Learning to Keep the Peace? UN Multidimensional Peacekeeping in Civil Wars," Ph.D. diss., University of California, Berkeley, 2001, pp. 1–2 (emphasis in original). Howard terms the ability to learn "during" the mission "first-level learning"; the ability to learn "between" missions "second-level learning."

6. 'UN Says East Timor Can Serve as Afghanistan Model," Reuters, Oslo, 11 December 2001. Available online at http://www.igc.topica.com (accessed 12 December 2001).

7. The number of nations contributing to the PKF varied, but throughout 2000–2001, it remained consistently around thirty to thirty-four.

8. Chris Seiple, *The US Military/NGO Relationship in Humanitarian Interventions* (Carlisle, PA: Peacekeeping Institute, Center for Strategic Leadership, U.S. Army War College, 1996), pp. 103–108, 175.

9. ROE matters were discussed briefly in Chapter 3, and are discussed further in Chapter 5.

10. Brahimi report, p. xiii. As of mid-2000, the report notes: "There is currently no integrated planning or support cell . . . that brings together those responsible for political analysis, military operations, civilian police, electoral assistance, human rights, development, humanitarian assistance, refugees and displaced per-

sons, public information, logistics, finance and recruitment." On staff shortages in the DPKO, it states that "it is clearly not enough to have 32 officers providing military planning and guidance to 27,000 troops in the field, nine civilian police staff to identify, vet and provide guidance for up to 8,600 police, and 15 political desk officers for 14 current operations and two new ones, or to allocate just 1.25 percent of the total costs of peacekeeping to Headquarters administrative and logistics support."

11. A *stovepipe* is a metal tube that extends vertically out of a fuel-burning stove. It has a single task: to act as a kind of chimney for the stove, moving the smoke and ash along a narrow, rigid path. In a *stovepipe organization,* employees have a narrowly defined set of responsibilities, and their output and feedback "moves" along a set path in the chain of command.

12. Brahimi report, par. 169, pp. 28–29.

13. Ibid., par. 151, p. 26.

14. Alan Ryan, *Primary Responsibilities and Primary Risks: Australian Defence Force Participation in the International Force in East Timor.* Study Paper No. 304 (Duntroon: Land Warfare Studies Centre, 2000), pp. 65, 93–104.

15. Brahimi report, p. xi; par. 117, p. 20.

16. Cedric de Coning, "The UN Transitional Administration in East Timor," *International Peacekeeping* 6, no. 2 (2000): 84, highlights this point when he notes that INTERFET was able to deploy in only sixteen days, while the "standard response time for a UN peacekeeping force is between three to six months."

17. See Eirin Mobekk, *Policing Peace Operations: United Nations Civilian Police in East Timor* (London: King's College, October 2001).

18. Brahimi report, par. 119, p. 20, notes that 25 percent of the 8,641 police positions authorized for UN operations remained vacant.

19. The use of the term *policekeeping* has gained currency in highlighting the important role of police in peacekeeping operations.

20. Brahimi report, p. xii; para. 126, p. 21.

21. John McFarlane and William Maley, *Civilian Police in United Nations Peace Operations*, Australian Defence Studies Centre Working Paper No. 64, Canberra, April 2001, p. 4.

22. See Graham Day, "After War, Send Blue Force," *Christian Science Monitor*, 30 May 2001.

23. Brahimi report, pars. 128–132, pp. 22–23.

24. Fetherston, *Towards a Theory of United Nations Peacekeeping*, pp. 218, 209.

25. Ian Martin, *Self-Determination in East Timor: The United Nations, The Ballot, and International Intervention* (Boulder, CO: Lynne Rienner, 2001), p. 39.

26. The term *language assistants* is used here to refer generically to interpreters and translators of varying standards and responsibilities.

27. The Civil Service Campus in Dili, inaugurated by the SRSG on 8 May 2000, housed the Public Service Commission offices, the East Timor administration's central recruitment office, and the Civil Service Academy.

28. Brahimi report, par. 92, p. 16.

29. Ibid., para. 95, p. 16.

30. The terms *war crimes* and *crimes against humanity,* while sharing some common features, are separate concepts under international law and were treated as such in UNTAET Regulation 2000/15, promulgated 6 June 2000.

31. Brahimi report, p. xiii; par. 244, p. 41.

5

Military Lessons

Peacekeeping is not a job for soldiers—but only soldiers can do it.
—Dag Hammarskjöld[1]

In East Timor, the military was the largest and most expensive component of UNTAET and was mandated to use force to maintain security. Two soldiers were killed in combat, while more died from illness or accident. Given the size and importance of the military component, and the reality that soldiers may be required to fight for peace, it is important that lessons are considered and problems rectified for future operations. Overall, the PKF performed well and achieved its tasks, being highly respected within the mission and by the East Timorese. This chapter examines the key military lessons that were learned—or relearned—in East Timor.

WARFIGHTING AND CONSTABULARY-CMA SKILLS

The complex nature of the training required for the modern peacekeeper is evident in current debate and studies on the issue, which show that balancing warfighting and constabulary-CMA requirements is not easy. A. B. Fetherston acknowledged in her study that training for military personnel was generally more developed than for civilians,[2] but she emphasized that the military still required better training to achieve the status of professional peacekeepers. In noting that "the peacekeeping profession deserves as much attention and professionalism as the military profession," she asserted that "the development of a professional peacekeeper is impeded by a military attitude which sees peacekeeping as a temporary deviation from the norm and an interruption of their primary function to train for war."[3] This is to take but one view of the role to be undertaken by the peacekeeper in this new age of complex peace operations.

121

General Sir Michael Rose, commander of the UN Protection Force in Bosnia in 1994–1995, acknowledged that "the traditional activities of peacekeeping—chiefly persuasion, persistence and pressure,"[4] still have a purpose to serve. But he argued that peacekeepers must now possess more skills in undertaking their current multipurpose role than are required of either a traditional soldier or traditional peacekeeper. Commenting on the qualities required of UN peacekeepers, Rose pointed out that the situation "demanded of them the same fighting qualities that soldiers need in battle: guile, courage, determination and endurance; but, without the clarity of purpose of a war." He suggested then that "perhaps peacekeeping demanded more of them than warfighting ever did."[5] Franz Kernic, on the other hand, has pointed out that "recent sociological studies in countries as varied as the United States, Canada, Italy, France, Norway, Sweden and the Netherlands indicates an inappropriateness of combat units for peacekeeping."[6]

In East Timor, the same troops were required to perform warfighting and constabulary-CMA tasks in fulfilling the central purpose of the PKF mission to maintain security. This experience demonstrated that in peace enforcement there is often little alternative to the use of combat forces, and that these same troops must also be experienced in peaceful third-party intervention where presence, tolerance, respect, and cross-cultural expertise are as important as professional combat skills. In essence, it is the melding of the warfighting and constabulary-CMA qualities, used in the right proportion and at the appropriate time, that is the distinguishing feature of complex peace operations. This is the overarching lesson learned from East Timor, and military establishments that continue to ignore it are likely to suffer more fatalities in future complex peace operations.

Military peacekeeping lessons can be categorized in different ways. Over the past twenty years, it has become fashionable in many defense forces to consider military operations at the strategic, operational, and tactical levels. These levels, however, can be somewhat artificial, tending often to focus on the role of various headquarters and on the distinction between politico-military considerations and the actual implementation of operations on the ground. But seldom can operations be analyzed so clinically, and the military success or failure of an operation depends on the whole rather than the part. In most operations, tactical action influences decision-making at the strategic and operational levels, and to view these levels in isolation can create considerable distortion. For example, the incidence of casualties and the realization of body bags as a result of tactical operations is likely to have a significant impact on political and strategic decisionmakers. As well, the actions of commanders and soldiers can have political consequences.

In this chapter, the military lessons are therefore analyzed within two main categories: (1) military planning and preparation—primarily the responsibility of the DPKO force commander, and the troop contributing nations; and (2) the conduct of operations—primarily the responsibility of the force commander and the deployed forces.

LESSONS ON MILITARY PLANNING AND PREPARATION

Continuing Need for MNFs

A key lesson relearned from East Timor is the distinction between MNFs and PKFs and the continued requirement for both types of forces. Even though both military forces conducted similar operations in East Timor and had similar capabilities, there were some critical differences. First, INTERFET assembled and deployed far more quickly than the PKF, and, second, INTERFET came with an operational force headquarters trained and equipped to conduct military operations (whereas the PKF headquarters took time to assemble and train). An important third difference was that INTERFET's size and composition was more elastic and not required to comply with UN regulations and fiduciary arrangements, which afforded its force commander greater flexibility and independence of action than was available to the PKF commander. The reestablishment of the UN's presence depended on the success of INTERFET's military operation, and General Cosgrove's authority was complete. He cooperated closely with Ian Martin and subsequently with Sergio Vieira de Mello, but he answered to the Australian defense headquarters in Canberra. By comparison, the PKF was part of UNTAET. It supported and was subordinate to the civil administration. Appropriately, the force commander reported to and through the SRSG. Another important distinction between the two forces was the longevity of their missions. INTERFET was an interim force designed to restore security and to remain for only a short period—five months as events transpired. The PKF had to maintain security and the support of the local population for a period of two to five years.

Notwithstanding the UN's desire to improve its capability to deploy PKFs quickly as and when required,[7] it is unlikely that the UN will be able to assemble forces as capable as INTERFET in the foreseeable future. This is due, in part, to the fact that many member states remain unwilling to permanently allocate their forces on standby arrangements for unspecified contingencies. Another reason is that current bureaucratic UN procedures (enforced by the same member states for justifiable reasons of probity) are not conducive to quick military action. Moreover, the creation of effective UN standby forces seems problematic as long as critical member states (such as the United States and Great Britain) remain reluctant to commit combat forces under UN command, although they remain more willing to do so for specific MNF missions. The failure of key member states to assign their forces to UN operations demonstrates a desire to maintain sovereign control over national forces, but it also conveys a lack of confidence and trust in the UN's ability to mount military operations successfully. Arguably, this practice presents the biggest hurdle to improving the capability of the UN to perform its military peacekeeping duties.

In terms of military planning, East Timor provides a useful case study. Before the ballot, and in accordance with the requirements of the 5 May Agreements, DPKO began contingency planning for the deployment of a PKF to replace the TNI in an orderly transition of power (in the event that the East Timorese rejected Indonesia's offer of special autonomy). This planning was transparent and included early negotiations with prospective troop-contributing nations. Australia's role in the planning process is instructive. There was considerable concern in Canberra, given the Australian assessment that the parlous state of DPKO manning would severely impede effective military planning. Accordingly, working through the Australian military attaché in New York,[8] in conjunction with a series of visits by senior military officers, Australian defense authorities provided advice to the DPKO in an effort to assist the department in its planning for a PKF. When the postballot violence and destruction of East Timor necessitated the rapid deployment of INTERFET, the planning for the PKF thus undertaken provided the baseline for INTERFET's planning. In establishing the coalition, Australia made changes to the original DPKO force structure, but the essential requirement for seven maneuver battalions did not change. Although heavily committed to the MNF, Australia continued to assist the DPKO with transition planning for the PKF, and before INTERFET's deployment, a small planning team was sent to New York.[9] This team supplemented the military attaché's staff and helped keep the DPKO advised of INTERFET's progress and helped plan the transition from INTERFET to the PKF. Notwithstanding the considerable improvements in DPKO staffing as a result of the Brahimi report,[10] it is possible that this example might prove to be a useful model for future UN operations.

The UN's intervention in Haiti, 1994–1995, is also considered a successful UN-mandated MNF operation. In examining both Haiti and INTERFET as case studies for planning purposes, there were some notable differences, particularly in the size of the force. In September 1994, the U.S.-led coalition deployed a large force of over 20,000 to restore security quickly. By March 1995, the United States had reduced this MNF to 6,000 in order to allow a seamless transition to the UN Mission in Haiti (UNMIH) PKF. In East Timor, this strategy was beyond the capability of Australia's much smaller defense force. Rather, Australia decided to deploy with approximately the same strength and capability as that required by the PKF after transition.

There is little doubt that the UN will continue to rely on MNFs for security restoration and stabilization operations. MNFs will then transition into UN PKFs. A key lesson from East Timor is that this strategy requires that early and effective planning mechanisms be established from the outset between the DPKO and the MNF.

Early Appointment of the Force Commander

The early selection of a capable PKF force commander is fundamental to good planning and preparation. There are a number of reasons why this is important. Politically, many countries are unwilling to confirm their PKF contributions until they know the nationality and caliber of the force commander. More practically, establishing early teamwork between the force commander and the SRSG is important, as the maintenance of a peaceful environment is fundamental to the mission's broader achievements. In close collaboration with DPKO staff, the SRSG and force commander need to plan together from the earliest possible moment. Initial planning is necessarily done by the Military Planning Service in New York, but it is essential that this planning is consistent with the force commander's concept for operations.

The early appointment of the PKF force commander is no less important in situations where an MNF precedes the deployment of a PKF. Indeed, it is critical in such circumstances because the transition must be planned in detail. This is the period when the new force is likely to be most vulnerable, and it is essential that both commanders have jointly planned and fully agreed on the conditions for handover. In this respect, the Haiti operation provides a better model for transition than East Timor. In Haiti's case, the incoming force commander (Major General Joseph Kinzer from the United States) was appointed early. Together with the SRSG (Lakhdar Brahimi), he participated fully in DPKO planning. He insisted that his headquarters be assembled and trained in theater and that the communications systems be fully tested before transition. Indeed, transition was postponed until Kinzer was willing to certify that his headquarters and the force were operationally ready.

Given the sound lessons on transition learned in Haiti, it is difficult to understand why circumstances should differ so greatly in East Timor. Lieutenant General de los Santos was not appointed until 30 December 1999. Following briefings in New York and reconnaissance, he deployed to Dili on 25 January 2000, by which time the transition plan had been prepared by INTERFET and was presented as a fait accompli. Six days later, de los Santos assumed command of Sector East, and then the remaining three sectors progressively, assuming total command from General Cosgrove on 23 February. The PKF headquarters had not been assembled and commenced operations on 1 February with only a small, disparate, multinational staff.[11] The headquarters was poorly equipped, and no provision had been made for force protection. This situation was not the fault of de los Santos, who was given inadequate preparation time. Much of the work done by the Australian liaison team in the DPKO had not been actioned following their departure in November 1999, and an unrealistic workload was given to a small PKF advance party that was established in Dili later that month. This advance party, headed initially by an Australian logistics colonel and later by the Korean chief of staff,[12] worked tirelessly with the SRSG, but they lacked the authority and presence of the force commander and the support of a proper staff.

In order to effect successful MNF-PKF transitions, the lessons from East Timor are clear. The UN should adopt the Haiti model (or something closely akin) as the better option. The force commander should be appointed as soon as possible and be intimately involved in planning and preparation. The model is in fact appropriate regardless of whether an MNF is required. But where a transition from MNF to PKF is necessary, it is preferable to have the change of command occur at a specific moment in time, as occurred in Haiti, rather than sequentially, as was the case in East Timor. Failure to learn from a comparison of the Haiti/East Timor experiences will jeopardize the success of future missions and will place at greater risk the lives of peacekeepers who remain reliant on the effectiveness and professionalism of their force headquarters. The DPKO needs to continue its current efforts to develop an organizational model for force headquarters and a training package as a matter of priority.

Force Commander's Directive

Command and control issues are important in all organizations but particularly so for military forces where the use of lethal force can have enormous consequences. It is essential, therefore, that the force commander be given a clear and timely directive. It is current practice that this is provided by the Under-Secretary-General DPKO. However, given uncertain and insecure circumstances on the ground and the designated relationship between the head of mission and the leader of the military component, the directive should be from the SRSG. The force commander, reporting to and through the SRSG, is responsible for conducting military operations and for providing military advice to the SRSG. The force commander, while also maintaining close contact with the military adviser in New York, works directly for the SRSG and not for the Military Planning Service in New York. Any other system is liable to cause divisions within the mission and is fraught with danger. Differences of opinion between the SRSG and force commander on key military issues need to be confronted in situ, and where not reconciled it is essential that the force commander's view be accurately reflected in mission reporting.

In East Timor, not only was the directive not provided by the SRSG, it was not received before transition and required amendment. The final directive was promulgated on 8 May 2000, more than four months after appointment of the force commander.[13] The unsatisfactory nature of such a situation adds further weight to the necessity for appointing the force commander early. He or she is then able to assist in shaping the directive, and the SRSG has sufficient time to be comfortable with it. Effective military operations demand an iterative planning process culminating in the issue of a realistic and achievable directive to the force commander. The following sequence is recommended for future missions:

- The force commander is appointed as soon as possible. (Where feasible this should be done in advance of the Security Council mandate, with the SRSG and force commander in provisional appointments.)
- The force commander and key planning staff are briefed by the DPKO. This briefing should include limitations likely to be imposed by the Security Council mandate and the intended force composition and ROE.
- The force commander conducts reconnaissance and confirms his or her concept for operations, force requirements, and ROE. This planning is cleared with the SRSG and then with the DPKO and the Office of Legal Affairs.
- Based on the force commander's concept and advice, and within the limitations of the Security Council mandate the DPKO confirms the force structure and clears the ROE with troop-contributing nations.
- In consultation with the force commander, the DPKO prepares the force commander's directive for clearance and issue by the SRSG.

The force commander's directive should be concise and unambiguous, highlighting the mission and tasks, confirming the command and reporting chains, and providing reference to supporting regulations and procedures. It should highlight the key stakeholders and the need for the force commander to establish and maintain effective liaison with them. The directive should also insist that the PKF develop and adhere to a strict code of conduct, that ROE be properly applied, and that the force be continuously trained in these requirements. The force commander should be required to assess the performance of each troop-contributing nation and to assess their preparedness for operations and their entitlement for refunding under assessed contributions. Importantly, the directive should allow the force commander to remain flexible and retain the initiative to complete the mission. While the development of the directive is iterative, the final document must be presented to the force commander before deployment and/or transition from the MNF.

Worst-Case Planning

Given that the success or failure of a mission depends largely on maintaining a secure environment, it is essential that the military and police components for a mission be based on realistic but worst-case planning. It is too late and too difficult to adjust force levels after deployment. It is better to be initially overgenerous with force capabilities and then reduce them as the security situation improves. Indeed, this reasoning has underpinned most NATO deployments and other U.S.-led military coalitions such as the Gulf War. A thorough and honest threat assessment—the worst-case scenario—should be the real issue on which the composition and deployment of military and police forces are determined.

In the planning for complex peace operations, a significant weakness in the Secretariat is the lack of a viable intelligence unit capable of making thorough threat assessments on which the Security Council can properly base its judgments on force capabilities. More often than not, decisions on force composition are based on an assessment of what member states are prepared to support rather than what might be needed. The Brahimi report recognized this deficiency across a number of UN missions and recommended establishing an Information and Strategic Analysis Secretariat to serve the Executive Committee on Peace and Security.[14] It is arguable that such a secretariat would be able to prepare accurate threat assessments on which mission planning is based. Although it is possible to argue about the most efficient mechanisms for producing intelligence assessments, there can be no sustainable argument for committing peacekeepers into dangerous situations without a proper analysis of the threat environment. Until it develops this capability, the UN should request support from key member states and be prepared to act on this advice.

The failure to conduct worst-case security planning for UNTAET was reflected in the lack of preparation and caliber of CIVPOL and in the need to augment the PKF with additional capabilities following the militia infiltration in August 2000. Such infiltration could always have been expected, yet the PKF's original force composition did not provide for this possibility. Indeed, the pressure from some Security Council members to reduce the burden of assessed contributions had forced the PKF to begin force reductions only one month previously. The PKF was then augmented following this infiltration, in a reactive manner. Worst-case planning based on proper threat assessments would better inform decisionmaking, enhance the maintenance of a secure environment, and help save lives. This is an important lesson for the UN to heed if it is to have credibility in complex peace operations.

Integrated Planning

Notwithstanding the difficulties in staff shortages within the Secretariat, the UN's intervention in East Timor also revealed a lack of coordination between and within departments, as well as with other UN Agencies, the Bretton Woods institutions, and the East Timorese. Interdepartmental "tensions" between the DPA and the DPKO are acknowledged in Ian Martin's account of UNAMET.[15] But, as noted in the previous chapter, stovepipes affecting planning also existed between the DPKO and the Office of Legal Affairs and within the DPKO itself. In the former case, the preparation and clearance of the ROE, the status-of-forces agreements, and other legal issues all impacted on military operations and should therefore have been resolved before deployment and then adjusted quickly as the need arose. As already explained, this was not the case.[16] Organizational stovepipes also existed within the DPKO, particularly between the Military Planning Service and the Field Administration and Logistics Division (FALD). The former arranged the composition of the force to conduct military operations, whereas the latter arranged contracts and MOUs from service providers (nations and companies) ensuring the most cost-effective option to administratively support the entire mission. These demands were sometimes in competition, with decisions normally favoring FALD and thus subordinating military proficiency to the mission's broader administrative requirements.

Two important lessons can be identified from the nonintegrated planning undertaken for East Timor. The most obvious is that stovepipes are unnecessary obstacles that prevent and distort good planning. But these obstructions can be avoided by implementing the Brahimi report's recommendation for the early establishment of IMTFs. Better and earlier coordinated planning will resolve many problems. The second lesson is that any degradation of military capability must be based on a thorough risk assessment. Maritime, air, and logistics support are critical vulnerabilities in military operations and should not always be under civilian control. Administrative procedures designed for traditional peacekeeping missions will often be inappropriate for complex peace enforcement missions. In such situations, the military (and arguably CIVPOL) must be able to operate with the same flexibility as modern warfighting forces. There is a strong argument, therefore, to segregate critical military and civilian capabilities and to move away from the current practice of integrated support in all areas.

Unity of Command

A principle accepted by many defense forces is the operational importance of unity of command. In simple terms, this means that the force commander has effective authority over all military forces operating within the theater. Although it is not possible to achieve full command in multinational forces, because national authority is never divested to a foreign commander, strong coalitions respect the authority of the force commander and undertake to work in unity for a common purpose. The UN itself may have two different military forces within the same mission—military observers and armed peacekeepers—further complicating the achievement of unity of command.

As explained in Chapter 3, unity of command was achieved in East Timor by placing UNMOG and the PKF under the single authority of the force commander. But initially this command status was not universally welcomed by all military observers, particularly in light of their important contribution and unique status during the UNAMET and INTERFET periods, where they had deployed in advance of the PKF. An important lesson from UNTAET, however, is that the decision to unify the force under a single military commander was fully justified and should be the norm in future operations of this kind. Under UNTAET, both military components wore the blue beret, reported to the same SRSG, and served to maintain security. While the CMO retained special status and was a key member of the force commander's inner planning group, there was only one force commander.

Ensuring the Right Force Mix

The most important military planning requirement is to ensure the right force mix for the operation. In summary, this includes an efficient force headquarters, capable combat and combat support forces, and a responsive logistics system. These issues are the subject of later discussion but, fundamentally, the military force must be credible: that is, it must be capable of providing deterrence and of defeating actual threats. This means that force capabilities must be appropriate to achieve the mission and tasks. Because it is more difficult to make major corrections to force structure once operations have begun, detailed and realistic planning is required well in advance. In complex peace operations, rarely will it be possible for military forces to restrict their activities solely to either warfighting or constabulary-CMA duties. As already explained, multidimensional peace operations are more likely to be required within a single mission. The military force was successful in East Timor because core capabilities were based on warfighting proficiency, to which were added the constabulary-CMA requirements. This was because combat remained a real possibility, and a requirement existed for the military force to be prepared to fight for peace.

As well, the military threat from the militias, combined with the difficult operating environment in East Timor, required a high tempo of operations to maintain an active presence and demanded a force structure based primarily on mobile light infantry supported by air and maritime assets. Maintaining an active military presence to prevent militia action and to reassure the people was critical, and mobility and maneuver were important to prevent and quickly react to threats. The PKF in East Timor had less air capability than did INTERFET, requiring more permanent positions and increased reliance on foot and vehicle patrols. (The importance of air-ground operations is discussed later.)

For complex peace operations it is essential that troop-contributing nations possess the necessary capabilities, commensurate with the threat. This requires tough judgments by the DPKO on the selection of force elements. Complex peace operations require combat-ready forces appropriately trained and fully equipped. It is not feasible for nations to provide troops with the prime purpose of attracting funding and/or provisioning through the reimbursement of assessed contributions. The two most important factors in selecting the best military forces are professional capability and acceptance by the host country. Political factors will always be important, but force composition based primarily on political compromise will seldom provide the desired result. The UN, and the member states, must insist on quality forces.

Selecting the Best Force Multipliers

A number of key force multipliers need to be considered carefully as part of the force. These force multipliers will vary from mission to mission depending on the role of the PKF, the threat, and the physical environment in which the force will operate.

Force protection is a sensitive issue, and optimizing the safety and well-being of the force is one of the force commander's most important responsibilities. The needless onset of casualties may place at risk the long-term commitment of troop contributors and may significantly degrade morale within the force. Currently, force protection measures are not uniformly understood or practiced in multinational forces, and every effort must be taken to set and apply acceptable standards. Again, the early appointment of the force commander would ensure that these standards are quickly established and conveyed to the troop-contributing nations. Force protection involves more than preventing unnecessary battle casualties, hardening defensive positions, and correctly implementing the ROE, although these are obviously important. It also requires active patrolling and includes measures to minimize deaths and injuries through accident or illness; a code of conduct should also be developed to ensure the integrity and reputation of the force. Force protection does not prevent close relations from being established with the local community. Indeed, if the relationship is close and forged on mutual respect, the measures undertaken will be enhanced.

Force protection was emphasized in East Timor, and SOPs were quickly developed and promulgated to all contingents. Nonetheless, it took time for procedures to be properly understood and fully applied. A significant advantage for INTERFET and the PKF was the total absence of landmines in East Timor. The presence of mines would have complicated the operation and would have required special force protection measures. (Countermine operations require the inclusion of specific capabilities within the force structure and the thorough training of contingents before deployment.) INTERFET and the PKF did encounter instances of unexploded ordnance, resulting in PKF casualties and necessitating the establishment of a specialist cell. This was an oversight in premission planning and provides a useful lesson for future missions. The overarching lesson, however, is that the DPKO should prepare and disseminate doctrine and instructions on force protection measures and ensure that acceptable standards are reached as part of predeployment training. Countries failing to meet these standards, or failing to understand the increased requirements for force protection in complex peace operations (as compared with traditional peacekeeping), should not be selected for deployment. The terrorist attacks of September 11 have further heightened the need for force protection.

Depending on the operating environment, *air and maritime components* can prove critical to the success or failure of a mission. This was the case in East Timor, where military operations depended on the air and on maritime lines of communication. In the harshness of East Timor's climate and terrain, effective air-ground operations were critical in the restoration and maintenance of security, as was ably demonstrated by INTERFET. This requirement was no less important for the PKF but was made more difficult by the reduction in military aircraft, the multi-roling of air assets, and the UN's requirement that all air missions be authorized by the UNTAET director of administration (DOA).[17]

In complex peace operations there is a need to distinguish between administrative requirements for the mission and military operational requirements. Under current UN procedures, responsibility for all air tasking within the mission rests with the DOA. While this is appropriate for routine administration and for traditional peacekeeping missions, it is totally inappropriate for the conduct of military air-ground operations. As a result, the PKF suffered from two critical operational deficiencies: a limited ability to conduct airmobile operations by day and night, and night aeromedical evacuation. This capacity had existed under INTERFET, but the replacement of Australian Blackhawk helicopters with less capable UNcontracted aircraft reduced the PKF's operational flexibility.[18] The prosecution of airmobile operations is a dangerous and precise skill requiring considerable training between the air and ground components. It is unrealistic to expect military- and civilian-contracted aircraft to possess this capability. Following several militia attacks against the Australians at night, Australia made a unilateral decision to return its Blackhawk helicopters but restricted their use and retained them under Australian command and control, not allowing them to be part of the UN aviation component. This was an inefficient way of prosecuting coalition operations and placed unrealistic limitations on the force commander's freedom of maneuver.[19] Had a worst-case threat developed in East Timor, it is doubtful that air tasking could effectively have been optimized for military purposes. For complex peace operations that are highly reliant on air support, there is a strong case for reviewing the allocation of air assets for both military and civilian purposes and reassessing tasking procedures within the mission. A segregated military aviation component for military operations, controlled by the force commander, would seem the most appropriate (albeit more costly) solution for complex peace operations. The conduct of effective air-ground operations requires dedicated air assets and significant training. In peace enforcement operations that are heavily reliant on air (such as East Timor), it is inadvisable to divest this responsibility from the force commander, whose responsibility it is to maintain security.

The maritime forces were also important. Secretariat planning for the maritime component was complicated by the requirement in the mandate to establish a maritime police unit. This caused uncertainty regarding the maritime responsibilities for the PKF and CIVPOL—a matter that was clouded further with the creation of the Border Service, which was intent on establishing its own maritime element. To maintain logistics support, in light of INTERFET's experience, a small maritime logistic unit was included as part of the PKF, but there was no capability for offensive patrolling and interdiction. Better planning by the Secretariat could have averted these problems. Either a police maritime unit should have been established from the outset, or the PKF should have been assigned maritime patrol craft. Other UN missions have included such a capability, and its absence in East Timor reflected inadequate planning and preparation by the DPKO.

Reliable *force communications* are essential for the prosecution of military operations, and they must be planned in advance and tested before operations begin. The military communications system in East Timor was initially based on a commercial system installed by INTERFET, with redundancy provided by a Pakistani force communications unit. Over time, this commercial system was integrated within the mission's overall communications setup. Connectivity was provided from force to sector headquarters, with contingents responsible for internal communications.

Generally, the commercial system worked well but experienced degradation due to a lack of technical personnel when it was taken over by UNTAET. The UN's organic communications system is functional and has been well tested in many missions. It is installed and operated by UN technicians, but it takes time to mature and is primarily focused on the needs of the mission rather than on the conduct of military operations. A common mission system provides limited redundancy, takes time to establish, and is not always flexible for military operations. A lesson from East Timor is that commercial systems for military communications are preferable to including the military requirements in the overall UN communications system. A concomitant lesson is that military communications should be separated from the rest of the mission with redundancy systems in place and tested. Providing security for military communications is an important force protection issue, and commercial systems are available offering a high level of security at the tactical and operational levels. The DPKO should investigate the provision of secure commercial communications for future operations.

CMA involves the planning and utilization of civil and military capabilities in the most efficient and sustainable manner to provide essential humanitarian relief and to assist in societal reconstruction (nation building). Properly planned and conducted CMA also helps maintain a secure environment. Postoperational assessments from a number of peacekeeping missions have stressed the importance of CMA in complex peace operations. Nevertheless, as shown in Chapter 3, CMA was underestimated and uncoordinated in premission planning for East Timor.

A key lesson for future missions is that, wherever possible, the prime responsibility for humanitarian relief and rehabilitation should rest with the civil authorities. Only in extreme circumstances and for limited periods should military forces assume leadership. OCHA should play the leading role in planning and coordination, recognizing that close cooperation with military forces will be required to ensure security and the provision of scarce assets, particularly during the establishment phase. As the situation stabilizes, the military should continue to provide assistance to the transitional and/or national administration in accordance with an agreed overarching plan, with liaison remaining through OCHA or a humanitarian and rehabilitation pillar (such as was created in East Timor). Military support should be progressively reduced as civil capabilities develop, and care should be taken not to create unsatisfied dependencies on departure.

The CMA experience in East Timor also highlighted two important tactical lessons. The first was that good CMA enhanced force protection because it contributed to building trust and confidence with the local population. The second lesson was that CMA improved situational awareness because it provided valuable information. With trust and confidence came good human intelligence and a much better understanding of the actual situation. Information from CMA activities better enabled the PKF to be proactive in planning its operations. CMA, therefore, became a key platform in achieving the PKF's mission to maintain security.

CMA will continue to play a major role in future peace operations, and the UN should consider initiatives to enhance CMA awareness and training. This should include closer collaboration between OCHA and the DPKO and the development of CMA doctrine and SOPs for UN forces. To complement this, DPKO unit organizations for "standby" forces should be adjusted, where necessary, to include CMA capabilities in these structures. An enhanced CMOC should also be included in the organization charts for the force and sector headquarters. The UN might seek assistance from specific countries to progress this issue quickly.

Another key force multiplier is *military information.* Without good information the force commander is totally reactive. PKFs are not necessarily composed of forces familiar with the area of operations, but it is critical that they have access to good sources of military information. A number of actions, therefore, need to be undertaken by the Secretariat early in the planning phase. First, it is important that a military information handbook be produced, perhaps with assistance from the lead nations, for the use of all troops during their predeployment training.

A second important action is to ensure that the Military Information cell at force headquarters (and within each of the major contingents) is staffed with sufficient personnel trained in intelligence procedures. Personnel should be appointed from nations having awareness of the operational theater, or at least the ability to acquire this knowledge quickly. It is also essential that personnel in the Military Information cell be competent in the language of the mission and that some of these personnel have relevant local language skills. Many of the personnel initially assigned to the PKF for East Timor did not meet these requirements. It was several months before the understaffed Military Information cell could provide adequate military assessments, and in time additional personnel were added to the cell. Some units failed to acquire these skills and were therefore unable to provide valuable tactical assessments to force headquarters.

A third important action is to provide the military force with capable C4ISR[20] systems and to enable them to conduct information operations (IO). Suitable commercial C4ISR systems for multinational forces are available, and these could be contracted by the UN for training purposes and for standby deployment. Proper IO protects C4ISR systems and personnel from physical, psychological, and electronic attack and actively targets the opponent's C4ISR systems. In complex peace operations, IO is becoming increasingly important for commanders at all levels. When the PKF for East Timor was planned, little thought was given to this important dimension. As the operation continued, the PKF's capabilities improved, including the assignment of an electronic warfare squadron capable of monitoring militia communications. Nevertheless, IO capabilities remained very basic and below that required for modern peace enforcement. An important element of IO is the ability to conduct psychological operations to counter the opposition's propaganda and to provide timely and accurate information to the local community. The PKF did not have this capability, and this proved to be a critical deficiency, particularly during peak periods of militia infiltration. Again, this was an area where the availability of skilled interpreters and translators would have had a positive impact on improving performance.

Allied to IO, but separate from it, is the need for a professional PKF *public information* component. This is required to keep the force commander fully informed of media issues, but also to support the commander in activitating news and responding to media inquiries. As with the Military Information cell, the PKF's Public Information cell was poorly resourced initially, and it took considerable time for it to become fully operational. A major drawback was the initial allocation of untrained media personnel, some with only a limited knowledge of English (the mission language).

Other important lessons from East Timor in this area are the need for early planning between DPKO and OCPI and for the reinforcement of this partnership within the mission area. It is important that the military public information plan fully supports that of the mission, which should be articulated as the mission is established. In UNTAET, however, many months passed before a coherent public information plan was in place, during which time the PKF was largely left to run its own "campaign." This is inexplicable given the UN's good reputation in this area, which it demonstrated so well during UNAMET. Notwithstanding the more difficult situation facing UNTAET, the military and civilian public information performance would have been enhanced, as with most aspects of the operation, with better planning and preparation.

In all operations, *military engineers* are required to ensure force mobility and to undertake essential construction. In postconflict situations, military engineers can also contribute to the civil reconstruction program. The inclusion of military engineering units as part of the PKF in East Timor was a significant force multiplier, but their subsequent contribution was limited due to the UN's procurement processes. East Timor was totally destroyed following the August 1999 ballot, and reconstruction was an obvious and high priority. It was disappointing to see the inadequate utilization of valuable engineering skills in beginning this task. The military contribution to nation building in postconflict environments needs to be reconsidered by the Secretariat to enhance flexibility and optimize reconstruction efforts.

A number of military engineering lessons were learned from East Timor. The first is that military engineers need to be incorporated into the overall reconstruction plan, with greater flexibility being exercised in the use of assessed and development funds for reconstruction purposes. Clearly, in situations where massive destruction has occurred, the contribution of the military engineers is critical, particularly if they are able to commence operations in advance of civil engineers. While the force commander must always have first call on engineer assets for military priority tasks, military engineers' assistance on civil tasks will benefit the force as well. This was demonstrated in the priority given to road maintenance in East Timor, with military engineers being tasked to keep open some of the main supply routes. Had these routes closed, elements of the force would have been isolated and the PKF's mobility would have been severely restricted, thereby jeopardizing the maintenance of security. Equally, these same roads were vital for commerce and governance. In postconflict situations, therefore, it is inadvisable to draw too fine a distinction on the tasks assigned to military engineers. Above all, however, is the importance of fidelity of coordinated premission planning within the Secretariat and the understanding that military engineers must be properly provisioned for their tasks.

Recognizing the difficulties in liberalizing current funding arrangements, a second lesson is that the DPKO should select engineering units from nations capable of providing much of their own matériel. This can hardly be expected from developing countries. Pakistan and Bangladesh provided capable engineer units, but their efforts were constrained by a slow matériel procurement system and draconian restrictions on tasking approvals. By comparison, the work rate of smaller self-funded engineer units from Portugal, Korea, and Australia was much higher. A lack of understanding during the planning process, and the failure to integrate military engineering as part of the civil reconstruction plan, meant that windows of opportunity were lost and that engineers were not always fully employed.

A third lesson is that military engineer units must be capable of providing their own force protection. This reflects the dual combat role of all engineer units and differentiates them from civil engineers. Rarely in peace enforcement operations, and particularly in low-intensity conflict, will it be feasible for scarce infantry assets to be reassigned to protect engineer units. Rather, engineer units will be expected to look after their own security, and they must come appropriately armed and trained for this task.

Political and Anthropological Advice

In complex peace operations, force commanders must continually operate in three separate dimensions. The first is the professional military dimension, where they are responsible for ensuring that the force conducts successful military operations. In this dimension, they should be able to rely on their training and experience and the support of professional subordinate commanders and staff. For most senior commanders this is the most comfortable, yet professionally challenging, dimension.

The second is the political dimension, where force commanders must ensure that all military action is in concert with political ends, or at least that military action does not jeopardize political outcomes. In complex peace operations, discussions between force commanders and their military counterparts will almost always have political implications. In postconflict environments, it is often the local or former military commanders who have the greatest influence. In East Timor, for example, the force commander was frequently engaged in important political discussions with his Indonesian counterpart and with the UNTAET and East Timorese political and military leadership. Reporting directly to the SRSG, the force commander was also involved in political decisions related to matters of national security. Generally, senior military commanders are less prepared for this dimension than for the professional military dimension. Recognizing the critical importance of this responsibility, the United States has for some years appointed experienced political advisers to assist its senior military commanders. It is recommended that the UN replicate this practice and that from commencement of operations a senior political adviser be appointed to assist the force commander and to foster the important relationship between force headquarters and the mission's political section.

The third is the social and cultural dimension. Here force commanders must be cognizant of the social and cultural issues within the host country. Peacekeeping is about building trust and confidence between UN international transients and the true inhabitants within the mission area. This requires military forces to understand the social, historical, and cultural issues that underpin the society and to operate in a way that earns the respect and confidence of the local population. Both INTERFET and the PKF achieved this in East Timor but more by default than design. A consistent complaint against UNTAET from some influential East Timorese and international staff was the lack of understanding by UN personnel of East Timor and its people. A weakness with most occupying military forces is that they have little opportunity to understand and fully appreciate the important cross-cultural issues. Many basic problems can be overcome with adequate predeployment and induction training, but it is not until commanders and troops are confronted with actual situations that they are able to focus clearly on the best course of action. Effectiveness would be enhanced by assigning anthropologists within the mission for continuation training and advice. The importance of building trust between the PKF and the community should not be underestimated. In East Timor, no effort was made to employ anthropologists to aid in this process. The assistance of a small team of experienced anthropologists in theater seems a small price to pay for enhancing relations between the UN and the local community.

Rules of Engagement and Other Legal Issues

ROE are essential both to enhance the protection of friendly forces and personnel and to leave the adversary in no doubt that necessary force will be used against them if and when required. Moreover, each mission requires ROE relevant to its particular circumstances, and rarely will it be appropriate simply to transplant ROE from other missions. ROE should be promulgated early; they should be understood, agreed upon, and practiced by all coalition partners; and they should provide the force commander with sufficient authority and flexibility to adjust them quickly when necessary. It is not always possible for all coalition partners to agree fully with all aspects of the ROE, and exemptions are often required to meet national requirements. Minor differences can normally be accommodated.

While robust ROE applied to INTERFET and the PKF, there are lessons to be learned for future UN missions. First, again comparing East Timor and Haiti, the ROE planning process for the latter emerges as the more efficient model for the UN to adopt in subsequent UN operations. As with the planning for transition, in the case of Haiti, the early and direct involvement of the force commander and SRSG in the preparation of ROE, and their clearance with coalition partners before deployment, avoided many of the difficulties experienced by the UNTAET PKF. A second lesson is the need to give the SRSG and force commander more authority and flexibility to adjust or amplify the ROE as required. While Secretariat and coalition approval must always be sought to strengthen the ROE and liberalize the use of lethal force, there is a case for delegating the tightening of ROE to the mission, particularly as the security environment improves. A further lesson is that ROE training must be completed before deployment and regularly conducted during operations. To assist, the DPKO should ensure that training packages, aide-mémoirs, and soldiers' cards (authorizing the conditions under which soldiers can open fire) are prepared before deployment.

The UN intervention in East Timor also revealed other legal lessons separate from the ROE. A clear policy is needed on arrest and detention procedures by military personnel; also needed are directives to ensure that this policy is in accordance with civil justice and the rule of law. It is important for military personnel to have unambiguous guidelines on arrest and detention and of the handover arrangements from military to civilian jurisdiction. Within UNTAET, problems were encountered between the PKF, CIVPOL, and the Legal Office largely because procedures had not been coordinated in advance. Another lesson concerned the status of forces agreement for the military component. This is normal for UN missions, but despite the wishes of most coalition partners, little progress was made because the UNTAET Legal Office argued that it was not possible for a UN PKF to have a status of forces agreement with a UN transitional administration. This was a moot point, but its absence failed to provide express safeguards that would normally apply to military personnel on such missions.

Improving Military-Police Coordination

As noted previously, UN military forces and CIVPOL operate in different ways to maintain a secure environment, but their actions are complementary and need to be coordinated. Each force should retain its own identity and chain of command, but coordination mechanisms are required to ensure that they work toward the same goal. This is particularly so in transitional administrations where the existence and performance of both forces is likely to be replicated in the new state. The difficulties experienced by UNTAET in military-police coordination were discussed in Chapter 3, and several lessons can be identified. The most important of these concerns the need for better coordination within the Secretariat during the mission-planning phase. As with the force commander, the police commissioner should also be appointed early. The opportunity then provided to develop operational concepts in close consultation will greatly enhance coordination and teamwork. Given the importance of CIVPOL in postconflict situations, consideration should also be given to elevating the status of the police commissioner and establishing CIVPOL as a separate component in its own right. Further, the UN needs urgently to develop doctrine and SOPs for military-police coordination in complex peace operations. While each mission will require its own directives to deal with specific circumstances, it should be possible to produce doctrine and SOPs that can be used in training and that can assist contingent preparation.

Having appropriate capabilities for internal security operations within each of the forces and better coordination between these elements is another lesson learned from the UNTAET experience. When the PKF is mandated to assist CIVPOL in maintaining law and order, it is important that it have relevant capabilities and that contributing states agree to this requirement. Wherever possible, the PKF should provide a supporting role, for use only in extremis, but on such occasions joint operations must be mounted professionally and successfully. This requires considerable training and preparation, suggesting advantages in the deployment of military and police forces from the same countries. Regardless of force composition, however, joint planning and training is required in theater to confirm interoperability and performance levels.

Overall, considerable work is yet to be done to improve military-police coordination in future complex peace operations. One area, however, that warrants particular consideration in determining force composition is the utility of employing military police. Military police are often able to help bridge the gap between military and police forces, particularly in the early phase of operations. They also play a useful role in preventing misunderstandings between the forces at the tactical level on the ground.

Responsive Logistics Support

It is a truism that efficient logistics is fundamental to the success of military operations. UNTAET demonstrated there is still the need to review current UN administrative procedures and to make them more responsive to military requirements. Most of the logistics problems encountered in East Timor reflected policy and procedures determined within the Secretariat. Accordingly, the resolution of these difficulties rests more with mission planning and preparation than it does with their application on the ground. The current UN logistics system is unsatisfactory for the conduct of military operations, and more so those in a harsh environment over tenuous lines of communication. The current system lacks detailed planning and is too centralized, too slow, and not sufficiently responsive to the force commander's requirements. In summary, UN logistics and administration are in need of major overhaul.

An important issue is that of ownership and accountability. Under current arrangements the force commander has little say over the logistics matters of his force, because the civilian DOA has full authority for all mission administration. While this system may be appropriate for traditional peacekeeping, it lacks responsiveness for peace enforcement operations. Moreover, UNTAET's experience would suggest that current UN policy requiring the establishment of a Joint Logistics Operations Centre (JLOC) to coordinate all logistics centrally within a mission is in need of review. In complex peace operations, there is a good case for segregating military and civilian logistics systems, including in the management of air and maritime assets. A clear delineation needs to be made between those assets and procedures required for the conduct of military operations and those required for the general administration and support of the whole mission.

The effect of unresponsive logistics on military operations can be stultifying. It is instructive to compare administrative support for INTERFET with that for the PKF. As explained, INTERFET deployed on short notice to East Timor in September 1999 and quickly established logistics support in the worst of possible environments. INTERFET's mandate was to restore and maintain security for an unspecified short duration until relieved by a PKF. Accordingly, the DPKO had ample warning and preparation time to arrange logistics support for the PKF that replaced INTERFET five months later. Despite this long lead time, significant logistics support from the INTERFET period had to be maintained for an additional six months until UN contracts could be put in place. Several examples of poor logistics planning by the DPKO serve to highlight the inefficiency of the UN system to support complex peace operations:

• Aviation. The withdrawal of Australian helicopters was contingent on the UN replacing this critical vulnerability. After several delays, replacement aircraft arrived only to be assessed as below the standard required for night aeromedical evacuation. Additionally, the contracting of a heavy lift helicopter failed to stipulate necessary seating arrangements, although troop movement was one of its major tasks. Reconfiguring the helicopter caused a significant delay.

• Rations. The contract for fresh rations was let to a new contractor at about half the cost of INTERFET rations. The initial provision of rations proved totally unacceptable, causing significant problems with morale and resulting in some commanders refusing to accept supplies and reverting to hard rations. This required a visit from the contracting authority in New York and an additional six weeks before the problems could be resolved. The provision of rations is a basic requirement for all defense forces, yet even with several months of preparation time, the UN initially failed to deliver. The contractor acknowledged the weaknesses and eventually remedied the problems, but this does not excuse improper planning by the UN.

• Telecommunications. Initially, the commercial telecommunications contract for INTERFET was extended by the UN for six months because an alternative system was not available. The service was then taken over by the UN, but the service deteriorated due to a lack of technicians, consequently causing increased reliance on alternate military radio communications. The perception was that the UN system was inferior for military purposes, yet the UN had ample time to plan and install it.

All military operations depend on administrative and logistics support, an increasing amount of which is contracted to the civil sector. For justifiable fiduciary reasons, the UN follows strict procedures and regulations, allowing little room for flexibility and requiring a long period for approval. It takes time to let contracts, and major contracts must meet rigorous standards in New York. A frequent complaint from mission staff in UNTAET was the slowness in letting contracts and the problems encountered in the process. The Secretariat needs to review current procedures. Consideration should be given to devolving greater authority to the mission and to contracting out the provision of complete services during the early stage of planning. The DPKO should confirm its logistics support plan as part of initial mission planning, and it must satisfy the force commander's requirements.

Current UN practice is for contingents to be fully self-sustaining, for which they are reimbursed through assessed contributions. Such a logistics concept is contingent on nations being able to properly sustain their forces, often in remote regions and a long way from home. A number of nations in East Timor had difficulty in meeting these requirements. One combat unit suffered illness and death resulting from a lack of medical supplies and from poor vehicle maintenance due to insufficient parts. The practice of self-sustainment should be contingent on nations proving a viable resupply system, and where this is not possible, the UN must make alternative arrangements, with appropriate adjustments made in reimbursement. Indeed, an important aspect in the selection of forces should include an assessment of the contributing nation's ability to meet its logistics responsibilities.

A final logistics lesson from UNTAET is the need to review current requirements to establish a JLOC. To be effective, a JLOC needs to be pre-planned, properly resourced, and reflective of a common culture between military and civilian members. For UNTAET, the JLOC was not preplanned by the DPKO, with much of the logistics responsibility falling to the PKF. Over time, the JLOC became established as more civilian personnel and facilities became operational; but initially there was some friction between civilian and military members. While both military and civilian logisticians stress accountability, this shared vocabulary actually masks very different approaches. The military are accountable for operational outcomes and focus on task completion in support of a particular operational objective. Civilian logisticians, however, tend to view accountability in a purely fiscal sense and focus on compliance with UN regulations. This difference in approaches is cultural and systemic and inevitably creates tension and friction between civilian and military staff in the mission. In such circumstances, integration is difficult to achieve, but polarization must be avoided at all costs. If JLOCs are to be the norm in complex peace missions, they must be planned in detail and jointly managed under authority of the DOA and force commander. If this is not possible, segregation of military-specific logistics will be required if security is to be effectively maintained.

Enhancing Training and Readiness

More than ever, the challenges facing contemporary peacekeeping forces are greater, and the demands on training are more acute. One of the most important military lessons from East Timor is the need to revamp and enhance military training for complex peace operations. Within the PKF, there was a noticeable difference in the professional standards and skill levels throughout the various contingents and between various staff officers and military observers. Clearly, training standards differed between troop-contributing nations. In an effort to improve standards, a Training cell was established by force headquarters to assist coalition partners. But this approach was too little too late, and the lesson is that better peacekeeping training standards need to be set by the DPKO and implemented by member states.

It is the responsibility of member states to ensure that their forces are properly trained for UN service. The DPKO cannot be expected to undertake the training of peacekeepers, but in consultation with member states it could set benchmarks and specify predeployment self-assessment standards to confirm readiness prior to deployment.[21] There are a number of important training categories for which military standards need to be set for complex peace operations. These include, but are not necessarily limited to:

- Force headquarters and staff officer preparation.
- Peace enforcement and internal security tasks.
- Peace monitoring and negotiation skills.
- Traditional peacekeeping constabulary duties.
- Military information and IO.
- Air and maritime operations.
- Public information.
- CMA.
- Humanitarian and disaster relief.
- Refugee management.
- Military-police operations.
- Gender affairs and local cultures.
- ROE.
- Codes of conduct.
- Force protection.
- Administration and logistics support.

Training for specific missions normally falls into four distinct phases: predeployment training, induction training on arrival in the mission area, continuation training during deployment, and redeployment (to home) training. By setting standards and benchmarks, the DPKO could subcontract training to member states and peacekeeping centers. The approach that Nordic countries use to standardize training (with each country taking prime responsibility for a different training course) provides a useful model for proliferating peacekeeping training and raising standards. The DPKO should encourage the extension of the Nordic model to peacekeeping centers throughout other regions.

To improve force readiness, the DPKO also needs to review the organizational models of its standby military structures. These charts provide a useful guide to contributing countries, but each mission requires the selection of specific military capabilities. Accordingly, the organizational structures need to be reviewed on a case-by-case basis, with adjustments made as necessary. The current organizations are being used too literally for reimbursement of assessed contributions. A preferred option would be for these existing models to be taken as a useful starting point for planning each mission and then adjusted to meet specific operational requirements. The final agreed organization should be used as the basis for reimbursement purposes, noting that further adjustments might be required as the mission continues. It is important that these military organizations include the right force multipliers (as noted earlier) to enhance the prospects of success.

Summary

The military lessons from East Timor discussed above mainly reflect inadequate planning and preparation before the establishment of the mission. Although problems were encountered and worked through on the ground, at the time it seemed that many of these dilemmas could have been averted had better planning and preparation occurred within the Secretariat following the signing of the 5 May Agreements. The recommendation of the Brahimi report to establish IMTFs (now being implemented) is a positive step toward ensuring that military considerations are incorporated more fully within overall mission planning. A common factor has emerged that would have averted many of the difficulties experienced by the PKF—that is, the early appointment of a highly capable force commander and the establishment of the mission team under the SRSG. For various reasons, sometimes political and sometimes practical (time constraints, for example) the UN has found it difficult to implement this procedure for a number of missions. The cause for this situation continues to be puzzling for East Timor, where there appeared to be no obvious constraints preventing the early assembly of mission leaders and their involvement in premission planning. In addition to the military aspects of the lessons that emerged from the need for thorough premission planning and preparation, the PKF also learned a number of major lessons during the conduct of its operations in East Timor. These lessons are discussed below.

LESSONS ON THE CONDUCT OF OPERATIONS

Military Reporting

In East Timor, the PKF found that there was a need for effective military reporting, both within the PKF and from the mission to the Secretariat.

Internal reporting issues were the easier to solve, although not without some difficulty. Not all contingents in multinational coalitions necessarily have the same approach to the collection and passage of information. Although SOPs dictate a common reporting schedule and format, they cannot overcome the problems of language or cultural sensitivities regarding the content of reports. This, added to the problems arising from an untrained and untested force headquarters, meant that considerable effort and patience was required before a professional reporting system could mature. This is an important consideration for future missions, because in crisis situations the passage of information must be timely and accurate. Several months passed in East Timor before reporting procedures within the PKF achieved a level of fidelity necessary for the conduct of efficient peace enforcement operations. The importance of command and staff visits in achieving an acceptable standard of reporting, and in developing teamwork, was also confirmed in East Timor. The high turnover of staff officers, combined with the frequency of contingent rotations, meant that continuous attention needed to be given to this particular issue. The UN preference for staff officers and military observers to serve a tenure of twelve months, thereby providing greater stability and knowledge within the force, was also vindicated. Many nations, however, provided personnel on much shorter tenure—a practice that should not be encouraged in future missions.

External military reporting to the Secretariat was a more difficult issue. It is essential that military information from a mission to the Secretariat be honest, timely, and unambiguous. The complex nature of the UN encourages considerable information exchange (particularly by fax, e-mail, and telephone), sometimes including comment on sensitive issues that may not always be visible to or have the agreement of the SRSG. On military matters, continuous staff action occurs between the force headquarters and the DPKO and between national contingent commanders and their home capitals. While routine staff action and liaison is to be encouraged, matters affecting policy or having political implications should be cleared through the SRSG. Care must be taken to ensure that information is not misunderstood or that troop-contributing nations are not alarmed or offended. For this reason, the system of UN code cables is the safest and most sensible means for conducting and recording important military business. This system was used by the PKF in East Timor, although it was not implemented instantaneously, and it proved effective and secure. Important military issues were compiled in these code cables and cleared by the SRSG before dispatch. This ensured that the SRSG was always fully informed of key military issues and that he was in agreement with military recommendations. It also permitted national contingent commanders to brief their national defense headquarters on action being considered on important military issues without subverting the role of the DPKO in liaising with national capitals. The UN code cable system is the SOP for reporting, but variations can occur from mission to mission depending on the personalities of the SRSG and force commander and on the size of the mission. Nonetheless, in complex peace operations (such as UNTAET), it is important that all senior military personnel fully understand the procedures to be used and that this is reflected clearly in the directives to the SRSG and force commander. The use of video conferencing between the mission and New York is highly beneficial and should be encouraged. There was scope for more frequent use of this mechanism in East Timor. Time spent in gaining an informed understanding of important issues and in determining appropriate courses of action in consultation is time well spent. The system of code cables can then be used as authority to confirm and record discussions.

In addition to code cables and video conferencing, regular military reporting was also required. Important military issues were covered in regular UNTAET situation reports, and the PKF also provided weekly and monthly situation reports, the latter providing a detailed record of military activities and statistics as well as confirming future military intentions. This system worked well but would have benefited from more feedback from the DPKO. Seldom did UN Headquarters acknowledge these reports, and the impression in the field, unfortunately, was that considerable staff effort was expended in the compilation of these reports, the exact purpose and value of which remained uncertain.

Improving Joint Operations

As in any complex operation, the military was only one component of the multidimensional mission in East Timor. This required the PKF to establish partnerships with the other stakeholders, to be a supportive team player, and to take the lead when the security situation so demanded. For most of the time, the PKF was able to maintain an active but benign presence, reassuring the East Timorese population and providing support to the transitional administration and other agencies. In each district, the PKF and UNMOG established close relations with the district administration, subordinating military to civil authority, maintaining security, and assisting in the reestablishment of governance and social order.

The relationship between the PKF and CIVPOL has already been discussed and the lesson noted that mechanisms enabling better coordination between the forces are required for future missions. By contrast, INTERFET and the PKF worked more closely with UNHCR in the management of displaced people. To this end, a joint command center was established under UNHCR leadership, and contingency plans to handle refugee returns were rehearsed. For many months the PKF played a key role in facilitating large family reunion meetings and, with UNHCR agreement, was instrumental in having these canceled when security was jeopardized. The mechanisms implemented by the PKF and UNHCR worked well and provide a useful model for future UN operations.

On border issues, the PKF worked closely with the Political Branch, district administrators, CIVPOL, and the Border Service. This ensured that tactical border arrangements did not contravene broader political objectives and that modalities were consistent with customs and immigration regulations. The careful and successful management of the border provided a stabilizing factor and helped build a positive relationship between Indonesia and the new nation of East Timor. Again, these are useful lessons for future operations.

In the areas of humanitarian relief and nation building, the military component sought to work cooperatively with relief agencies and assisted with planning and development projects to rebuild the East Timorese infrastructure. The tasks were many and varied. The PKF worked alongside USGET, forging a close relationship and ensuring that efforts between the two military forces were not duplicated. The PKF also cooperated with the Human Rights Office and participated in gender training through the Office of Gender Affairs. As well, the military aided the management of Falintil and the establishment of the ETDF. It liaised with UN Security Coordination in relation to security issues and evacuation planning and with the DSRSG's office on matters of disaster relief. The PKF also provided significant advice on establishing a national security framework and helped bring it into existence. All these joint endeavors were successful, but, more important, they highlighted that the maintenance of security in complex peace operations demanded more from the PKF than a mere military presence. The need for close teamwork and partnership between a diverse range of stakeholders is one of the most important elements for success in postconflict environments.

Military Leadership and Direction

Mention has already been made of the importance of careful and early selection of the force commander. To be equipped to provide the capable military leadership essential to mission success, a force commander should have professional skill, intellect, integrity, personality, and the ability to build a cohesive team. The PKF's first force commander, Lieutenant General Jaime de los Santos, was significantly disadvantaged because of his late appointment and the consequent limited latitude he was afforded in shaping the transition from INTERFET. His overall impact was also constrained because of his decision to depart the mission after only six months.

Nevertheless, de los Santos ensured that INTERFET's fine reputation was continued by the PKF, and he established a sound foundation on which the PKF could continue to develop. De los Santos was replaced at short notice by Lieutenant General Boonsrang Niumpradit from Thailand, who made it clear to all under his command that his appointment was for the long term, and this proved highly beneficial in consolidating PKF operations and enhancing force morale. An intelligent and dedicated commander, Boonsrang asserted his presence quickly and melded the force with greater unity of purpose. His arrival coincided with an intensification in militia infiltration and a heightening of security concern, and he worked tirelessly to turn this situation around. His efforts boosted morale and confidence throughout the force. Boonsrang also gave special attention to improving the welfare of the force, encouraging greater interaction with the community, emphasizing the need for sport and fitness, and actively encouraging social gatherings. Clearly understanding the need for personal contact and teamwork, he led by example.

Both force commanders employed similar mechanisms to provide unambiguous direction. Each articulated a simple vision and concept of operations. These were backed by a series of Commander's Directives and Operations Orders that clearly stated the PKF's mission and tasks as well as the desired endstate. These documents were backed by SOPs and by the promulgation of a strict code of conduct. Regular conferences were held with sector commanders; after-action reviews were conducted to confirm lessons from each major operation; and the force commander, his deputy, and the CMO maintained a busy program of regular visits to each of the sectors. Teamwork was established and emphasized between the unarmed UN military observers (UNMOs) and the armed peacekeepers, and each component was given specific tasks and reporting requirements. Recognition was given to individual achievements, care was taken to promote UN Medal ceremonies, and encouragement was given to celebrate national days and to acknowledge the contribution of contingents before they departed the mission area. The tragic deaths of PKF members were afforded special attention through religious services and farewell ceremonies, which were carried out with great dignity and honor. These deaths were spread across almost all of the major contingents, which, together with the public recognition of the soldier's ultimate sacrifice, helped forge greater commitment and solidarity within the PKF. The universal code of the warrior proved a deeply binding force and helped provide greater focus and determination by all to succeed as a multinational team.

Particular recognition was given to each of the national contingent commanders, each of whom was afforded unrestricted access to the force commander and deputy commander. They and their staffs were encouraged to meet regularly with the senior military staff at force headquarters, affording the opportunity to confer on operational issues, provide updates, and pass on relevant information. This had the additional benefit of enabling the commanders to provide timely and accurate information to their national capitals without subverting the more formal lines of communication from New York on matters of policy. They were also encouraged to raise concerns and were frequently consulted to resolve (or prevent) specific problems. With their support and diligence, the PKF maintained an excellent discipline record with few instances of misconduct. A significant lesson is that national contingent commanders play an important role in helping force commanders fulfill their missions, but at the same time, these contingent commanders must be prepared to assist and not obstruct the conduct of operations.

Establishing the Force Headquarters

Mention has already been made of the need for the force headquarters to be assembled, trained, and tested before the commencement of operations. An inoperable headquarters is a critical vulnerability that places the performance of the entire PKF and the success of the mission in jeopardy. If the UN is serious about deploying military forces quickly, it needs, as a matter of urgency, to develop SOPs for force headquarters and to provide for an emergency "fly-away kit" to enable the headquarters to become established quickly, even in a temporary location. This kit could be based on a standard layout, with the provision of essential command and control equipment and basic fittings.

An equally important consideration is the accommodation and rationing required for headquarters personnel. Ideally, this should occur as close to the headquarters as possible, enabling better force protection and encouraging the development of teamwork in a multinational environment. Most particularly, the accommodation should not be lavish, as this sends a poor message to the local inhabitants and causes friction over differences in standards between the headquarters and deployed troops. Emphasis needs to be on functionality rather than comfort, with enhancement occurring over time. In East Timor, a different situation eventuated. Until a proper camp was constructed adjacent to the headquarters, PKF personnel were accommodated for five months with civilian staff on a well-appointed barge, which attracted adverse comment from the East Timorese leaders and caused problems with weapons security. Military team building and productivity were adversely affected, and force protection was seriously jeopardized (resulting in injury and almost death to one operations shift officer). When the camp was eventually completed (three months behind schedule), morale, productivity, and force protection of the headquarters greatly improved. The UNTAET experience highlights the need in future missions for force commanders to confirm their requirements for accommodation and rationing well in advance of deployment.

The East Timor experience also revealed a number of issues to be considered regarding operational command. Each headquarters develops its own tempo of operations based largely on the character and drive of the senior staff, and this in turn influences what happens throughout subordinate commands. But it is essential that the headquarters lead by example and fully support continuous operations throughout the mission area. This approach was adopted by the force headquarters in East Timor. Morning and evening briefings were conducted for the force commander to hone staff procedures and develop situational awareness. The force commander also conducted formal meetings with his senior staff three times a week, and following General Boonsrang's arrival, informal discussions with the deputy and CMO occurred almost daily (depending on visit schedules). Most of the branches developed internal training packages, and the Operations Branch conducted a number of command post exercises. Overall, following a slow and painful birth, the force headquarters improved in stature and capability.

Avoiding Mission Creep

The principal military mission in peace enforcement operations is to maintain security and to assure everyone that the PKF is professionally capable of doing so. The force must be credible, otherwise it will be unable to gain the confidence and trust of the population or deter and defeat hostile incursions. To this end, the mission must be constantly reinforced so that all troops never lose sight of their primary objectives, and they must be assessed in their ability to produce results. Not to do so allows for mission creep.

Mission creep occurs when the PKF's central purpose (i.e., its mission) is replaced in importance by tasks of lower priority or when the opportunity costs of performing these other tasks prevents the proper execution of the original primary mission. There was the potential for this to occur in East Timor had the maintenance of security by the PKF been replaced in importance by the provision of humanitarian relief or by nation building. Mission creep did not happen, but the force commander had to be vigilant in guarding against it. Operating in a devastated territory, among a traumatized people, the temptation existed for the PKF to undertake too many tasks and thus establish dependencies that could not be maintained after military drawdown and withdrawal.

A key lesson for future UN missions is that all military commanders should remain focused at all times on the primary purpose for the PKF being in situ. They must be aware of the consequences of mission creep and constantly guard against the dangers of its effect on the military component's mission.

Developing Relations with the Key Protagonists

To maintain security in East Timor, it was extremely important for INTER-FET and the PKF to develop professional relations with two key protagonists—Falintil and the TNI. As shown in Chapters 2 and 3, the conditions under which this had to be achieved were conducive to success. Falintil's actions were highly responsible, and the TNI honored the ballot outcome once INTERFET arrived. Moreover, the physical separation of these entities and of the militia remnants in West Timor better enabled INTERFET and the PKF to establish separate professional relations with both. This situation is unlikely to be replicated in many postconflict situations, but a number of lessons seem no less relevant.

The first is that senior military commanders have considerable influence in these circumstances, and their actions can impact directly on political outcomes. This requires MNF and PKF commanders to be tough-minded and politically astute. A second lesson is that the key to success depends as much on the capability and integrity of the interventionist force as it does on the ability of armed groups to engage in conflict. At all times, peace enforcement missions must be capable of fighting for and winning the peace they have been sent to preserve. Militarily incompetent interventionist forces will jeopardize security more than they will ensure it. Although the MNF and the PKF brokered agreements with both Falintil and the TNI aimed at preventing conflict, the protagonists were never in doubt that strong military action would be taken quickly to resolve any incident that jeopardized security. The third lesson is that, together with this firm but professional approach, military interventionist forces should, wherever possible, assist cooperating armed combatants to meet their responsibilities and resolve their problems. The PKF's decision to utilize Falintil's experience to counter the militia threat, to press for improved living conditions in the cantonment, and to assist Falintil in its transition into a legitimate defense force are examples of such action. At the same time, the PKF was persistent in its efforts to encourage the TNI to take greater responsibility to prevent the arming of militias in West Timor and to coordinate border procedures to help prevent militia infiltration. These examples provide firm evidence of the positive results that can be achieved by this approach.

CONCLUSION

The PKF performed to a high standard in East Timor, but important lessons were relearned on which the UN and member states should take immediate action. Most of these lessons related to inadequate planning and preparation by the Secretariat and to the late appointment of the force commander. If implemented, the initiatives of the Brahimi report will address many of the problems experienced in these areas and greatly improve the Secretariat's capability to plan for UN missions in the future. This is essential, as the successful implementation and funding of these initiatives will depend upon the support and backing from member states, and these states will insist that the lives of their peacekeepers not be jeopardized because of incomplete preparation. Sound military planning is imperative and thus an important element in overall mission planning. Once deployed to East Timor, the PKF experienced a number of difficulties and learned a number of important tactical lessons. Generally, corrective action was taken over time and force enhancement occurred. As the operation continued, this was assisted by the establishment of a more rigorous training regime to help improve force capability. In summary, critical PKF weaknesses included:

- An untrained and understaffed force headquarters at the beginning of operations.
- A lack of mobility (particularly at night and by air).
- The absence of a maritime enforcement capability.
- Variable standards of force protection between contingents.
- An initial lack of capability in CMA, military information and IO, and public information.
- An inability of some contingents to satisfactorily meet their self-sustainment commitments.
- A lack of language assistants.
- A lack of coordination and planning between the PKF and CIVPOL.
- The limited capability of combat units to assist CIVPOL in internal security tasks.

The overall military conclusion for complex peace operations is clear: PKFs and MNFs require multiskilled personnel and units to be trained across the full spectrum of warfighting and constabulary-CMA tasks. This is an enormous challenge for the UN and member states. The obvious solution would seem to rest with the establishment of more clearly focused regional peacekeeping training centers, operating to meet more specific benchmarks provided by the Secretariat. Finally, the military experience in East Timor highlights an important lesson for future military intervention:

how a force starts will largely determine the culture of the whole operation, and it is far more difficult to pick up the pieces from a bad start than it is to continue to operate effectively and improve. This emphasizes the need for thorough planning and preparation and a high level of readiness to enable forces to respond quickly and decisively.

NOTES

1. Dag Hammarskjöld, UN Secretary-General from 1953 to 1961. Awarded the Nobel Prize for Peace in 1961.
2. See Chapter 4, p. 111.
3. A. B. Fetherston, *Towards a Theory of United Nations Peacekeeping* (London: Macmillan, 1994), p. 228.
4. General Sir Michael Rose, *Fighting for Peace: Lessons from Bosnia,* 2d ed. (London: Warner Books, 1999), p. 11. Rose was commander of the UN Protection Force in Bosnia 23 January 1994–23 January 1995.
5. Ibid., p. 4.
6. Franz Kernic, "The Soldier and the Task: Austria's Experience of Preparing Peacekeepers," *International Peacekeeping* 6, no. 3 (1999): 124.
7. As first argued in Boutros Boutros-Ghali, *An Agenda for Peace* (New York: UN Department of Public Information, 1992), and recommended again in *Report of the Panel on United Nations Peace Operations* (Brahimi report), UN General Assembly Security Council, A/55/305–5/2000/809, 21 August 2000, par. 117, p. 20.
8. Colonel (subsequently Brigadier) Gary Bornholt. An experienced and highly respected infantry commander with previous UN experience, Bornholt played an important role in assisting with UN military thinking and planning for East Timor.
9. The team was commanded by the author and included a senior logistics officer (Colonel Craig Boyd), an operations officer (Lieutenant Colonel Graeme Phillips), and an administrative officer (Captain Trent Scott). The latter three officers deployed to Dili as part of the PKF advance party in November 1999.
10. As a result of the implementation of the Brahimi report, DPKO initially received ninety-three staff and subsequently received an additional ninety-two (as of December 2001).
11. See Chapter 3, pp. 67–68, for further details on the inadequacies of the initial PKF headquarters.
12. Colonel Craig Boyd and Brigadier General Haing Keown Kwon.
13. *Directive for the Force Commander of the United Nations Transitional Administration in East Timor*, Department of Peacekeeping Operations, Military Planning Service, MPS/3636, 8 May 2000.
14. Brahimi report, pars. 65–75, pp. 12–13.
15. Ian Martin, *Self-Determination in East Timor: The United Nations, the Ballot, and International Intervention* (Boulder, CO: Lynne Rienner, 2001), p. 126, notes that obstacles to effective joint planning arose as a result of uncertainty about when the responsibility for a full-scale peacekeeping operation would pass from the DPA to the DPKO.
16. See Chapter 3, p. 71.

17. In smaller missions, administration is the responsibility of the chief administrative officer (CAO).

18. The Australian Blackhawk helicopter assistance to the PKF was withdrawn on 23 April 2000.

19. These same helicopters could have been used to quickly evacuate UN staff from Atambua in West Timor—following the murder of UNHCR international staff on 6 September 2000—but Australia's complex chain of command necessitated the use of less capable helicopters from New Zealand over a much longer distance, thus requiring more time to conduct the mission.

20. C4ISR refers to command, control, communications, computers, intelligence, surveillance, and reconnaissance.

21. The need for CIVPOL personnel to also meet UN-set standards is discussed in Chapter 4, pp. 107–108.

6

The Future

The UN can only become effective in its principal role of peacekeeping if there is a will in the international community to make it so. The UN represents the collective political will of all nations, and it is pointless blaming the UN as if it were some autonomous organisation. The UN represents all of us. Its peacekeepers belong to all of us.

—General Sir Michael Rose, 1998[1]

FUTURE CHALLENGES

Since the end of the Cold War, peace operations have become more numerous and more complex. Traditional peacekeeping—based on the principles of consent, impartiality, and the nonuse of lethal force—has given way to peace enforcement, stabilization, and humanitarian operations, usually in hostile and insecure environments and often without clear end-dates or exit strategies. The prospect of interstate conflict remains, but the reality of brutal intrastate and transnational violence has demanded action by the UN and international coalitions. At its zenith in the mid-1990s, the number of UN troops, military observers, and CIVPOL peaked at almost 80,000, with UN expenditure levels of about U.S.\$3.5 billion per year.[2] A quieter period followed, but by mid-2000 UN military numbers had again increased to around 37,000, with almost 12,000 civilian personnel and an annual expenditure of more than U.S.\$2 billion.[3] The UN can claim success of varying degree in Namibia, Cambodia, Haiti, Mozambique, Nicaragua, El Salvador, and Eastern Slavonia/Croatia, but these are eclipsed by UN failures in Somalia, Rwanda, and Bosnia. Regardless of these successes or failures, many of the same lessons were relearned by each of these missions with only incremental improvement to UN procedures, planning, and readiness. Secretary-General Boutros-Ghali's declared commitment to enhance the UN's capacity for peacekeeping (as reflected in his two Agendas for Peace,

in 1992 and 1993) were only partially implemented, and many of the recommendations from the Brahimi report of 2000 have been slow to take
root. The cause of this seemingly over-bureaucratic approach to implementing change, however, lies only in part with the Secretariat itself. More
important, it is ironic that in an increasingly violent world, where the UN's
presence is needed more than ever, the UN remains constrained from acting
as effectively as it should because of the continued intransigence of member states, including members of the P-5, to fully support its work.

The UN's intervention in East Timor proved its greatest challenge to
that date, and overall each of its three missions was successful. The specific
purpose of each of the mandates for each of these missions enables East
Timor to provide a useful case study for both traditional and complex
peacekeeping. Traditional peacekeeping principles were applicable in East
Timor for the UNAMET ballot, but following Indonesia's failure to ensure
security, these principles did not apply to INTERFET or UNTAET.
Operating under Chapter VII mandates, these two missions were required
to restore and maintain security, while UNTAET was further mandated to
begin the arduous task of reconstructing and preparing the country for independence. The UNTAET mission was truly multidimensional and was
forced to operate well beyond the bounds foreseen in the original UN
Charter. UNTAET's responsibilities extended even beyond those of the UN
in Namibia, Cambodia, Eastern Slavonia, and Haiti. In these cases, the UN
had limited transitional responsibilities, but in East Timor UNTAET was
mandated to perform the full tasks of an interim government, to shepherd a
nation to independence from ground zero, and to provide the conditions for
sustainability beyond independence.

Two particular challenges emerge from the UN's intervention in East
Timor. The first relates to the future prospects for East Timor's survival as
a viable nation-state. The second concerns the future prospects for peacekeeping itself. This study on the UN's intervention in East Timor does not
provide categorical answers to either of these challenges, but it helps identify many of the key factors that need to be considered to enhance the
prospects for both.

EAST TIMOR'S SURVIVAL

The future of East Timor is uncertain and unpredictable. Since the early
1940s, the East Timorese people have suffered considerable oppression.
Their journey to freedom has been long, arduous, and painful, marked by
massive loss of life, by a measure of internal dissent and disagreement, and
by their opposition to foreign (non-Portuguese) intervention. They are a
small population located in a harsh but remote and beautiful part of the

world. The country is one of the poorest on earth and the people among the most illiterate. It is a heterogeneous population in language and culture, unemployment is high, and major reforms in agriculture and fishery are long overdue. The country boasts no major industries that promise economic salvation, including the expected revenues from oil and gas in the Timor Sea. The infrastructure is poorly developed, and its human resources have limited experience and little depth in governance, public administration, commerce, and business. Strategically, East Timor shares a long and porous land and maritime border with Indonesia. A large number of East Timorese refugees are still to be relocated from neighboring West Timor, from where anti-independence militias continue to operate. Security from external aggression depends largely on the future stability of Indonesia, which itself remains unpredictable. Internal security problems could easily arise in the early years of independence, stemming from political differences and local or transnational criminal activity. In summary, the difficulties facing the new country are considerable and should not be ignored.

Yet, despite these many hurdles, the prospects for East Timor's survival seem no worse than for some other small states. Indeed, they appear much better. The new country boasts a committed team of leaders who, although lacking the experience of office, have devoted most of their lives to the survival of their country. These leaders are politically astute and mature. They understand the challenges confronting the newly independent country and are aware of their responsibilities in ensuring its sustainable development. They remain fully committed to honoring the legacy of those who have died in the struggle for freedom. Lawlessness and internal security problems, feared and even prophesied by some international observers, have yet to transpire. Overall, the East Timorese people have heeded the advice of their bishops and priests and their political leaders, who have all advocated peace and forgiveness. East Timor's inner strength comes from the resolution of its people, but, together with continued international support, the territory's survival also rests on its domestic political stability following independence. Provided the international community continues to support East Timor, the prospects for economic and social development appear reasonably good, as does deterrence against external aggression. East Timor's current low level of development notwithstanding, its small population presents opportunities denied to many overpopulated Third World states: relatively little improvement is required to break the poverty cycle and to establish a more viable economy. Thus, the UN and the Bretton Woods institutions will need to continue to assist East Timor. Politically, the United States and the European Union should maintain their moral and economic support and insist that democratic governance and human rights be upheld. Good relations will also need to be maintained with Indonesia and Australia and closer contact established with the

ASEAN, Asian, and South Pacific countries. Portugal and the other Lusophone countries also have an important role to play in helping East Timor maintain its history and language and in providing the new state with wider contacts throughout the world community.

Current and future generations of East Timorese leaders can be inspired by examining the recent history of the Singaporean people. Notwithstanding the latent economic potential of Singapore's having been a major entrepôt for 100 years, this was "a small country with no natural resources . . . cut off from its natural hinterland and [which] had to survive in a tough world of nationalistic new states in Southeast Asia."[4] They can see how a tiny new state, with more people but fewer resources than East Timor, could transform itself in less than forty years into a vibrant society and economic powerhouse through sheer hard work and determination. In comparison, the East Timorese can reflect on the abundance of their own untapped natural resources and the less perilous strategic situation in which they find themselves. They might also, like the Singaporeans for whom former Prime Minister Lee Kuan Yew wrote his memoirs, heed the lessons behind the stated purpose of his book: "Our people should understand how vulnerable Singapore was and is, the dangers that beset us, and how we nearly did not make it. Most of all, I hope that they will know that honest and effective government, public order and personal security, economic and social progress did not come about as the natural course of events."[5] East Timor and its people have earned their freedom, but they must now earn their place among the community of nations. The longevity of this independence is not guaranteed and must not be taken for granted. At a time when the East Timorese deserve a rest from their long struggle, they must now work harder than ever to preserve their freedom and statehood. This second journey, as with the first, will not be easy—but as with the first, it is also achievable.

Equally vital are the responsibilities of the UN to continue to assist East Timor. In his report to the Security Council in October 2001, Secretary-General Kofi Annan highlighted the continuing support required of the UN's follow-on mission to ensure acceptable standards of governance, security, and social and economic development. The report advised that funding from the assessed budget would provide for a reduced force of some 5,000 troops,[6] and 1,250 police by independence. It was not foreseen that East Timor would be in a position to take full responsibility for maintaining security against external and internal threats until mid-2004 at the latest.[7] Importantly, while noting the efforts of the Indonesian authorities to improve security in West Timor, the report "assessed that a core of hardline militia in West Timor will continue to pose a potential threat to East Timor after independence."[8] Additionally, the report "identified 100 core functions for which local expertise does not exist, but which are essential to the stability and functioning of government" in the civil administration.[9] Key areas included the management of public finances and the justice system. This comprehensive study also assessed that the premature withdrawal of international assistance from the former would risk the "mismanagement of public finances [and] threaten the overall functioning of the administration, as well as donor confidence in East Timor."[10] Likewise, given the nascent state of the justice system, "any precipitous withdrawal of this support would be prejudicial to security as it would be likely to seriously undermine the judicial process and the rule of law, with adverse consequences for refugee return and reconciliation."[11] From voluntary contributions, and additional to the significant support provided through the East Timor Trust Fund, the report identified an additional 135 functions "as being crucial to the effectiveness of the new State."[12] While noting improvements in social and economic development under UNTAET, it assessed that rural recovery had been slower than in urban areas and would be a major ongoing concern. Significant difficulties existed with infrastructure development—particularly with deteriorating road conditions and with inadequate air services—and the report contended that funding of these critical areas would be beyond the capacity of the East Timor government for some years. In summing up the responsibilities of the East Timorese and the international community, the Secretary-General's comments are equally relevant for future missions of this nature:

> The essential requirement in the case of East Timor is to ensure that the enormous sacrifices of the East Timorese, the substantial investments of the international community, and the cooperation of the parties required to bring about a successful transition to independence are not squandered for lack of international attention and support for the new State. At the same time, it is important to move towards a normal development assistance framework as quickly as is responsibly possible.[13]

If this advice is followed, then the future prospects for East Timor are encouraging.

THE FUTURE OF PEACEKEEPING

The short history of the UN does not engender optimism in its ability to resolve many of the world's future security problems and thereby further the cause of global peace. Born in the shadow of World War II and constructed to operate within the confines of the Cold War, the organization has been forced beyond the original intentions of its founders. Traditional peacekeeping has given way to complex peace operations characterized more by prevention, intervention, and reconstruction than by merely monitoring or upholding a peace agreement, although the two original requirements still remain. With the increased demands on its overstretched capabilities since the end of the Cold War, the main effort of the UN in the field has changed, but many of its procedures and processes have struggled to adapt proactively to meet the new challenges. In part, this is because the UN remains hamstrung by its own procedures; but more culpable are the member states that have been reluctant to let the organization move too quickly.

The success of the UN's intervention in East Timor does not necessarily herald a new era in UN operations. Most of the lessons discussed in this case study were lessons relearned from previous missions—lessons on which firm action had not been taken, despite the considerable commentary and weight of evidence that to be more effective the organization must be reformed. While all involved in the UN's intervention in East Timor can be rightly proud of the outcome, success was never preordained and was often a "close run thing." A number of factors at work in East Timor combined to provide the conditions for success that supported the UN's ability to conduct complex peace operations rather than cause it to be overtaxed. Any assessment of the UN's success must consider the value to the outcome provided by the relatively benign security situation on the ground, the continued commitment of the international community, Indonesia's compliance, and the overwhelming support of the East Timorese people.

On a realistic note, an examination of the Peacekeeping Baker's Dozen for the UN's intervention in East Timor reveals that much more needs to be done before the UN can intervene with confidence of success in future trouble spots. Better mechanisms are required to plan and integrate missions and to adequately fund and resource them. Moreover, the need for more comprehensive training for all civilian and military components stands out as a necessary beacon to improve the UN's credibility and effectiveness. This cannot be achieved without the full support of member states, which must agree to standards and benchmarks set by the Secretariat and then ensure that these are met. This highlights the need for the further development of more integrated regional peacekeeping training centers, along the Nordic and Canadian models.

A significant lesson for military forces, demonstrated yet again in East Timor, is that professional warfighting skills provide the foundations necessary for effective peace enforcement operations, but that these need to be supplemented by peacekeeping constabulary skills and CMA. The burden in preparing national defense forces for complex peace operations is therefore greater than ever. Not only must professional military forces be able to conduct combat operations, but they must also perform as an integral part of the mission and in a manner that will give confidence to the people they protect and not contravene local customs and traditions. Coalition forces of such caliber have proved difficult for the UN to assemble at short notice, and the reliance on MNFs for rapid stabilization operations is likely to continue. Notwithstanding the UN's likely dependency on "coalitions of the willing," more work is required by the Secretariat and member states to improve the standby arrangements for peacekeeping forces and to assemble and train force headquarters personnel quickly prior to the commencement of operations. The earliest possible appointment of a capable force commander and his or her active participation in integrated mission planning is one of the keys to success.

CONCLUSION

The UN's requirements for modern peacekeeping have been clearly articulated in the Brahimi report, which followed the start-up of UN operations in East Timor. The experiences and lessons from the UN's intervention in East Timor add further weight to the findings of this report. The consequences of not implementing the necessary reforms recommended will be severe: more failed states, increased insecurity, higher numbers of refugees and displaced people, increased levels of poverty, and more dead peacekeepers. Indeed, the UN's inability to intervene successfully in future trouble spots will jeopardize the viability of the system of states that the UN was created to defend and on which it depends for its support and effectiveness. As the Brahimi report noted, and as evidenced by the UN's intervention in East Timor, "Without renewed commitment on the part of Member States, significant institutional change and increased financial support, the United Nations will not be capable of executing the critical peacekeeping and peacebuilding tasks that the Member States assign to it in coming months and years."[14]

The UN's intervention in East Timor provides an example of the positive contribution that can be made to peace and security, to the establishment and survival of a new state, and to the alleviation of poverty. The question raised from this study, therefore, is not so much whether UN intervention was successful in East Timor, but rather how much more successful it might have been had many of the lessons from previous missions been acted upon fully. And more the pity if the UN and member states do not address the lessons from East Timor and implement more purposely the recommendations of the Brahimi report. In closing its deliberations on the future of the UN, the Brahimi panel provided a vision that few would contest. Presciently they noted:

> We have also come to a shared vision of a *United* Nations, extending a strong helping hand to a community, country or region to avert conflict or

to end violence. We see an SRSG ending a mission well accomplished, having given the people of a country the opportunity to do for themselves what they could not do before: to build and hold onto peace, to find reconciliation, to strengthen democracy, to secure human rights. We see, above all, a United Nations that has not only the will but also the ability to fulfil its great promise, and to justify the confidence and trust placed in it by the overwhelming majority of humankind.[15]

It remains to be seen if the member states truly share this vision and are prepared to ensure its realization.

NOTES

1. General Sir Michael Rose, *Fighting for Peace: Lessons from Bosnia,* 2d ed. (London: Warner Books, 1999), p. 14.

2. Michael Renner, "UN Peacekeeping: An Uncertain Future," *In Focus* 5, no. 28 (September 2000). Reproduced in K. C. Eyre and Kiril Sharapov, eds., *Pro Pace Paratus: An Anthology of Readings in Modern Peacekeeping* (Cornwallis Park, Nova Scotia: Pearson Peacekeeping Centre, May 2001), p. 345.

3. Ibid.

4. Lee Kuan Yew, *The Singapore Story* (Singapore: Times Editions, 1998), p. 8.

5. Ibid.

6. Including 120 military observers.

7. Kofi Annan, *Report of the Secretary-General on the United Nations Transitional Administration in East Timor,* S/2001/983, 18 October, 2001, pars. 56, 65, pp. 8, 9.

8. Ibid., par. 29, p. 4.

9. Ibid., par. 76, p. 10. These positions were primarily in the areas of public finance and banking, justice, human rights, infrastructure, and administrative services.

10. Ibid., par. 16, p. 3.

11. Ibid., pars. 20, 22, p. 3.

12. Ibid., par. 80, p. 11.

13. Kofi Annan, *Report of the Secretary-General "No Exit Without Strategy: Security Council Decision-Making and the Closure or Transition of United Nations Peacekeeping Operations,"* S/2001/394, 20 April 2001, par. 43, p. 8.

14. *Report of the Panel on United Nations Peace Operations* (Brahimi report), UN General Assembly Security Council, A/55/305–S/2000/809, 21 August 2000, p. viii.

15. Brahimi report, p. xv. Emphasis in original.

Annex A
Pro-Integration Militias and Paramilitary Groups

ABLAI: Struggle for Integration, based in Same and led by Nazario Cortereal.

AHI: Fire, based in Aileu.

AITARAK: Thorn, based in Dili and led by Eurico Guterres.

BESIH MERAH PUTIH: Red and White Iron, based in Liquiça and led by Manuel de Sousa.

DADURUS MERAH PUTIH: Red and White Tornado, based in Maliana (Bobonaro), leader unknown.

DARAH MERAH: Red Blood, based in Ermera and led by Lafahek Saburai.

HALI LINTAR: Thunder, based in Maliana and led by João Tavares.

HAMETIN: Bobonaro, leader unknown.

JATI MERAH PUTIH: Real Red and White, based in Los Palos, leader unknown.

LAKSAUR: Flying Eagle, based in Suai and led by Olivio "Moruk" Mendonça.

MAHADOMI: based in Manatuto and led by Vital Doutel Sarmento and Aquino Caldas.

MAHIDI: Live or Die for Integration, based in Ainaro, Cassa, and Sumalai and led by Cançio Lopes de Carvalho.

NARA MERAH: Red Dragon, based in Emera and led by Miguel Soares Babo.

PANA: based in Liquiça, leader unknown.

RAJAWALI: leader unknown.

SAKUNAR: based in Oecussi and led by Simão Lopes.

SERA: Sera Malik, leader unknown.

TEAM 59/75 JUNIOR: named after the unsuccessful rebellion against the Portuguese administration in 1959, based in Viqueque.

PARAMILITARY GROUPS

TEAMS ALPHA, SERA, and SAKA: based in Baucau and Los Palos, formed by Kopassus to serve as auxiliary groups with the TNI against Falintil; fully armed and trained by the TNI.

Sources: James J. Fox and Dionisio Babo Soares, eds., *Out of the Ashes* (Adelaide: Crawford House, 2000), pp. 67–68; John Martinkus, *A Dirty Little War* (Sydney: Random House, 2001), pp. xviii–xix.

Annex B

UN Security Council
Resolution 1272

The Security Council,

Recalling its previous resolutions and the statements of its President on the situation in East Timor, in particular resolutions 384(1975) of 22 December 1975, 389(1976) of 22 April 1976, 1236(1999) of 7 May 1999, 1246(1999) of 11 June 1999, 1262(1999) of 27 August 1999 and 1264(1999) of 15 September 1999,

Recalling also the Agreement between Indonesia and Portugal on the question of East Timor of 5 May 1999 and the Agreements between the United Nations and the Governments of Indonesia and Portugal of the same date regarding the modalities for the popular consultation of the East Timorese through a direct ballot and security arrangements (S/1999/513, annexes I to III),

Reiterating its welcome for the successful conduct of the popular consultation of the East Timorese people of 30 August 1999, and *taking note* of its outcome through which the East Timorese people expressed their clear wish to begin a process of transition under the authority of the United Nations towards independence, which it regards as an accurate reflection of the views of the East Timorese people,

Welcoming the decision of the Indonesian People's Consultative Assembly on 19 October 1999 concerning East Timor,

Stressing the importance of reconciliation among the East Timorese people,

Commending the United Nation in East Timor (UNAMET) for the admirable courage and determination shown in the implementation of its mandate,

Welcoming the deployment of a multinational force to East Timor pursuant to resolution 1264(1999), and *recognizing* the importance of continued cooperation between the Government of Indonesia and the multinational force in this regard,

Noting the report of the Secretary-General of 4 October 1999 (A/1999/1024),

Noting with satisfaction the successful outcome of the trilateral meeting held on 28 September 1999, as outlined in the report of the Secretary-General,

Deeply concerned by the grave humanitarian situation resulting from violence in East Timor and the large-scale displacement and relocation of East Timorese civilians, including large numbers of women and children,

Reaffirming the need for all parties to ensure that the rights of refugees and displaced persons are protected, and that they are able to return voluntarily in safety and security to their homes,

Reaffirming respect for the sovereignty and territorial integrity of Indonesia,

Noting the importance of ensuring the security of the boundaries of East Timor, and the importance of ensuring the security of the boundaries of East Timor, and *noting* in this regard the expressed intention of the Indonesian authorities to cooperate with the multinational force deployed pursuant to resolution 1264(1999) and with the United Nations Transitional Administration in East Timor,

Expressing its concern at reports indicating that systematic, widespread and flagrant violations of international humanitarian and human rights law have been committed in East Timor, *stressing* that persons committing such violations bear individual responsibility, and *calling* on all parties to cooperate with investigations into these reports,

Recalling the relevant principles contained in the Convention on the Safety of United Nations and Associated Personnel adopted on 9 December 1994,

Determining that the continuing situation in East Timor constitutes a threat to peace and security,

Acting under Chapter VII of the Charter of the United Nations,

1. *Decides* to establish, in accordance with the report of the Secretary-General, a United Nations Transitional Administration in East Timor (UNTAET), which will be endowed with overall responsibility for the administration of East Timor and will be empowered to exercise all legislative and executive authority, including the administration of justice:

2. *Decides also* that the mandate of UNTAET shall consist of the following elements:

    (a) To provide security and maintain law and order throughout the territory of East Timor;

    (b) To establish an effective administration;

    (c) To assist in the development of civil and social services;

    (d) To ensure the coordination and delivery of humanitarian assistance, rehabilitation and development assistance;

    (e) To support capacity-building for self-government;

    (f) To assist in the establishment of conditions for sustainable development;

3. *Decides further* that UNTAET will have objectives and a structure along the lines set out in part IV of the report of the Secretary-General, and in particular that its main components will be:

    (a) A governance and public administration component, including an international police element with a strength of up to 1,640 officers;

    (b) A humanitarian assistance and emergency rehabilitation component;

    (c) A military component, with a strength of up to 8,950 troops and up to 200 military observers;

4. *Authorizes* UNTAET to take all necessary measures to fulfil its mandate;

5. *Recognizes* that, in developing and performing its functions under its mandate, UNTAET will need to draw on the expertise and capacity of Member States, United Nations agencies and other international organizations, including the international financial institutions;

6. *Welcomes* the intention of the Secretary-General to appoint a

Special Representative who, as the Transitional Administrator, will be responsible for all aspects of the United Nations work in East Timor and will have the power to enact new laws and regulations and to amend, suspend or repeal existing ones;

7. *Stresses* the importance of cooperation between Indonesia, Portugal and UNTAET in the implementation of this resolution;

8. *Stresses* the need for UNTAET to consult and cooperate closely with the East Timorese people in order to carry out its mandate effectively with a view to the development of local democratic institutions, including an independent East Timorese human rights institution, and the transfer to these institutions of its administrative and public service functions;

9. *Requests* UNTAET and the multinational force deployed pursuant to resolution 1264(1999) to cooperate closely with each other, with a view also to the replacement as soon as possible of the multinational force by the military component of UNTAET, as notified by the Secretary-General having consulted the leadership of the multinational force, taking into account conditions on the ground;

10. *Reiterates* the urgent need for coordinated humanitarian and reconstruction assistance, and *calls upon* all parties to cooperate with humanitarian and human rights organizations so as to ensure their safety, the protection of civilians, in particular children, the safe return of refugees and displaced persons and the effective delivery of humanitarian aid;

11. *Welcomes* the commitment of the Indonesian authorities to allow the refugees and displaced persons in West Timor and elsewhere in Indonesia to choose whether to return to East Timor, remain where they are or be resettled in other parts of Indonesia, and *stresses* the importance of allowing full, safe and unimpeded access by humanitarian organizations in carrying out their work;

12. *Stresses* that it is the responsibility of the Indonesian authorities to take immediate and effective measures to ensure the safe return of refugees in West Timor and other parts of Indonesia to East Timor, the security of refugees, and the civilian and humanitarian character of refugee camps and settlements, in particular by curbing the violent and intimidatory activities of the militias there;

13. *Welcomes* the intention of the Secretary to establish a Trust Fund available for, *inter alia,* the rehabilitation of essential infrastructure, including the building of basic institutions, the functioning of public services and utilities, and the salaries of local civil servants;

14. *Encourages* Member States and international agencies and organizations to provide personnel, equipment and other resources to UNTAET as requested by the Secretary-General, including for the building of basic institutions and capacity, and *stresses* the need for the closest possible coordination of these efforts;

15. *Underlines* the importance of including in UNTAET personnel with appropriate training in international humanitarian, human rights and refugee law, including child and gender-related provisions, negotiation and communication skills, cultural awareness and civilian–military coordination;

16. *Condemns* all violence and acts in support of violence in East Timor, *calls* for their immediate end, and *demands* that those responsible for such violence be brought to justice;

17. *Decides* to establish UNTAET for an initial period until 31 January 2001;

18. *Requests* the Secretary-General to keep the Council closely and regularly informed of progress towards the implementation of this resolution, including, in particular, with regard to the deployment of UNTAET and possible future reductions of its military component if the situation in East Timor improves, and to submit a report within three months of the date of adoption of this resolution and every six months thereafter;

19. *Decides* to remain actively seized of the matter.

*   *   *

UN SECURITY COUNCIL REPORT OF THE SECRETARY-GENERAL ON THE SITUATION IN EAST TIMOR, 4 OCTOBER 1999

IV. Proposed United Nations Transitional Administration

29. To implement this mandate UNTAET will have the following objectives:

i. Assist and protect East Timorese displaced or otherwise affected by the conflict;

ii. Facilitate emergency rehabilitation and reconstruction of services and infrastructure;

iii. Administer the territory of East Timor and create the basis for good governance;

iv. Develop mechanisms for dialogue at the national and local levels;

v. Assist the East Timorese in the development of a constitution;

vi. Organize and conduct elections, and build the institutional capacity for electoral processes;

vii. Undertake confidence-building measures and provide support to indigenous processes of reconciliation;

viii. Create non-discriminatory and impartial institutions, particularly those of judiciary and police, to ensure the establishment and maintenance of the rule of law and to promote and protect human rights;

ix. Promote economic and social recovery and development, including in the fields of education and health;

x. Coordinate assistance to East Timor;

xi. Develop administrative institutions that are accountable, transparent and efficient;

xii. Facilitate the strengthening and development of civil society, including the media;

xiii. Ensure that the development of any indigenous structures for security conform to the standards of civilian oversight, democratic accountability, and international human rights norms and standards;

xiv. Create conditions of stability through the maintenance of peace and security, including through programmes for disarmament, demobilization and reintegration, as may be necessary.

Annex C

Summary of PKF/UNMOG Force Contributions (as of December 2000)

TOTAL personnel 7,893: 7,771 PKF and 122 UNMOG

AUSTRALIA
1,595 personnel (from February 2000)
UNMOG: 15 officers
Headquarters PKF: deputy force commander, 32 staff
National Command Headquarters: 51 staff
Sector West: commander and 1,102 personnel, including Headquarters Sector West, 1 battalion group, 4 Blackhawk utility helicopters, 2 light observation helicopters
Maritime: 4 landing craft (2 heavy, 2 medium)
Force Logistics Squadron (Dili): 195 personnel
UN Military Hospital (Dili): 60 personnel
Aviation and Airfield Group (Dili): 138 personnel

BANGLADESH
551 personnel (March 2000–March 2002)
UNMOG: 7 officers, including chief military observer until July 2000
Headquarters PKF: 15 staff
Engineer Battalion (Dili and Oecussi): 529 personnel

BOLIVIA
2 personnel (from February 2000)
UNMOG: 2 officers

BRAZIL
84 personnel (from March 2000)
UNMOG: 13 officers, including chief military observer from July 2001
Headquarters PKF: 1 staff officer
Sector West: 20 military police
Sector Central: 50 military police

CANADA
3 personnel (March 2000–February 2001)
Headquarters PKF: 3 staff officers

CHILE
33 personnel (from May 2000)
Headquarters PKF: 1 staff officer
Aviation and Airfield Group (Dili): 32 personnel, 2 Puma utility helicopters, 1 light observation helicopter

DENMARK
4 personnel (from February 2000)
UNMOG: 2 officers
Headquarters PKF: 2 staff officers

EGYPT
75 personnel (from February 2000)
UNMOG: 2 officers
Headquarters PKF: 2 staff officers
UN Military Hospital (Dili): 71 personnel

FIJI
191 personnel (from February 2000)
Headquarters PKF: 3 staff
National Command Element: 5 staff
Sector West: 183 personnel (1 infantry company as part of New Zealand [composite] battalion)

FRANCE
3 personnel (February–December 2000)
Headquarters PKF: 3 staff officers

IRELAND
44 personnel (from February 2000)
UNMOG: 2 officers
Headquarters PKF: 3 staff
Sector West: 39 personnel (1 infantry platoon as part of New Zealand [composite] battalion)

JORDAN
723 personnel (February 2000–January 2002)
UNMOG: 4 officers
Headquarters PKF: 11 staff
National Command Headquarters: 4 staff
Sector Oecussi: 704 personnel (Headquarters Sector Oecussi and 1 infantry battalion group)

KENYA
250 personnel (February 2000–November 2001)
Headquarters PKF: 12 staff
National Command Headquarters: 6 staff
Sector Central: 232 personnel (1 infantry company and 1 engineer platoon)

KOREA, REPUBLIC OF
444 personnel (from February 2000)
Headquarters PKF: 12 staff
National Command Headquarters: 3 staff officers
Sector East: 429 personnel (1 infantry battalion group)

MALAYSIA
33 personnel (from June 2000)
UNMOG: 13 officers
Sector Oecussi: 20 military language assistants (to the Jordanian battalion)

MOZAMBIQUE
12 personnel (from July 2000)
UNMOG: 2 officers
Sector Central: 10 military police

NEPAL

162 personnel (from April 2000)

UNMOG: 3 officers

Headquarters PKF: 4 staff

National Command Headquarters: 3 staff

Sector West: 152 personnel (1 infantry company as part of New Zealand [composite] battalion)

NEW ZEALAND

697 personnel (from February 2000)

UNMOG: 9 officers, including chief military observer, July 2000–July 2001

Headquarters PKF: 7 staff

National Command Headquarters: 9 staff

Sector West: 672 personnel (1 battalion group and 4 Iriquois utility helicopters)

NORWAY

6 personnel (from February 2000)

Headquarters PKF: 6 staff officers

PAKISTAN

788 personnel (April 2000–April 2002)

UNMOG: 15 officers

Headquarters PKF: 15 staff

Force Communications Unit: 142 staff

Sector East: 23 communications personnel

Sector West: 72 communications personnel

Sector Oecussi: 9 communications personnel

Engineer Battalion (Sector West): 512 personnel

PERU

23 personnel (from July 2000)

Aviation and Airfield Group (Dili): 23 personnel and 1 MI 26 heavy lift helicopter

PHILIPPINES

645 personnel (from February 2000; battalion departed December 2001)

UNMOG: 8 officers
Headquarters PKF: 7 staff
National Command Headquarters: 6 staff
Force Headquarters Support Unit (Dili): 90 personnel
Sector East: 534 personnel (one infantry battalion group)

PORTUGAL
769 personnel (from February 2000)
Headquarters PKF: 9 staff
Sector Central: Commander and 730 personnel (Headquarters Sector
    Central and 1 infantry battalion group)
Aviation and Airfield Group (Dili): 29 personnel and 3 light observation
    helicopters

RUSSIA
2 personnel (from February 2000)
UNMOG: 2 officers

SINGAPORE
24 personnel (from February 2000)
Headquarters PKF: 3 staff
UN Military Hospital (Dili): 21 personnel
Note: In mid-2001, Singapore also provided an infantry platoon of 50 per-
    sonnel as part of the New Zealand (composite) battalion.

SWEDEN
2 personnel (from February 2000)
UNMOG: 2 officers

THAILAND
714 personnel (from February 2000)
UNMOG: 7 officers
Headquarters PKF: force commander, 16 staff
National Command Headquarters: 3 staff
Sector East: commander and 687 personnel (Headquarters Sector East and
    1 infantry battalion group)

TURKEY
2 personnel (from February 2000)
UNMOG: 2 officers

UNITED KINGDOM
4 personnel (from February 2000)
UNMOG: 4 officers

UNITED STATES
3 personnel (from February 2000)
UNMOG: 3 officers

URUGUAY
5 personnel (from February 2000)
UNMOG: 5 officers

Annex D PKF Organization (as of December 2000)

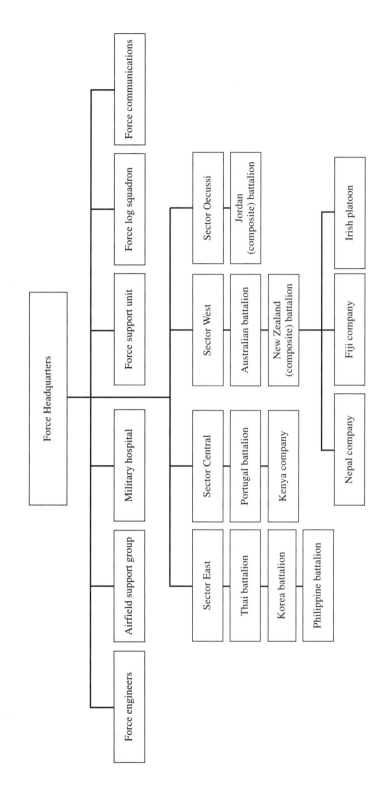

Annex E   PKF Force Headquarters (as of December 2000)

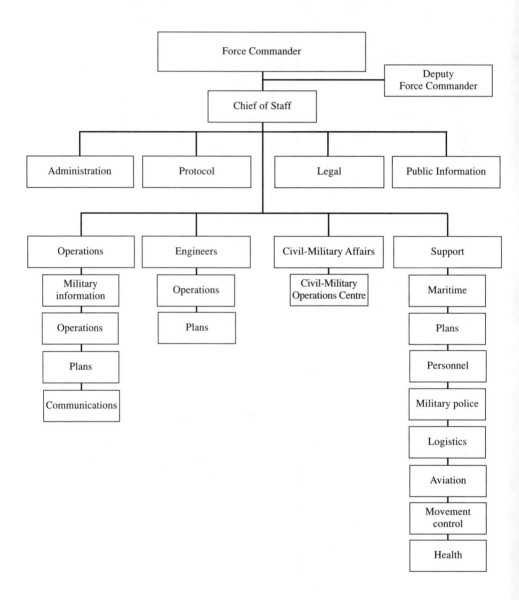

Acronyms and Abbreviations

Apodeti	Timorese Popular Democratic Association (Associação Popular Democrática Timorense)
CIVPOL	civilian police (UN)
CIMIC	civil-military cooperation
CMA	civil-military affairs
CMOC	Civil-Military Operations Centre
CNRT	National Council of Timorese Resistance (Conselno Nacional de Resistência Timorense)
CNS	Council for National Security
DOA	director of administration
DOC	District Operations Centre
DPA	Department of Political Affairs (UN Secretariat)
DPKO	Department of Peacekeeping Operations (UN Secretariat)
DSRSG	Deputy Special Representative to the Secretary-General
ETDF	East Timor Defence Force
ETPS	East Timor Police Service
ETTA	East Timor Transitional Administration
FALD	Field Administration and Logistics Division, DPKO
Falintil	Armed Forces for the National Liberation of East Timor (Forças Armadas de Libertação Nacional de Timor-Leste)
Fretilin	Revolutionary Front for an Independent East Timor (Frente Revolucionária de Timor Leste Independente)
GPA	Governance and Public Administration, UNTAET
HAER	Humanitarian Assistance and Emergency Rehabilitation, UNTAET
IDP	internally displaced person
IMTF	Integrated Mission Task Force
INTERFET	International Force in East Timor
IO	information operations

IOM	International Organization for Migration
JAM	Joint Assessment Mission
JLOC	Joint Logistics Operations Centre
JOC	Joint Operations Centre
MLO	military liaison officer
MNF	multinational force
MOU	memorandum of understanding
MPR	People's Consultative Assembly (Majelis Permusyawaratan Rakyat) (Republic of Indonesia)
NATO	North Atlantic Treaty Organization
NC	National Council
NCC	National Consultative Council
NGO	nongovernmental organization
NOC	National Operations Centre
NSA	national security adviser
OCHA	Office for the Coordination of Humanitarian Affairs (UN)
OCPI	Office of Communications and Public Information (UN)
ODFD	Office of Defence Force Development
OHCHR	Office of the High Commissioner for Human Rights (UN)
PKF	peacekeeping force (UN)
POLRI	Indonesian police force (Polisi Republik Indonesia)
PRSG	Personal Representative of the Secretary-General
ROE	rules of engagement
SOP	standard operating procedures
SRSG	Special Representative of the Secretary-General
TCL	tactical coordination line
TFET	Trust Fund for East Timor
TNI	Indonesian National Military (Tentara Nasional Indonesia)
UDT	Timorese Democratic Union (União Democrática Timorense)
UNAMET	United Nations Mission in East Timor
UNDP	United Nations Development Programme
UNHCR	United Nations High Commissioner for Refugees
UNHOC	United Nations Humanitarian Operations Centre
UNMIH	United Nations Mission in Haiti
UNMO	United Nations military observer
UNMOG	United Nations Military Observer Group
UNOSOM	United Nations Operation in Somalia
UNSCR	United Nations Security Council Resolution
UNTAC	United Nations Transitional Authority in Cambodia
UNTAET	United Nations Transitional Administration in East Timor
UNTAG	United Nations Transitional Assistance Group in Namibia
USG	Under Secretary-General
USGET	United States (Military) Support Group East Timor
WFP	World Food Programme

Chronology

1975–1998
August 1975	Civil war breaks out in East Timor. Falintil formed.
December 1975	Indonesian troops land in East Timor 7 December. UN General Assembly (12 December) and Security Council (22 December) adopt Resolution 384(1975) reaffirming East Timor's right to self-determination and urging Indonesia to withdraw its troops.
22 April 1976	Security Council adopts Resolution 389(1976) calling again for Indonesian forces to be withdrawn from East Timor.
15 July 1976	East Timor integrated into Indonesia by the People's Representative Council (DPR). President Suharto declares the territory Indonesia's twenty-seventh province on 17 July. Integration decree passed by the People's Consultative Assembly (MPR) in 1978.
1 December 1976	UN begins its yearly reaffirmation on the right of East Timorese people to self-determination.
1982	General Assembly resolution requesting Secretary-General to hold discussions with governments of Indonesia and Portugal. Secretary-General begins informal discussions with these countries directed toward achieving a solution to the problem.
1983	First Tripartite Talks held between Indonesia and Portugal under the auspices of the UN Secretary-General.
20 August 1987	Falintil restructured into a national army.
12 November 1991	150–270 East Timorese killed by Indonesian troops at Santa Cruz Cemetery in Dili.

1975–1998

1992	Xanana Gusmão captured in Dili and imprisoned in Cipinang Prison, Jakarta.
March 1993	UN Human Rights Commission censures Indonesia's poor human rights record in East Timor.
1996	José Ramos-Horta and Bishop Carlos Belo awarded Nobel Peace Prize.
1997	Kofi Annan becomes UN Secretary-General (January) and appoints Jamsheed Marker as his Personal Representative (PRSG) for East Timor (February).
23–27 April 1998	National Council of Timorese Resistance (CNRT) is formed at a meeting of resistance representatives held in Portugal. Xanana Gusmão appointed president of CNRT in absentia.
21 May 1998	President Suharto resigns and B. J. Habibie assumes presidency.
9 June 1998	President Habibie makes first public mention that Indonesia is considering possible autonomy proposal for East Timor.
18 June 1998	Indonesia's foreign minister, Ali Alatas, presents broad outline of proposal to Secretary-General.
16–23 July 1998	PRSG Marker visits Jakarta and East Timor for high-level discussions.
4–5 August 1998	High-level talks held in New York between Secretary-General and Indonesian and Portuguese foreign ministers.
5 August 1998	Portugal and Indonesia issue a joint communiqué agreeing to negotiate "special status" for East Timor within the Tripartite Talks framework.
October 1998	UN submits blueprint for self-administration of East Timor to the 6–8 October Tripartite Talks.
19 November 1998	Further round of Tripartite Talks.

1999

January	Clashes intensify between pro-integration and pro-independence elements in East Timor.
27 January	President Habibie decides to offer East Timorese a choice on their future: integration as a special autonomous region, or independence.
7–8 February	Near-final text of autonomy proposal agreed upon at ministerial Tripartite Talks in New York.
11 February	Xanana Gusmão transferred from prison to residential detention in Jakarta.

1999

11 March	Agreement reached at UN Headquarters on use of a direct ballot to consult the East Timorese on the autonomy proposal.
6, 17 April	Killings in Liquiça and Dili.
21–23 April	Agreement reached at UN Headquarters on terms of the autonomy package and "Popular Consultation," pending approval by Lisbon and Jakarta.
27 April	President Habibie gives public commitment to acceptance of the tripartite agreement and to creating stable conditions for the consultation.
4–15 May	UNAMET assessment team deployed to East Timor.
5 May	Secretary-General's report on the question of East Timor (S/1999/513). Signing of the tripartite "5 May Agreements." Indonesia put on notice with the UN Secretary-General's memorandum on security.
7 May	Security Council adopts Resolution 1236(1999) welcoming 5 May Agreements and stressing Indonesia's responsibility to ensure security in East Timor for the ballot.
24 May	Secretary-General's report on question of East Timor (S/1999/595).
1 June	Special Representative of the Secretary-General (SRSG), Ian Martin, arrives in Dili to head UNAMET.
11 June	Security Council adopts Resolution 1246(1999) authorizing the establishment of UNAMET and endorsing its mandate.
22 June	Secretary-General's report on question of East Timor (S/1999/705).
23 June	Secretary-General announces a delay in the ballot of two weeks due to the security situation.
29 June	Militia attacks on UNAMET facilities begin at Maliana. Subsequent attacks occur at Viqueque and Liquiça.
16 July–6 August	451,792 voters register throughout East Timor.
20 July	Secretary-General's report on question of East Timor (S/1999/803).
28 July	Secretary-General delays date of ballot to 30 August.
3 August	Security Council adopts Resolution 1257(1999) extending mandate of UNAMET.

1999

9 August	Secretary-General's report on question of East Timor (S/1999/862).
27 August	Security Council adopts Resolution 1262(1999) further extending UNAMET mandate.
30 August	Ballot day: 98.6 percent of those registered vote.
September	Estimated 250,000 refugees are relocated to West Timor.
1 September	Violence erupts in Dili.
4 September	Ballot results announced: 21.5 percent accept autonomy and 78.5 percent reject it (opting for independence).
5–8 September	Security situation deteriorates. Foreign nationals and UNAMET staff begin to depart. Indonesia introduces martial law. Worldwide condemnation of situation.
8–12 September	Security Council Mission visits Jakarta and Dili.
10 September	Secretary-General calls on Indonesia to agree to a multinational force (MNF).
12 September	President Habibie agrees to deployment of an MNF to restore security.
15 September	Security Council adopts Resolution 1264(1999) authorizing an MNF to restore security in East Timor.
20 September	MNF (INTERFET) troops begin deploying to East Timor. SRSG Ian Martin and senior UNAMET staff return to Dili.
4 October	Secretary-General's report on situation in East Timor (S/1999/1024).
20 October	Indonesian MPR recognizes result of ballot and revokes 1978 decree incorporating East Timor into Indonesia.
21 October	Xanana Gusmão returns to Dili.
25 October	Security Council adopts Resolution 1272(1999) establishing UNTAET.
29 October	Bretton Woods–UN Joint Assessment Mission arrives in Dili.
1 November	Last TNI troops depart East Timor.
17 November	SRSG UNTAET and transitional administrator, Sergio Vieira de Mello, begins duties in East Timor.
2 December	East Timor National Consultative Council is established.

1999

13 December	Secretary-General's progress report on question of East Timor to the General Assembly (A/54/654).
30 December	Secretary-General appoints Lieutenant-General Jaime de los Santos (Philippines) as UNTAET force commander, and Major General Mike Smith (Australia) as deputy force commander.

2000

12 January	INTERFET-TNI Memorandum of Technical Understanding (MOU) on border management signed.
24 January	U.S. dollar becomes official currency. Central Payments Office opened.
25 January	Lieutenant General de los Santos and Major General Smith arrive in Dili.
26 January	Secretary-General's report on UNTAET (S/2000/53). SRSG attends UN Security Council.
1 February	INTERFET begins handover of military authority to UNTAET PKF in Sector East.
14 February	President of Portugal, Jorge Sampaio, visits. PKF assumes responsibility for Sector Central from INTERFET.
15 February	PKF assumes responsibility for Oecussi enclave sector.
17–18 February	Visit of UN Secretary-General Kofi Annan.
21 February	Grant agreement signed in Dili between World Bank, UNTAET and CNRT. PKF assumes responsibility for Sector West.
23 February	Full military authority is officially transferred from INTERFET to UNTAET.
24 February	National Consultative Council approves formation of Border (immigration and customs) Service.
29 February	President Wahid visits Dili.
March	Increased militia infiltration along the border and in Ermera district.
March	Negotiations begin between East Timor (UNTAET) and Australia on revenue sharing from oil and gas reserves in Timor Sea.
8 March	High-level discussions held between UNTAET and Indonesia in Jakarta on security situation in the border region.
14 March	More than 150,000 of the 250,000 East Timorese refugees in West Timor have returned.

2000

22 March	Portuguese Police Riot Control Unit commences operations in Dili.
24 March	UNTAET inaugurates Public Service Commission.
27 March	Police training college opens in Dili.
30 March	SRSG meets with President Wahid in Jakarta.
5 April	UNTAET and Indonesia conclude MOU on legal, judicial, and human rights cooperation. UNTAET announces decision to appoint East Timorese to top administrative positions and to establish District Advisory Councils.
11 April	MOU for tactical coordination in the border area signed by PKF and TNI in Dili, updating 12 January agreement.
22–25 April	Visit by Portuguese prime minister, Antonio Guterres.
29 April	East Timor postal service opens.
May	PKF force reductions commence in Sector East.
8 May	Civil service campus opens.
11 May	Dili District Court opens its first public proceeding.
29 May	SRSG meets with President Wahid in Jakarta.
30 May	Conference on Reconstruction of East Timor held in Liquiça. Falintil Company 5 rebellion in Aileu resolved.
6 June	Special Panels for Serious Crimes of the Dili District Court established.
7 June	Police commissioner, José Luis da Coste é Sousa, arrives.
8 June	Governor of West Timor, Piet Tallo, visits Dili.
12 June	UNTAET and CNRT agree on new composition and structure of National Consultative Council.
16 June	60 Falintil break Aileu cantonment but return peacefully.
17 June	Jordanian police riot control unit deploys to Baucau.
22–23 June	Donor Conference on East Timor, Lisbon.
27 June	SRSG attends UN Security Council.
July	Militia infiltration across border increases.
July	Updated estimate of refugees returned and resettled given as 170,000.
8–20 July	King's College, London, study on security force options for East Timor.

2000

11 July	Graduation of first police cadets from Police Training College.
12 July	UNTAET Governance and Public Administration pillar transitioned into East Timor Transitional Administration. Cabinet of the First Transitional Government in East Timor is established.
13 July	National Consultative Council authorizes its transformation into the National Council.
15 July	Swearing in of First Transitional Cabinet members.
17 July	Inaugural meeting of First Transitional Cabinet held in Dili.
19 July	Lieutenant General Boonsrang Niumpradit (Thailand) assumes command of UNTAET PKF from Lieutenant General de los Santos.
24 July	First combat-related death of UN peacekeeper (Private Leonard Manning [NZ] in Cova Lima district).
26 July	Secretary-General's report on UNTAET (S/2000/738).
5–7 August	Visit of the UN Human Rights Commissioner.
8 August	King's College London submits report on security options.
10 August	Private Devi Ram Jaisi (Nepal) killed in militia attack in Cova Lima district.
20 August	Xanana Gusmão relinquishes command of Falintil to Taur Matan Ruak during twenty-fifth anniversary celebrations.
21–30 August	CNRT National Congress held in Dili.
31 August	Due to increased militia activity, SRSG recommends PKF force enhancement (subsequently agreed to by Secretary-General).
September	Portuguese battalion in Sector Central conducts Operations Cobra and Crocodilo—successful sweep-and-find operations to counter militia infiltration in Manufahi and Ainaro districts.
6 September	Three UNHCR workers murdered at Atambua. UN personnel withdrawn from West Timor.
8 September	Security Council adopts Resolution 1319(2000) calling on Indonesia to disband militias and improve security in East Timor.

2000

12 September	Transitional Cabinet approves the establishment of East Timor Defence Force (ETDF).
14 September	High-level security discussions between UNTAET and Indonesia held in Denpasar. Joint Border Committee established to oversee border activities.
29 September	SRSG attends UN Security Council.
23 October	Inauguration of National Council.
27 October	National Planning and Development Agency established.
12–17 November	UN Security Council Mission visits Indonesia and East Timor to assess security situation in West Timor and progress of UNTAET.
17 November	50 ex-milsas and families (total 400) return from West Timor.
21–23 November	ETDF donor meeting in Dili.
23 November	Office of Defence Force Development set up within ETTA.
30 November	Preliminary Joint Border Committee meeting in Denpasar.
5–6 December	Donor Conference on East Timor in Brussels.
13 December	Transitional Cabinet agrees to establishment of a Commission for Truth, Reception and Reconciliation.

2001

January	Civil Registration commences.
13–14 January	Visit by President of UN General Assembly.
16 January	Secretary-General's report on UNTAET (S/2001/42).
26 January	SRSG attends UN Security Council.
29 January	National Council authorizes establishment of ETDF.
30 January	Falintil Veterans Association established.
30–31 January	First formal meeting of Joint Border Committee in Denpasar.
31 January	Security Council adopts Resolution 1338(2001) extending UNTAET mandate until 31 January 2002.
February	Training of ETDF maritime officers with the Portuguese Navy begins in Portugal.
February	Updated estimate of refugees returned and resettled given as 176,000, an increase of only 6,000 since July 2000.

2001

1 February	Falintil disbanded and ETDF inaugurated. Brigadier General Taur Matan Ruak appointed as first commander. Transitional Cabinet regulates against possession, sale, and use of firearms, ammunition, and explosives.
19 February	Training of ETDF commences in Aileu.
26 February– 2 March	Visit of Under-Secretary-General DPKO.
27 February	PKF hand over Dili airport to civilian authorities.
3 April	Construction of ETDF camp at Metinaro begins.
2 May	Secretary-General's interim report on UNTAET (S/2001/436).
8 May	National Security Adviser position established in ETTA.
29 May	Five civilians killed and forty wounded when hand grenades are thrown among Timorese in a crowded market on the border, 7 km southeast of Balibo.
9 June	CNRT dissolved.
14–15 June	Donor Conference on East Timor in Canberra.
25–26 June	ETDF donor meeting in Dili.
26 June	Inauguration of ETDF headquarters at Metinaro.
2–5 July	Deputy Secretary-General Louise Fréhette visits East Timor.
5 July	Timor Sea Arrangement between Australia and East Timor initialed in Dili by Australian ministers for foreign affairs and industry and by East Timor First Transitional Cabinet members Peter Galbraith and Mari Alkatiri.
5–6 July	ETDF relocates from Aileu to new training facilities at Metinaro.
13 July	UNTAET Regulation 2001/10 establishes Commission for Reception, Truth and Reconciliation in East Timor.
19–20 July	Joint Border Committee meeting in Jakarta.
31 July	SRSG attends UN Security Council.
28 August	PKF-TNI Military Technical Agreement signed, updating 11 April 2000 argreement.
30 August	Democratic election for Constituent Assembly.
31 August	Lieutenant General Winai Phattiyakul (Thailand) assumes command of PKF from Lieutenant General Boonsrang Niumpradit.

2001

September	UNHCR reestablishes permanent presence in West Timor.
6 September	Final meeting of First Transitional Cabinet.
12 September	SRSG and East Timorese leaders meet with President Megawati Sukarnoputri in Jakarta.
14 September	Large group of East Timor refugees returns from West Timor as a result of peaceful security situation and successful election process.
15 September	Swearing in of the eighty-eight-member East Timor Constituent Assembly.
20 September	Swearing in of the all-Timorese "Second Transitional Government."
17 October	Return of key ex-militia figure Nemésio Lopes de Carvalho to East Timor.
18 October	Secretary-General's report on UNTAET (S/2001/984). Advises that approximately 186,000 refugees had returned to East Timor and that an estimated 60,000 to 80,000 remain in Indonesia.
26 October	Inauguration of first battalion of ETDF.
31 October	Security Council reviews East Timor situation.
19–21 November	Joint Border Committee meeting in Dili.
26 November	Gradual downsizing of PKF begins (from 8,000 to 5,000 by independence). Kenyan contingent departs.
26–29 November	Xanana Gusmão undertakes three-day reconciliation visit to West Timor encouraging refugees, including former militia, to return.
1 December	First battalion of ETDF completes basic training.
10–11 December	Joint Border Committee meeting in Jakarta.
11 December	Portuguese government delivers two modified Albatross patrol boats as part of Portuguese aid to ETDF naval component.
11–12 December	Donor Conference on East Timor in Oslo.
15 December	PKF downsizing continues: Philippine battalion departs.
21 December	East Timor Transitional Government and Phillips Petroleum reach an understanding on allowing gas development in the Timor Sea to proceed.

2002

11 January	PKF downsizing continues: Jordanian battalion hands over to Korean battalion and departs Oecussi enclave. ETDF replaces Koreans in Lautem district.

2002

12 January	Patrol boats *Oecussi* and *Atauro* formally offered to the ETDF naval component by Portugal.
17 January	Secretary-General's report on UNTAET (S/2002/80).
30 January	SRSG attends UN Security Council.
22 March	East Timor constitution is authorized.
14 April	Presidential election.
20 May	Independence.

Bibliography

Annan, Kofi. *Report of the Secretary-General on the Situation in East Timor*, Part IV. S/1999/1024, 4 October 1999.

———. *Report of the Secretary-General "No Exit Without Strategy: Security Council Decision-Making and the Closure or Transition of United Nations Peacekeeping Operations."* S/2001/394, 20 April 2001.

———. *Report of the Secretary-General on the United Nations Transitional Administration in East Timor.* S/2001/983, 18 October 2001.

Ball, Desmond, and Hamish McDonald. *Death in Balibo, Lies in Canberra.* Sydney: Allen and Unwin, 2000.

Bartu, Peter. "The Militia, the Military, and the People of Bobonaro District." *Bulletin of Concerned Asian Scholars*, 32, nos. 1–2 (2000): 35–42.

Boutros-Ghali, Boutros. *An Agenda for Peace: Preventive Diplomacy, Peacemaking and Peacekeeping.* New York: UN Department of Public Information, 1992.

Bowman, Steve. "'Historical and Cultural Influences on Coalition Operations." In Thomas Marshall, Phillip Kaiser, and Jon Kessmeier, eds., *Problems and Solutions in Future Coalition Operations.* U.S. Army War College, Strategic Studies Institute, December 1997, pp. 1–21.

Brahimi, Lakhdar. *Report of the Panel on United Nations Peace Operations.* UN General Assembly Security Council. A/55/305–S/2000/809, 21 August 2000.

Breen, Bob. *Mission Accomplished East Timor.* Sydney: Allen and Unwin, 2000.

Budiardjo, Carmel, and Liem Soei Liong. *The War Against East Timor.* London: Zed Books, 1984.

Callinan, Sir Bernard. *Independent Company: The 2/2 and 2/4 Australian Independent Companies in Portuguese Timor, 1941–1943.* Melbourne: Heinemann, 1953.

Carey, Peter, and G. Carter Bentley, eds. *East Timor at the Crossroads: The Forging of a Nation.* London: Cassell, 1995.

Centre for Defence Studies, King's College London. "Independent Study on Security Force Options and Security Sector Reform for East Timor," 8 August 2000.

Chopra, Jarat. "The UN's Kingdom of East Timor." *Survival* 42, no. 3 (2000): 27–39.

Cliffe, Sarah. "The Joint Assessment Mission and Reconstruction in East Timor." In James J. Fox and Dionisio Babo Soares, eds., *Out of the Ashes: Destruction*

Bibliography

and Reconstruction of East Timor. Adelaide: Crawford House, 2000, pp. 252–261.

Coning, Cedric de. "The UN Transitional Administration in East Timor (UNTAET): Lessons Learned from the First 100 Days." *International Peacekeeping* 6, nos. 2–3 (2000): 83–90.

Cosgrove, Peter. "The Night Our Boys Stared Down the Barrel." *The Age* (Melbourne), 21 June 2000, p. 15.

Cotton, James, ed. *East Timor and Australia.* Canberra: Australian Defence Studies Centre, 1999.

———. "'Part of the Indonesian World': Lessons in East Timor Policy-Making, 1974–76." *Australian Journal of International Affairs* 55, no. 1 (2001): 119–131.

Crouch, Harold. "The TNI and East Timor Policy." In James J. Fox and Dionisio Babo Soares, eds., *Out of the Ashes: Destruction and Reconstruction of East Timor.* Adelaide: Crawford House, 2000, pp. 151–179.

Day, Graham. "After War, Send Blue Force." *Christian Science Monitor*, 30 May 2001.

Dee, Moreen. "'Coalitions of the Willing' and Humanitarian Intervention: Australia's Involvement with INTERFET." *International Peacekeeping* 8, no. 3 (2001): 1–20.

Department of Foreign Affairs and Trade. *Documents on Australian Foreign Policy, Australia and the Indonesian Incorporation of Portuguese Timor 1974–1976.* Melbourne: Melbourne University Press, 2000.

———. *East Timor in Transition 1998–2000: An Australian Policy Challenge.* Canberra: Brown and Wilton, 2001.

Dunn, James. "Crimes Against Humanity in East Timor, January to October 1999: Their Nature and Causes." Unpublished UN Report, 2001, p. 20. Available online at http://www.eban.org/news/2001a/dunn1.htm (accessed 9 January 2002).

———. *The East Timor Situation: Report on Talks with Timorese Refugees in Portugal.* Canberra: Legislative Research Service, Australian Parliament, 1977.

———. *Timor: A People Betrayed.* Sydney: ABC Books, 1996.

"East Timor Revisited: Ford, Kissinger and the Indonesian Invasion, 1975–76." In William Burr and Michael L. Evans, *National Security Archive Electronic Briefing Book No. 62*, December 2001. Available online at http://www.gwu.edu/~nsarchiv (accessed 8 January 2002).

Evans, Benjamin. "Australian Operations in Timor 1942–1943." *Wartime*, no. 10 (autumn 2000): 28–29.

Fetherston, A. B. *Towards a Theory of United Nations Peacekeeping.* London: Macmillan, 1994.

Fox, James J. "Tracing the Path, Recounting the Past: Historical Perspectives on Timor." In James J. Fox and Dionisio Babo Soares, eds., *Out of the Ashes: Destruction and Reconstruction of East Timor.* Adelaide: Crawford House, 2000, pp. 1–29.

Gunn, Geoffrey C. "The Five-Hundred-Year Timorese *Funu*." In Richard Tanter, Mark Selden, and Stephen R. Shalom, eds., *Bitter Flowers, Sweet Flowers: East Timor, Indonesia and the Word Community.* Sydney: Rowman and Littlefield, 2001, pp. 3–14.

Haseman, John B. "East Timor: The Misuse of Military Power and Misplaced Military Pride." In James J. Fox and Dionisio Babo Soares, eds., *Out of the*

Ashes: Destruction and Reconstruction of East Timor. Adelaide: Crawford House, 2000, pp. 180–191.

Hayden, Bill. "Defence After Timor." *Quadrant* 44, no. 78 (2000): 18–23.

Howard, Lise Morje. "Learning to Keep the Peace? UN Multidimensional Peacekeeping in Civil Wars. Ph.D. diss., University of California, Berkeley, 2001.

Kernic, Franz. "The Soldier and the Task: Austria's Experience of Preparing Peacekeepers." *International Peacekeeping* 6, no. 3 (1999): 113–128.

Kinzer, Maj. Gen. Joseph W. *Success in Peacekeeping: United Nations Mission in Haiti: The Military Perspective.* Carlisle, PA: U.S. Army Peacekeeping Institute, 1996.

Lee Kuan Yew. *The Singapore Story.* Singapore: Times Editions, 1998.

Liu, F. T. "Evolution of United Nations Peacekeeping Operations." In Kevin Clements and Christine Wilson, eds., *UN Peacekeeping at the Crossroads.* Canberra: Peace Research Centre, Australian National University, 1994, pp. 60–75.

Martin, Ian. *Self-Determination in East Timor: The United Nations, the Ballot and International Intervention.* International Peace Academy Occasional Paper. Boulder, CO: Lynne Rienner, 2001.

Martinkus, John. *A Dirty Little War.* Sydney: Random House, 2001.

McBeth, John. "Whose Future Is It Anyway?" *Far Eastern Economic Review,* 9 November 2000, pp. 68–69.

McFarlane, John, and William Maley. *Civilian Police in United Nations Peace Operations.* Australian Defence Studies Centre Working Paper No. 64, Canberra, April 2001.

Mobekk, Eirin. *Policing Peace Operations: United Nations Civilian Police in East Timor.* Kings College London, October 2001.

Neuffer, Elizabeth. "Slaughter Suspects Elude UN's Reach." *Boston Globe,* 9 February 2001, p. A6.

Parliament of the Commonwealth of Australia. *Final Report of the Senate Foreign Affairs, Defence and Trade References Committee: East Timor.* December 2000.

Ramos-Horta, José. "Democracy and Diplomacy in the Asia–Pacific Region." In Jeffrey Hopkins, ed., *The Art of Peace*: *Nobel Peace Laureates Discuss Human Rights, Conflict and Reconciliation.* New York: Snow Line, 2000, pp. 32–49.

Renner, Michael. "UN Peacekeeping: An Uncertain Future." *In Focus* 5, no. 28 (September 2000). Reproduced in K. C. Eyre and Kiril Sharapov, eds., *Pro Pace Paratus: An Anthology of Readings in Modern Peacekeeping.* Cornwallis Park, Nova Scotia: Pearson Peacekeeping Centre, May 2001, pp. 345–349.

Rose, General Sir Michael. *Fighting for Peace: Lessons from Bosnia,* 2d ed. London: Warner Books, 1999.

Ryan, Alan. *Primary Responsibilities and Primary Risks: Australian Defence Force Participation in the International Force in East Timor.* Study Paper No. 304. Duntroon: Australian Army Land Warfare Studies Centre, November 2000.

Schwarz, Adam. *A Nation in Waiting: Indonesia in the 1990s.* Sydney: Allen and Unwin, 1994.

Seiple, Chris. *The US Military/NGO Relationship in Humanitarian Interventions.* Carlisle, PA: U.S. Army Peacekeeping Institute, 1996.

Soares, Dionisio Babo. "Political Developments Leading to the Referendum." In James J. Fox and Dionisio Babo Soares, eds., *Out of the Ashes: Destruction and Reconstruction of East Timor.* Adelaide: Crawford House, 2000, pp. 57–76.

Suhrke, Astri. "Peacekeepers As Nation-Builders: Dilemmas of the UN in East Timor." *International Peacekeeping* 8, no. 4 (2001): 1–20.

Taylor, John. *Indonesia's Forgotten War: The Hidden History of East Timor.* London: Zed Books, 1991.

Thakur, Ramesh. "Cambodia, East Timor and the Brahimi Report." *International Peacekeeping* 8, no. 3 (2001): 115–124.

Traub, James. "Inventing East Timor." *Foreign Affairs* 79, no. 4 (2000): 74–89.

Trust Fund for East Timor. Update No. 14, 15 January 2002. Available on line at http://www.worldbank.org/eap (accessed 19 January 2002).

UN Department of Peacekeeping Operations. *Directive for the Force Commander of the United Nations Transitional Administration in East Timor.* Military Planning Service, MPS/3636, 8 May 2000.

"UN Says East Timor Can Serve as Afghanistan Model." Reuters, Oslo, 11 December 2001. Available online at http://www.igc.topica.com (accessed 12 December 2001).

UNTAET daily press releases. September 1999–January 2002. Available online at http://www.un.org/peace/etimor (accessed December 2001 and January 2002).

UNTAET Regulations 1999–2001.

Van Creveld, Martin. *The Transformation of War.* New York: Free Press, 1991.

Warner, Nick. "Cambodia: Lessons of UNTAC for Future Peacekeeping Operations." In Kevin Clements and Christine Wilson, eds., *UN Peacekeeping at the Crossroads.* Canberra: Peace Research Centre, Australian National University, 1994, pp. 116–131.

Index

199

About This Publication

The UN intervention in East Timor amply illustrates the type of complex operation that the United Nations increasingly is being asked to undertake. Michael Smith analyzes the successes and failures of the UN Transitional Administration in East Timor (UNTAET), which was designed to work in partnership with the East Timorese in guiding the country to independence following the 1999 vote to secede from Indonesia.

Continuing the compelling narrative begun by Ian Martin in *Self-Determination in East Timor*, Smith gives a lucid first-hand account of a UN mission in the unfamiliar role of interim government—a mission dealing with critical requirements for good governance, sustainable development, and effective military and police forces. Evaluating the lessons learned from the experience, he highlights the urgent need for reforms within the UN. The absence of those reforms, he believes, will lead to more failed states, more refugees, more poverty, and more dead peacekeepers.

Major General Michael G. Smith (recently retired from the Australian army after 34 years of distinguished service) was deputy force commander of the UNTAET peacekeeping force from January 2000 through March 2001. Moreen Dee is a diplomatic and military historian contracted to the Australian Department of Foreign Affairs and Trade.

The International Peace Academy

The International Peace Academy (IPA) is an independent, international institution dedicated to promoting the prevention and settlement of armed conflicts between and within states through policy research and development.

Founded in 1970, the IPA has built an extensive portfolio of activities in fulfillment of its mission:

- Symposiums, workshops, and other forums that facilitate strategic thinking, policy development, and organizational innovation within international organizations.
- Policy research on multilateral efforts to prevent, mitigate, or rebuild after armed conflict.
- Research, consultations, and technical assistance to support capacities for peacemaking, peacekeeping, and peacebuilding in Africa.
- Professional-development seminars for political, development, military, humanitarian, and nongovernmental personnel involved in peacekeeping and conflict resolution.
- Facilitation in conflict situations where its experience, credibility, and independence can complement official peace efforts.
- Outreach to build public awareness on issues related to peace and security, multilateralism, and the United Nations.

The IPA works closely with the United Nations, regional and other international organizations, governments, and nongovernmental organizations, as well as with parties to conflicts in selected cases. Its efforts are enhanced by its ability to draw on a worldwide network of government and business leaders, scholars, diplomats, military officers, and leaders of civil society.

The IPA is a nonprofit organization governed by an international Board of Directors. The organization is funded by generous donations from governments, major philanthropic foundations, and corporate donors, as well as contributions from individuals and its Board members.

International Peace Academy Publications

Available from Lynne Rienner Publishers, 1800 30th Street, Boulder, Colorado 80301 (303-444-6684), www.rienner.com.

From Promise to Practice: Strengthening UN Capacities for the Prevention of Violent Conflict, edited by Chandra Lekha Sriram and Karin Wermester (2003)

The Chittagong Hill Tracts, Bangladesh: On the Difficult Road to Peace, Amena Mohsin (2003)

Peacekeeping in East Timor: The Path to Independence, Michael G. Smith with Moreen Dee (2003)

From Cape to Congo: Southern Africa's Evolving Security Challenges, edited by Mwesiga Baregu and Christopher Landsberg (2003)

Ending Civil Wars: The Implementation of Peace Agreements, edited by Stephen John Stedman, Donald Rothchild, and Elizabeth M. Cousens (2002)

Sanctions and the Search for Security: Challenges to UN Action, David Cortright and George A. Lopez, with Linda Gerber (2002)

Ecuador vs. Peru: Peacemaking Amid Rivalry, Monica Herz and João Pontes Nogueira (2002)

Liberia's Civil War: Nigeria, ECOMOG, and Regional Security in West Africa, Adekeye Adebajo (2002)

Building Peace in West Africa: Liberia, Sierra Leone, and Guinea-Bissau, Adekeye Adebajo (2002)

Kosovo: An Unfinished Peace, William G. O'Neill (2002)

From Reaction to Conflict Prevention: Opportunities for the UN System, edited by Fen Osler Hampson and David M. Malone (2002)

Peacemaking in Rwanda: The Dynamics of Failure, Bruce D. Jones (2001)

Self-Determination in East Timor: The United Nations, the Ballot, and

International Intervention, Ian Martin (2001)

Civilians in War, edited by Simon Chesterman (2001)

Toward Peace in Bosnia: Implementing the Dayton Accords, Elizabeth M. Cousens and Charles K. Cater (2001)

Sierra Leone: Diamonds and the Struggle for Democracy, John L. Hirsch (2001)

Peacebuilding as Politics: Cultivating Peace in Fragile Societies, edited by Elizabeth M. Cousens and Chetan Kumar (2001)

The Sanctions Decade: Assessing UN Strategies in the 1990s, David Cortright and George A. Lopez (2000)

Greed and Grievance: Economic Agendas in Civil War, edited by Mats Berdal and David M. Malone (2000)

Building Peace in Haiti, Chetan Kumar (1998)

Rights and Reconciliation: UN Strategies in El Salvador, Ian Johnstone (1995)